Tong Li

An Approach to Modelling
Software Evolution Processes

Tong Li

An Approach to Modelling Software Evolution Processes

With 72 figures and 6 tables

AUTHOR:

Tong Li
School of Software
Yunnan University
Kunming 650091, P.R. China
Email: tli@ynu.edu.cn

ISBN 978-7-302-17537-7 **Tsinghua University Press, Beijing**
ISBN 978-3-540-79463-9 **Springer Berlin Heidelberg New York**
e ISBN 978-3-540-79464-6 **Springer Berlin Heidelberg New York**

Library of Congress Control Number: 2008925346
Co-published by Tsinghua University Press, Beijing and Springer-Verlag GmbH Berlin Heidelberg

Springer is a part of Springer Science+Business Media
springer.com

Cover design: Frido Steinen-Broo, EStudio Calamar, Spain
Printed on acid-free paper

To my daughter, Yixiao, my wife, Lixia and my parents with all my love.

Contents

Preface

The importance and popularity of software evolution increase as more and more successful software systems become legacy systems. For one thing, software evolution has become an important characteristic in the software life cycle; for another, software process plays an important role in increasing efficiency and quality of software evolution. Therefore, the software evolution process, the inter-discipline of software process and software evolution, becomes a key area in software engineering. A well-managed software evolution process can effectively support a successful software evolution; however, a poor software evolution process will lead to the failure of the corresponding software evolution.

What Is the Uniqueness of This Book?

This book aims to model and describe formal software processes that effectively support software evolution. For this purpose, progress has been made in the following aspects:

Firstly, five important properties of software evolution processes are analysed. It is indicated that iteration, concurrency, interleaving of continuous and discontinuous change, feedback-driven systems and multi-level frameworks play important roles in software evolution processes.

Secondly, a Petri Net is extended with object-oriented technology and Hoare Logic. Based on the extended Petri Net and according to the preceding properties, a formal evolution process meta-model EPMM is designed. EPMM can define software evolution process models with a four-level framework and can embody some important properties, such as iteration, concurrency, interleaving of continuous and discontinuous change and feedback-driven systems.

Thirdly, based on EPMM, an object-oriented evolution process description language EPDL is designed. It is more detailed and easier to implement in computers than EPMM.

Fourthly, based on EPMM, the framework of software evolution processes is discussed. According to the framework, a semi-formal approach to modelling and describing software evolution processes is proposed. The approach is used to design software evolution processes at the global level (designing global models), at the process level (designing software processes), at the activity level (designing activities) and at the task level (designing tasks), each corresponding to the levels in the framework. At the process level, the approach supports top-down white box modelling and top-down black box modelling, which are proved to preserve the interface consistency over refinement hierarchies. The approach also supports process reuse by means of three different reuse methods. At the task level, by repeatedly decomposing the function of a task into one of three basic control structures, the function can be decomposed into a code segment consisting of finer functions, which can be easily realised. If the executions of all the decomposed finer functions terminate, the decomposition is proved to be totally correct. Using EPDL, software evolution processes can be described in detail.

Fifthly, according to the dependence analysis between activities and between tasks, an approach is proposed to capture and extend concurrency in an inefficient process segment dug down from an evolution process model. After its efficiency is improved, the process segment is put back into the original model to improve the efficiency of the corresponding evolution process.

Sixthly, a CASE environment EPT that supports the proposed approach is designed and a prototype system of EPT is also implemented.

Finally, four case studies of various complexities and scales indicate that the proposed approach is feasible and effective.

In summary, a semi-formal approach is proposed to construct formal software evolution process models and the corresponding descriptions to effectively support software evolution.

Acknowledgements

The work described in this book has been supported by the National Science Foundation of China under Grant No. 60463002 and by the Science Foundation of Yunnan Province, China under Grant No. 2007F008M.

This book is based on my Ph.D. thesis accomplished in February 2007 at De Montfort University, U.K. I would like to thank all the people who have helped me in different ways since I undertook the work described in this book.

Firstly and foremost, I would like to thank Professor Hongji Yang, De Montfort University, U.K. Although it was certainly not always easy during I undertook the work, I think that I have evolved over the years. Professor Yang, more than anybody else, was extremely important in this evolution. It is mainly through the interaction with Professor Yang that I developed a deeper understanding of my research project. I feel so lucky to have so many opportunities to discuss with him.

I am very happy that I have had the chance to research on software evolution processes in the Software Technology Research Laboratory at De Montfort University, U.K. The laboratory has such a unique academic atmosphere that I had numerous opportunities to interact with many excellent staff and Ph.D. students. My thanks must go to Professor Hussein Zedan, the Director of the laboratory, for this atmosphere, his valuable advice and the experienced guidance that he had provided along the way. In addition, I would like to thank Professor Hong Zhu, Oxford Brookes University, U.K., Dr. Martin Ward and Dr. Antonio Cau, De Montfort University, U.K. for their valuable suggestions concerning my research work.

I also wish to express many thanks to Dr. Juan F. Ramil, Open University, U.K. and Dr. Douglas R. Smith, Kestrel Institute and Stanford University, U.S.A. for providing me with their papers "Software Evolution and Software Evolution Processes" and "Top-Down Synthesis of Divide-and-Conquer Algorithms" respectively, by e-mail.

I would like to thank all of the colleagues in the Software Technology Research Laboratory at De Montfort University, U.K. and the colleagues in the School of Software and in the School of Information Science and Engineering at Yunnan University, China, such as Professor Hongzhi Liao, Professor Hua Zhou, Professor Degao Zhang, Dr. Shaoyun Li, Dr. Feng Chen, Professor Zhihong Liang, Professor Qing Liu, Dr. Helge Janicke, Mr. Tony Chen, Mr. Wei Wang, Mr. Howard Billam, Miss Jinzhuo Liu, Miss Niwen Ma, Mr. Hengrui Zhang, Mr. Fei Li, Mr. Jiang Zheng, Mr. Zhao Dong, Ms. Lingxiao Zheng, Miss Xikun Pan and Mr. Zhan Chen. I would like to thank them for their valuable suggestions, discussion and assistance over all these years.

I would also like to thank Professor Shuzhen Yao, Beijing University of Aeronautics and Astronautics, China, Professor Hujie Huang, Harbin Institute of Technology, China, Professor Jiliu Zhou, Sichuan University, China, Ms. Ling Ding and Ms. Hui Xue, Tsinghua University, China for their recommendation and valuable suggestions.

Finally, I wish to express thanks to my daughter, Yixiao Li, my wife, Lixia Wang, and my parents for all their love, encouragement, patience and support over the years. This book is dedicated to them.

Tong Li
January, 2008

List of Figures and Tables

1 Introduction

Tong Li

School of Software, Yunnan University, Kunming, 650091, China
Software Technology Research Laboratory, De Montfort University, Leicester, LE1 9BH, U.K
tli@ynu.edu.cn

Abstract   The roadmap to evolving a legacy software system into a high quality software system is the software evolution process. Making use of the formalisms of Petri Nets, Hoare Logic and Backus-Naur Form, a semi-formal approach is proposed to construct formal software evolution process models and the corresponding descriptions to effectively support software evolution. The approach is expected to be adopted by software managers, software engineers and stakeholders. In this chapter, besides the concepts of software evolution process and software evolution process model, the advantages of modelling and describing software evolution processes are discussed. The motivations, research methods and the original contributions of the work described in this book are also presented. Furthermore, the success criteria and validation methods for the proposed approach are also given. Finally, an outline is listed to describe the framework of this book. This chapter aims to give an introduction to the research work described in this book.

Key Words   motivation, software evolution process, software evolution process model, contribution, research method, success criterion, validation, outline.

1.1   Motivation

As more and more successful software systems become legacy systems, software evolution becomes more and more important. Twenty years ago, software just needed to be corrected occasionally and a new software release was issued perhaps once a year. The term *maintenance* could be used to imply that software engineers were working to enable their software to continue to do what it used to do. Ten years ago, software needed a major release with new functionality twice a year, and the term *reengineering* was used to imply that software engineers were adding new user-required functions to the software (Yang and Ward 2003).

Nowadays, software systems change continuously in step with the changes in techniques and requirements. These changes improve the software systems from the less-mature to the mature and are described by the technical term *evolution* which refers to the progressive change in their properties whilst the process of change leads to new properties or new improvements. Software evolution has become an important characteristic in the software life cycle (Aoyama 2001; Bennett and Rajlich 2000; Lehman and Ramil 2002).

A *software evolution process* is a set of interrelated software processes under which the corresponding software is evolving. The software evolution process constructs a framework to support software evolution and is also the workflow of software evolution. Obviously, it is different from the traditional software process. During software evolution, the following questions must be answered: What is a software evolution process? What software processes can effectively support software evolution? How is a software evolution process modelled and described? This book tries to provide solutions to these questions.

The roadmap to evolving a legacy software system into a high quality software system is the software evolution process. Software evolution processes are adopted to meet the needs of the software engineers and the managers. A well-managed software evolution process will lead to high quality and efficient evolution of software systems on time and under budget. However, an undefined or even chaotic software evolution process will be dangerous when success depends on individual effort, which can be unreliable and unpredictable.

A *software evolution process model* denotes a static and abstract representation of a software evolution process. A *software evolution process description* denotes a detailed and concrete representation of a software evolution process. When a process is enacted by means of executing its description, the corresponding software is evolved. The advantages of modelling and describing the software evolution process are obvious. Some of them are discussed as follows:

(1) This leads to software evolving according to a roadmap of the defined software evolution process so that the well-managed software evolution process can be applied to software evolution.

(2) A software evolution process model and the corresponding description can simulate behaviour patterns which reflect those of a real-world evolution process. Executing the model and description can provide significant insights into the domain being modelled and described.

(3) A software evolution process model and the corresponding description can provide a basis to manage, control, schedule, analyse and measure the software evolution process, which otherwise can get out of control easily.

(4) The software evolution process improvement can be carried out by means of optimising the corresponding software process model and its description, which is easier than making the direct improvement to an executing software evolution process.

(5) A software evolution process is very complex because it includes a lot of

iteration and concurrency. In some cases, the coordination may be very difficult. A rigorous process model and the corresponding description prescribe these behaviours in advance so that the executing process keeps going in the correct order and avoids confusion.

(6) A well-defined software evolution process model and the corresponding description can ensure that all resource configurations are in order.

In addition to the advantages stated above, a formal process model and its description are more rigorous and more precise than an informal one and are more easily implemented in computers. They are expected to greatly promote successful software evolution.

1.2 Contributions

This book aims to construct software process models and the corresponding process descriptions to effectively support software evolution. Compared to previous published works, although many aspects of software evolution and software processes have been researched, the formal software evolution process model, its description and the corresponding construction approach are rarely addressed. Concretely, the original contributions of this book are as follows:

(1) Five properties of software evolution processes are summarised according to the analysis of software evolution and the published works in the area of software evolution.

(2) A Petri Net is extended with object-oriented technology and Hoare Logic. Abstract data types and inheritance are added in order to describe activities; Hoare Logic is added in order to describe tasks.

(3) Based on the extended Petri Net, a formal evolution process meta-model, EPMM, and an EPMM-based evolution process description language, EPDL, are proposed. EPDL is an extension of EPMM. EPMM embodies the important properties of software evolution processes and supports the construction of evolution process models (EPMs for short) with a four-level framework. An evolution process description (EPD for short) defined by EPDL is more concrete than an EPM defined by EPMM so that the detailed information in software evolution processes can be described.

(4) Based on EPMM, a semi-formal approach to modelling and describing software evolution processes at the global level (designing global models), at the process level (designing software processes), at the activity level (designing activities) and at the task level (designing tasks) is proposed. At the process level, the approach supports top-down white box modelling and top-down black box modelling, which are proved to preserve the interface consistency over refinement hierarchies.

(5) The preceding approach supports process reuse by means of three different reuse methods.

(6) For designing tasks, three rules which decompose a pair of assertions based on Hoare Logic into one of three basic control structures are proposed and the correctness of the decompositions is proved. Based on a knowledge base, an approach which decomposes a function into a series of finer functions is also proposed.

(7) A set of algorithms to transform an activity dependence graph into a process segment is proposed in order to capture concurrency in a software evolution process. Another set of algorithms to transform an inefficient process segment into an efficient process segment is also proposed in order to extend concurrency from the local to the global. Based on these algorithms, an approach which improves the efficiency of a software evolution process is proposed by means of replacing inefficient process segments with efficient ones. The approach is proved to preserve the interface consistency between before and after the replacement.

In summary, making use of the formalisms of Petri Nets, Hoare Logic and Backus-Naur Form, this book proposes a semi-formal approach to constructing formal software evolution process models and the corresponding descriptions to support software evolution. The approach is expected to be used by software managers, software engineers and stakeholders.

1.3   Research Methods

While pursuing the research outlined in this book, the methodologies of metaphysics and positivism are utilised. Concretely, the following research methods are applied:

(1) Observation and analysis: By comparing and contrasting software evolution with traditional software development, the properties of software evolution and software development are observed. By analysing the similarities and differences between them, the properties of software evolution processes are summarised.

(2) Hypothesis: Any software evolution process is hypothesised to meet the properties summarised. If a software evolution process meta-model and the corresponding description language can model and describe these properties, then they can be regarded as supporting software evolution.

(3) Choice and extension: An appropriate formalism (Petri Net) is chosen to model software evolution processes. If the formalism, called *main formalism*, cannot meet all the preceding properties and requirements of defining software evolution processes, it should be extended and another appropriate formalism (Hoare Logic) should be added and combined into the main formalism.

(4) Design: A software evolution process meta-model and a software evolution process description language are designed to model and describe software evolution processes. The meta-model is defined by means of mathematical methods and the syntax of the language is defined with the Extended Backus-Naur Form.

(5) Methodology: A methodology is proposed to model, describe and improve software evolution processes at different abstract levels.

(6) Validation: By means of case studies, the research is validated to reflect the degree of satisfaction of the requirements of the software evolution processes.

1.4   Success Criteria

A main criterion for the success of software evolution processes is how well they support software evolution. The following criteria are given to judge the success of the research described in this book:

(1) Can the software evolution process models defined by EPMM embody the important properties of software evolution processes?

(2) Can EPDL effectively describe software evolution processes defined by EPMM in detail?

(3) Is the framework of the software evolution processes reasonable? Does it support the descriptions of the software evolution processes at different levels and from different points of view?

(4) Can the approach effectively construct software evolution processes? Does it support the construction of industrial-scale processes? Can the interface consistency of the software processes over hierarchies be preserved?

(5) Can the approach support the reuse of software processes?

(6) Can the functions of tasks be further decomposed so that they are easily realised? Is the correctness of the decompositions preserved?

(7) Does the approach support the efficiency improvement of the software evolution processes? Can the concurrency in software evolution processes be captured and extended?

(8) Is the approach feasible and effective?

1.5   Validation Methods

The following methods are given to validate the proposed approach described in this book:

(1) To judge whether or not the proposed approach meets the success criteria given in Section 1.4;

(2) To compare the results of this research with the work of two of the most influential researchers in the areas of software processes and software evolution processes, Osterweil and Lehman, to judge whether or not the proposed research is innovative;

(3) To judge whether or not the proposed approach reflects the requirements of software evolution processes by means of case studies.

1.6 Outline

The rest of this book is organised as follows:

In Chapter 2, an overview of software processes and software evolution is given. The areas include the software process modelling approach, the software process modelling language, software process improvement, CMM, software process reuse, the process-centred software engineering environment, software reengineering and software evolution.

In Chapter 3, the related work is discussed. This includes the software evolution process, Petri Nets, concurrency in software processes, data dependence analysis and formal functional decomposition.

In Chapter 4, five important properties in software evolution processes are discussed. Iteration and concurrency are analysed in depth. A Petri Net is extended with object-oriented technology and Hoare Logic. According to these analyses, a formal software evolution process meta-model, EPMM, based on the extended Petri Net is designed to define software evolution process models.

In Chapter 5, based on EPMM, an object-oriented software process description language, EPDL, is designed. EPDL extends the descriptive powers of EPMM. The syntax of EPDL is defined with the Extended Backus-Naur Form. The semantics of EPDL are described informally.

In Chapter 6, the framework of the software evolution processes is discussed. The steps of modelling software evolution processes are proposed. An approach to modelling software evolution processes at the global level is proposed. The descriptions of software evolution processes are also discussed.

In Chapter 7, an approach to designing processes and an approach to designing activities are proposed. Three different process reuse techniques are also presented.

In Chapter 8, an approach to designing tasks is proposed. The approach decomposes the function of a task into finer functions, which are easily carried out. Three decomposition rules are proposed and a knowledge base to support decomposition is also designed.

In Chapter 9, in order to improve the efficiency of a software evolution process, an approach to capturing concurrency in a software process is proposed. Furthermore, an approach to extending a local concurrency into a global concurrency is proposed. Finally, based on these results, an approach to reconstructing a software process is also presented.

In Chapter 10, in order to effectively support software evolution processes, a CASE environment EPT (Evolution Process Tool) is designed and a prototype system of EPT is also implemented. The functionality, architecture and data structures of EPT are discussed.

In Chapter 11, four case studies are given to evaluate the proposed approach.

In Chapter 12, the success criteria are revisited and evaluations are discussed by means of comparing the proposed approach with those of Osterweil and Lehman. Based on these discussions, the conclusions of this book are drawn.

Finally, the limitations of the proposed approach and directions for future work are also discussed.

References

[1] Aoyama M (2001) Continuous and discontinuous software evolution: aspects of software evolution across multiple product lines. In: Proceedings of the 4th international workshop on principles of software evolution. ACM Press, New York, pp 87 – 90

[2] Bennett K, Rajlich V (2000) Software maintenance and evolution: a roadmap. In: Proceedings of the conference on the future of software engineering. ACM Press, New York, pp 73 – 87

[3] Lehman MM, Ramil JF (2002) Software evolution and software evolution processes. Annals of Software Engineering 14: 275 – 309

[4] Yang H, Ward M (2003) Successful evolution of software system. Artech House, London

2 Overview of Software Processes and Software Evolution

Tong Li

School of Software, Yunnan University, Kunming, 650091, China
Software Technology Research Laboratory, De Montfort University, Leicester, LE1 9BH, U.K
tli@ynu.edu.cn

Abstract   In this chapter, an overview of the research progress both in software processes and software evolution are presented from the viewpoints of methodologies, technologies, tools and management. Firstly, the basic concepts related to software processes are discussed. In addition, an overview of the research progress in the areas of software process modelling and descriptions, software process modelling languages and description languages, software process improvement, CMM, software process reuse and process-centred software engineering environments is presented. Furthermore, the basic concepts related to software evolution are discussed. Finally, the work in the areas of software evolution and software reengineering is also discussed. The research outlined in this chapter shows that both software evolution and software process have become the hot spots in software engineering. The combination of software evolution and software process will promote smooth and effective software evolution.

Key Words   overview, software process, software evolution, activity, task, software process model, software process description, modelling, modelling language, process improvement, CMM, process reuse, process-centred environment, software reengineering.

Objectives

- To discuss the basic concepts related to software processes and software evolution
- To present an overview of software processes
- To present an overview of software evolution, and
- To give the background of software evolution process

2.1 Introduction

The area of software evolution processes is related to both software evolution and software processes. Software evolution and software processes are two important areas in software engineering. Much progress has been made in these two areas. The research topics include methodologies, technologies, tools and management.

In this chapter, the basic concepts related to software processes are firstly discussed. In addition, the research progress in the areas of software process modelling and descriptions, software process modelling languages and description languages, software process improvement, CMM, software process reuse and process-centred software engineering environments are outlined respectively. Furthermore, the basic concepts related to software evolution are discussed. Finally, the work in the areas of software evolution and software reengineering is also discussed. The research progress gives the background of software evolution process.

2.2 Software Processes

Software processes denote a set of interrelated processes in the software life cycle. A software process provides a framework for managing activities that can very easily get out of control in software development. Different software projects require different software processes. The software development's work products (programs, documentation and data) are produced as consequences of the activities defined by the software processes (Pressman 2000). Boehm indicated that the concept of software process exposed a rich duality between practices that are good for developing products and practices that are good for developing processes. Initially, this focus was primarily on process programming languages and tools, but the concept has been broadened to yield highly useful insights into software process requirements, process architectures, process change management, process families and process asset libraries with reusable and composable process components, enabling more cost-effective realisation of higher software process maturity levels (Boehm 2006).

2.2.1 Concepts of Software Process

The Standard for Information Technology—Software Life Cycle Processes (ISO/IEC 12207 Standard) defines a *software process* as *a set of interrelated activities*, which transform inputs into outputs. Each process is further described in terms of its own constituent activities, each of which is further described in terms of its constituent tasks. An *activity* under a process is *a set of cohesive tasks*. A *task* is expressed in the form of self-declaration, requirement and recommendation or permissible action (ISO and IEC 1998).

The ISO groups the activities that may be performed during the life cycle of software into five primary processes, eight supporting processes and four organisational processes. Each life cycle process is divided into a set of activities; each activity is further divided into a set of tasks (ISO and IEC 1998). These processes are:

(1) Primary processes (ISO and IEC 1998): acquisition process, supply process, development process, operation process and maintenance process

(2) Supporting processes (ISO and IEC 1998): documentation process, configuration management process, quality assurance process, verification process, validation process, joint review process, audit process and problem resolution process

(3) Organisational processes (ISO and IEC 1998): management process, infrastructure process, improvement process and training process

In his pioneering paper (Osterweil 1987), which won the Most Influential Paper of ICSE9 Award in 1997 (Osterweil 1997), Osterweil presented a widely accepted view that *software processes are software too*. He suggested that it is important to create software process descriptions to guide key software processes, that these descriptions should be made as rigorous as possible and that the processes then become guides for the effective application of computing power in support of the execution of processes instantiated from these descriptions (Osterweil 1987).

A *software process model* is a static and abstract representation of a software process. A *software process description* is a detailed and concrete representation of a software process.

There is a key difference between a process and a process description. While a process is a vehicle for doing a job, a process description is a specification of how to do the job. The process itself is a dynamic entity and the process description is a static entity. From the point of view of a computer scientist, the difference can be seen as the difference between a type or class and an instance of that type or class (Osterweil 1987, 1997).

Furthermore, it was suggested that the development of a software product is actually the execution of a process by a collection of agents, some of which are human and some of which are tools. Humans must be employing some powerful process abstractions. The phrase "software process is software too" suggests that the processes by which software is created are a particular type of software, and presumably this is some sort of subtype of the larger universe of software (Osterweil 2003).

Constructing software process models using some approaches is called *software process modelling* (*SPM*). Software process models need to be defined by a meta-model or a modelling language. The former is called the *software process meta-model* and the latter is called the *software process modelling language* (*SPML*). A software process can also be described in detail by a *software process description language* (*SPDL*).

The Object Management Group (OMG) presented a four–layered architecture of modelling, as shown in Fig. 2.1 (OMG 2002), which describes the relationship stated above. A performing process—that is, the real-world production process—as it is enacted, is at level M0. The definition of the corresponding process is at level M1. The meta-model stands at level M2 and serves as a template for level M1. A meta-model is defined as an instance of the MOF (Meta-Object Facility) meta-meta-model (OMG 2002).

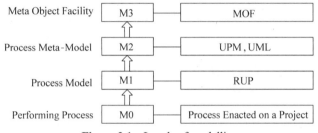

Figure 2.1   Levels of modelling

2.2.2   Software Process Modelling and Descriptions

The approaches to modelling software processes are various, but mainly include top-down and bottom-up approaches. The software process models include the informal, the semi-formal and the formal models. The description tools of software process models include graphs, tables, natural languages, computer languages and mathematical expressions. A process research suggests that graphical process models are useful in raising human awareness and intuition about process characteristics. Unsurprisingly, the most effective models incorporate high-level abstractions that support concise visualisation (Cobleigh *et al.* 2000).

Software process modelling as an effective abstract approach has been receiving more attention recently. Also, there have been a great number of studies in related areas into how various application software modelling formalisms model software processes. For example, Petri Nets, finite state machines and data flow diagrams have been used to model software processes (Bandinelli *et al.* 1993; Fuggetta 2000). Different types of process models are good for different things. In general, models, by their nature, abstract away details in order to focus on specific narrow issues, which are thereby made correspondingly clearer and more vivid (Osterweil 1997, 2003). Process models require articulate support for some characteristics that are not nearly sufficiently prominent in traditional programming languages. They must be articulate in specifying which activities are to be performed

11

by which kinds of agents (Osterweil 2003). Recent progress is discussed as follows:

Kirk's research focused on creating a model that inherently supports the structuring of processes from existing activities. The first contribution is an abstraction of the product that allows activities to be compared. The second is a reduction in problem space for the identification and quantification of the factors that influence how well engineers create and modify software products (Kirk 2004).

Mishali et al. defined aspects to support both software process management and software process modelling. The aspects can monitor, enforce or even partially implement compliance with desired development practices. They also provided a basis for a precise description of a software development process (Mishali and Katz 2006).

Viewing software processes as blueprints emphasises that design is separate from use, and thus that software process designers and users are independent. In Aaen's approach, software processes are viewed as recipes; developers individually and collectively design their own software processes through facilitation, reflection and improvisation (Aaen 2003).

Cangussu et al. presented an approach to modelling the system test phase of the software life cycle. This approach is based on concepts and techniques from control theory and is useful in computing the effort required to reduce the number of errors and the schedule slippage under a changing process environment. Their model might well be a significant milestone along the road to a formal and practical theory of software process control (Cangussu et al. 2002).

The Unified Process uses the Unified Modelling Language when preparing all blueprints of the software system. It is use-case driven, architecture-centric, iterative and incremental. The Unified Process repeats over a series of cycles making up the life of a system. The process has become more and more popular (Jacobson et al. 1999).

Doppke et al. investigated the use of virtual environments—in particular, MUDs (Multi-User Dimensions)—in the domain of software processes. They defined a mapping, or metaphor, that permits the representation of software processes within a MUD. The system resulting from this mapping permits the modelling and execution of software processes by geographically dispersed agents (Doppke et al. 1998).

Some researchers raise a number of questions including: "How can we raise the level of abstraction in which the framework instantiation is expressed, reasoned about and implemented?" "How can the same high-level design abstractions that were used to develop the framework be used during framework instantiation instead of using source code as is done currently?" "How can we define extended design abstractions that can allow framework instantiation to be explicitly represented and validated?" Oliveira et al. presented an approach to framework instantiation based on software processes that addresses these issues. They represented the framework design models in an explicit and declarative way, and supported changes to this design based on explicit instantiation tasks based on software processes while maintaining system integrity, invariants, and general constraints. In this way, the framework instantiation can be performed in a valid and controlled way (Oliveira *et al.* 2004).

Lardjane *et al.* presented an approach to integrate software process models in a distributed context. It is based on the fusion of process fragments (components) defined with the UML notation. The integration methodology allows unifying the various fragments both at the static level as well as at the dynamic level (behavioural). This integration approach provides multiple solutions for the integration conflicts and gives the possibility of improving and designing new software process models by the merging of reusable process fragments (Lardjane and Nacer 2003).

Zhao *et al.* proposed an approach for applying agent technology to software process modelling and process-centred software engineering environments. In their approach, software processes are viewed as the collaboration of a group of process agents that know how to manage the software development activities and can act in the way software developers go about planning, enacting and reflecting on their work (Zhao *et al.* 2005).

Zhang *et al.* presented an architecture-based software process model (ABSP). The ABSP model divides a software process based on the architecture into six sub processes: requirements, design, documentation, review, implementation and evolution. Compared with the traditional software process model, the ABSP model has many advantages such as an explicit structure, easy understandability, better portability and large, reusable granularity (Zhang and He 2003).

Kornstaedt *et al.* presented a concept and prototype tool implementation to systematically capture process knowledge in the form of annotations. These annotations are, upon analysis, integrated into the process model, thus incorporating experience and allowing users to learn from previous experiences (Kornstaedt and Reinert 2002).

The emergence of various software development methodologies raises the need to evaluate and compare their efficiencies. Germain *et al.* performed such a comparison by having different teams apply different process models in the implementation of multiple versions of common specifications (Germain and Robillard 2005).

Moreover, Lehman and his colleagues also made many contributions (Lehman and Ramil 2002) in this area, which will be discussed in the next chapter.

In summary, various efforts have demonstrated that the research into software process modelling and corresponding descriptions is rich and colourful with different aspects being investigated by researchers with different points of view. On the other hand, because of these different points of view, it can be observed that some of the same concepts have some differences in semantics.

2.2.3 Software Process Modelling and Description Languages

Software process modelling languages (*PMLs*) and *process description languages*

(*PDLs*) are the tools for defining software processes. Humans must employ some powerful process abstractions (Osterweil 2003).

Because software processes are complex entities, researchers have created a number of languages that make it possible to represent in a precise and comprehensive way a number of software process features and facets (Fuggetta 2000):

(1) Activities that have to be accomplished to achieve the process objectives (e.g. develop and test a module)

(2) Roles of the people in the process (e.g. the software analyst and project manager)

(3) The structure and nature of the artefacts to be created and maintained (e.g. requirements specification documents, code modules and test cases), and

(4) Tools to be used (e.g. CASE tools and compilers)

Processes must be articulate in specifying which activities are to be performed by which kinds of agents. In cases where humans are to be the agents, the process definition must be careful to present to the human considerable contextual information about the activity to be performed, and to accord the human considerable latitude and choice about how the activity is to be performed (Osterweil 2003). Fuggetta also noted that PML must be tolerant and allow for incomplete, informal and partial specification (Fuggetta 2000).

The area of process modelling and description languages which has been researched energetically by many researchers is discussed as follows.

Osterweil and his colleagues have many achievements in this area. Their first process modelling language based on Ada, APPL/A (Sutton *et al.* 1990, 1995) demonstrated that processes could be defined using a procedural language, but that it was necessary to also provide reactive control constructs in that language. They have adopted a somewhat different approach with the notion of process programming. This approach is based on the idea that processes can be described using the same kind of languages that are exploited to create conventional software. This view has been initially pursued with the development of APPL/A and another language, called Little-JIL (Cass *et al.* 2000), both of which incorporate constructs and concepts typical of different programming languages. Little-JIL is a language for programming coordination in processes and is an executable, high-level language with a formal (yet graphical) syntax and rigorously defined operational semantics. It attempts to resolve the apparently conflicting objectives of providing constructs to support a wide variety of process abstractions such as organisations, activities, artefacts, resources, events, agents, and exceptions and creating a language that is easy to use and understandable by non-programmers (Cass *et al.* 2000).

Cobleigh *et al.* described how FLAVERS, a finite state verification system, has been used to verify properties of processes that have been defined using Little-JIL. It is demonstrated that process abstractions can be quite effective in supporting precise process definitions, but the underlying semantic complexity poses challenges for static analysis (Cobleigh *et al.* 2000).

Lerner described how Little-JIL processes are translated into models and also reported on analysis results which have uncovered seven errors in the Little-JIL interpreter that were previously unknown as well as an error in a software process that had previously been analysed by using a different approach without finding the error (Lerner 2004).

Warboys *et al.* designed a second-generation process language which incorporates significant departures from conventional thinking. Firstly, a process is viewed as a set of mediated collaborations rather than as a set of partially ordered activities. Secondly, emphasis is given to how process models are developed, used and enhanced over a potentially long lifetime. In particular, the issue of composing both new and existing model fragments is central to the development approach (Warboys *et al.* 1999).

Jaccheri *et al.* presented a process modelling language E^3 and a support tool, which are conceived especially for process model elicitation. The E^3 language is an object-oriented modelling language with a graphical notation. In E^3, associations are a means to express constraints and facilitate reuse. The E^3p-draw tool supports the creation and management of E^3 models and provides a view mechanism that enables the inspection of models according to different perspectives (Jaccheri *et al.* 1998).

The work of Nitto *et al.* aims at assessing the possibility of employing a subset of UML as an executable process modelling language. They proposed a formalisation of the semantics of the UML subset and present the translation of UML process models into code, which can be enacted in a process-centred environment. They expected that process modelling by means of UML would be easier and available to a larger community of software process managers (Nitto *et al.* 2002).

Atkinson *et al.* discussed an evolutionary process modelling language that encourages evolutionary model development. They described a tool for performing model verification and used the language and tool on a model for distributed software development (Atkinson *et al.* 2004).

Chen presented a concurrent software process language (CSPL). CSPL takes an approach to integrating the object-oriented Ada95-like syntax (for its modelling power) with UNIX shell semantics (for its enactment capability) in a software process language. The language was specially designed for software processes such as work assignment statements, communication-related statements, role units, tool units and relation units (Chen 1997).

Cook *et al.* developed techniques for uncovering and measuring the discrepancies between models and executions, which is called *process validation*. Process validation takes a process execution and a process model, and measures the level of correspondence between the two. The techniques provide detailed information once a high-level measurement indicates the presence of a problem (Cook and Wolf 1999).

SPADE is an environment that supports the analysis, design and enactment of software processes. SPADE includes a language called SLANG which is a domain-specific language for software process modelling and enactment. A software process is viewed as a set of related activities that are executed concurrently according to their logical precedence and, at the same time, scheduled to meet some global deadlines. The concept of activity is central for the description of a software process (Bandinelli *et al.* 1993).

Sliski *et al.* proposed an approach where the tool utilisation model is specified by a process, written in a process definition language. Their approach incorporates a user-interface specification that describes how the user interface is to respond to, or reflect, progress through the execution of the process definition. It is easy to develop alternative processes that provide widely varying levels and styles of guidance and to be responsive to evolution in the processes, user interfaces or toolset (Sliski *et al.* 2001).

Moreover, Lehman and his colleagues have also made many contributions (Lehman and Ramil 2002) in this area, which will be discussed in the next chapter.

In summary, various software process modelling languages are developed to effectively support software processes and their execution, validation and analysis.

2.2.4 Software Process Improvement and CMM

Software processes cannot be defined once for all. Processes need to be continuously changed and refined to increase their effectiveness and quality to deal with software development. Therefore, software process improvement (SPI) has become a driving force in the software industry.

Process improvement is a comprehensive and continuous activity. It involves not only every basic activity during the process modelling and process implementation but also involves the process measurement, process assessment, process optimisation and control (Jalote 2000; Wang and Leung 2001). Among them, the method of process improvement determines the relevant technologies of implementing the process improvement.

In the areas of software process improvement, much progress has been achieved in the academic community and industry. Currently, there are mainly two kinds of modes to implement process improvement, one is model-driven and the other is measurement-driven (Xu and Qian 2003). The former, such as ISO 9000 and CMM, aims at improving the maturity of an organisation's process capability and implements top-down measurement. It launches relevant improvement activities based on a definite assessment model. The latter constantly collects feedback from the process measurement activities and takes improvement actions to solve the problems produced during the process execution (Conradi and Fuggetta 2002; Xu and Qian 2003).

In process improvement, the CMM (Capability Maturity Model) developed by the Software Engineering Institute (SEI) at Carnegie Mellon University plays an important role. To determine an organisation's current state of process maturity, the SEI uses an assessment that results in a five point grading scheme. The SEI approach provides a measure of the global effectiveness of a company's software engineering practices and establishes five process maturity levels in which the higher level denotes the process improvement in contrast to a lower level. The SEI has associated key process areas (KPAs) with each of the maturity levels. The KPAs describe those software engineering functions (e.g., software project planning, requirements management) that must be present to satisfy good practice at a particular level (Pressman 2000).

The CMMI (Capability Maturity Model Integration) project resulted from the success of the CMM for software. This expansion created challenges: organisations that wished to apply more than one model found that overlaps and conflicts in content and differences in architecture and guidance increased the cost and difficulty of organisation-wide improvement. In addition, new CMMI models have been developed that include supplier sourcing and integrated product and process development (SEI 2004).

CMM quality models and the ISO 9001 standard define the requirements of an ideal company, i.e., a reference model to be used in order to assess the state of a company and the degree of improvement achieved or to be achieved (Fuggetta 2000; Tingey 1997). Based on CMM, considerable progress has been made, discussed as follows.

Beecham et al. described how the requirements engineering (RE) process is decomposed and prioritised in accordance with maturity goals set by CMM. Their R-CMM builds on the SEI's framework by identifying and defining recommended RE sub-processes that meet maturity goals. This new focus tries to help practitioners to define their RE process with a view to setting realistic goals for improvement (Beecham et al. 2005).

Based on CMM, ISO/IEC 15504 and ISO 9000-3 etc., Wu et al. provided a methodology for benchmark-based adaptable software process improvement (MBASPI), and introduced the main components of its support environment (MBASPI/E). With the philosophy of "balance and optimum", through large granular software process reuse, using a software process modelling language to construct the unified models of practical development, and through the enactment of these models under the support environment combined with domain knowledge, software development organisations are forced to comply with some process standards so as to achieve a higher capability maturity level and realise a continuous software process improvement natively (Wu et al. 2004).

Manzoni et al. described an assessment of the Rational Unified Process based on CMM. For each key practice (KP) identified in each key process area (KPA) of CMM levels 2 and 3, the Rational Unified Process was assessed to determine whether it satisfied the KP or not. The assessment resulted in the elaboration of proposals to enhance the Rational Unified Process in order to satisfy the key process areas of CMM (Manzoni and Price 2003).

Knowledge management can be used to support process improvement. Falbo et al. presented the knowledge management approach adopted in an organisation at CMM level 3 to support organisational process tailoring to projects and process improvement based on metric data collected from past projects (Falbo *et al*. 2004).

The progress in the other areas of software process improvement is discussed as follows.

Tianfield proposed an autonomic framework for quantitative software process improvement. Such a framework embodies an autonomic mechanism, which brings forth self-organisation for software process improvement (Tianfield 2003).

Software process improvement could require changes of the process models. Therefore it is important to evaluate the maintainability of these models to facilitate their evolution. Garcia *et al*. presented the results obtained with the replication of an experiment to validate a set of metrics for software process models. As a result, a set of useful indicators of the understandability and modifiability of the software process models has been obtained (Garcia *et al*. 2005).

Jalote *et al*. pointed out that there is an increased interest in using control charts for monitoring and improving software processes, particularly quality control processes like reviews and testing. They developed a cost model for employing control charts for a software process using those optimum control limits that can be determined (Jalote and Saxena 2002).

Gray *et al*. suggested a framework containing a possible sequence of improvement steps. The main conclusion is that an incremental improvement path can be defined using process assessment that commences with questionnaires, then goes on to matrices, workshops, and finally reaches pro-formas. Furthermore, it seems quite plausible that all four types of assessment techniques should be employed on an ongoing basis in a staged fashion (Gray *et al*. 2005).

Nikula *et al*. reported the results of an investigation into the use of the model in a requirements engineering (RE) process improvement from three industrial case studies. A domain-specific method was constructed independently of the utilising companies, i.e. it was outsourced, and it was then used in SPI efforts in the companies to establish a solid infrastructure for basic RE in a short period of time, with limited resources and without previous expertise in RE (Nikula and Sajaniemi 2005).

Xu investigated and found that knowledge is most helpful in improving the effectiveness and efficiency of process tailoring. His study is valuable to the understanding of the role of knowledge in process tailoring, the understanding of the impacts of different types of knowledge on the effectiveness of decision-making in process tailoring and the understanding of the moderating effects of task complexity on the relationships between knowledge support and the performance of process tailoring (Xu 2005).

In summary, considerable efforts have been made to improve software processes in various ways. At the same time, CMM and the ISO 9001 Standard are also accepted in academic research and industry. All these achievements aim to develop software with high quality and high efficiency.

2.2.5   Software Process Reuse

In process reuse, process architecture plays an important role. The purposes of software process architectures include: describing the significant components, structure, internal and external relationships and interfaces; defining graceful evolution paths and the reuse variations required; guiding component selection, adaptation, composition and binding; allowing smooth assembly of the components and connecting them with the surrounding environment and providing compatibility across multiple instances. Architecture must allow the provision of the needed functionality and performance (Redwine 1991).

Aoyama presented a software process architecture that integrates concurrent and asynchronous processes, incremental and iterative process enaction, distributed multi-site processes and people-centred processes. It has the following properties: ① an incremental and evolutionary process, ② a modular and lean process, ③ a time-based process (Aoyama 1998).

Succi *et al.* described a model to define a set of standard reusable processes. They adopted Jacobson's use cases as a starting point and then generated scenarios and identified people and their roles. By adopting activity-based management, it is possible to validate the model directly. This forms the basis for the reengineering process (Succi *et al.* 1997).

Reis *et al.* discussed the need to provide better support for software processes reuse in process-centred software engineering environments. This discussion is influenced by the definition of a meta-model for process modelling, enaction and simulation in an integrated environment (APSEE). This model proposes templates and policies as basic constructs to store generic and reusable knowledge about process models, which are integrated with a search engine based on similarity measurement (Reis *et al.* 2001).

Henninger presented a method that embeds reusable information in a process model that is customised to the specific needs of development efforts. By reusing these processes, projects draw on the collective experiences of the organisation to apply known best practices to specific business requirements. To ensure continuous acquisition of reusable process information, deviations become part of the defined process so that future efforts with similar characteristics can use the same processes (Henninger 1998).

Keller *et al.* focused on the issue of connections among reusable software process elements and components. The difficulties become more severe in cases involving process technology, such as formal representation of processes in a process modelling language, the automated analysis and simulation of processes and automated execution support for processes. They addressed the connection issues that arise across all of these cases, particularly including the challenges that process reuse poses to process technology (Keller 1996).

In summary, the methods of reusing software processes have been attempted by some researchers. However, there are few systematic achievements reported. More attention should be paid to the problem of software evolution process reuse.

2.2.6 Process-Centred Software Engineering Environments

Tools and environments are very important to support software processes. An environment that supports the creation and exploitation of software process models is often called the *process-centred software engineering environment* (*PSEE*). Fuggetta considered that (Fuggetta 2000):

(1) PSEEs must be non-intrusive. It must be possible to deploy them incrementally

(2) A PSEE must tolerate inconsistencies and deviations

(3) A PSEE must provide the software engineer with a clear state of the software development process (from many different viewpoints)

The idea of using a process language to encode a software process as a process model and enacting this using a PSEE is now well established (Fuggetta 2000). Many prototype environments have been developed.

Pohl *et al.* presented the PRIME (Process-Integrated Modelling Environments) framework, which empowers method guidance through process-integrated tools. Process integration of PRIME tools is achieved through ① the definition of tool models, ② the integration of the tool models and the method definitions, ③ the interpretation of the integrated environment model by the tools, the process-aware control integration mechanism and the enactment mechanism, ④ the synchronisation of the tools and the enactment mechanism based on a comprehensive interaction protocol (Pohl *et al.* 1999).

Chou *et al.* described process program change control in the CSPL (Concurrent Software Process Language) environment. They provided an editor to guide the process program change with which the consistency between a change plan and the actual change can be enforced (Chou and Chen 2000). They also proposed a process engine called DPE/PAC (Decentralised Process Engine with Product Access Control). It can be embedded in a PSEE to decentralise the PSEE. In a decentralised PSEE, every site can enact process programs and therefore the workload of the PSEE's sites is balanced (Chou *et al.* 2005).

Serendipity is an environment which provides high-level, visual process-modelling and event-handling languages. Grundy *et al.* described Serendipity's visual languages, support environment, architecture, and implementation, together with experience of using the environment and integrating it with other environments (Grundy and Hosking 1998).

Scheduling a software project is extremely difficult because the time needed to complete a software development activity is hard to estimate. Padberg *et al.* showed how to use process simulation to support software project managers in scheduling. They presented a discrete-time simulator tailored to software projects which explicitly takes a scheduling strategy as input. The simulator provides quick feedback on the progress and completion time of a project (Padberg 2003).

Moreover, Lehman and his colleagues also made many contributions (Lehman and Ramil 2002) in this area which will be discussed in the next chapter. Many software process modelling languages have been realised in PSEEs, as discussed above.

In summary, various PSEEs have been developed to support software processes. The process models and process-based languages play important roles in PSEEs. These achievements have significantly promoted software process modelling, execution, improvement and management.

2.3 Software Evolution

In the context of software, due to the rapid development of software, the demands and costs of software changes are increasing continuously. Software needs to be changed on an ongoing basis with major enhancements required within short timescales (days or weeks rather than months or years). Software changes now comprise a major portion of software life-cycle costs (Yang and Ward 2003). Software evolution through iterative and agile development represents a fundamental departure from the previous waterfall-based paradigm of software engineering (Rajlich 2006).

2.3.1 Concepts of Software Evolution

The term *evolution* generally refers to progressive change in software properties or characteristics. This process of change in one or more of their attributes leads to the emergence of new properties or, in some sense, to improvements. In general, the change will be to adapt the elements of the class so that they maintain or improve their fitness within a changing environment. The change may make them more useful or meaningful or otherwise increase their value in some sense. At the same time, evolution may remove the properties that are no longer appropriate (Lehman and Ramil 2002).

The related concepts also include software reengineering and software maintenance. *Software reengineering* implies that new user-required functions are added to the existing software. Reengineering generally consists of three stages: reverse engineering, functional restructuring and forward engineering. Software evolution is the process of conducting continuous software reengineering. In other words, to a large extent, software evolution is repeated software reengineering (Yang and Ward 2003). Therefore, reengineering can be regarded as an important step and technology during software evolution.

Software maintenance is defined as the modification of a software product after delivery to correct faults, to improve performance or other attributes or to adapt the product to a changed environment (Yang and Ward 2003). Maintenance tries to keep the system performing its function effectively and efficiently. However, maintenance means simply fixing faults in the original implementation. This ignores the problems of rapidly changing environments and requirements. These considerations suggest that the word *maintenance* should be replaced by "*reengineering*" or "*evolution*" (Yang and Ward 2003). Some researchers and practitioners use evolution as a preferable substitute for maintenance (Bennett and Rajlich 2000). From the point of view of a software process, software maintenance can be regarded as fine-grained, local reengineering.

Lehman, who has researched into the topic of software evolution for near forty years, defined an *E-type program* as a computer program that solves a problem in some real-world domain (Lehman and Ramil 2000). He and his colleagues indicated that *E-type software* (E-type software is of particular relevance in the context of evolution since such evolution is inevitable for a program of the E-type as long as it is in regular use) supports *E-type applications* and the latter must also evolve (Lehman and Ramil 2002). Based on these E-type definitions, Lehman presented eight laws of software evolution (Lehman 1997), shown as follows:

Law 2.1 (Lehman 1997)   *Continuing Change*: An E-type program that is used must be continually adapted else it becomes progressively less satisfactory.

Law 2.2 (Lehman 1997)   *Increasing Complexity*: As a program is evolved its complexity increases unless work is done to maintain or reduce it.

Law 2.3 (Lehman 1997)   *Self Regulation*: The program evolution process is self regulating with close to normal distribution of measures of product and process attributes.

Law 2.4 (Lehman 1997)   *Conservation of Organisational Stability* (*Invariant Work Rate*): The average effective global activity rate on an evolving system is invariant over the product lifetime.

Law 2.5 (Lehman 1997)   *Conservation of Familiarity*: During the active life of an evolving program, the content of successive releases is statistically invariant.

Law 2.6 (Lehman 1997)   *Continuing Growth*: Functional content of a program must be continually increased to maintain user satisfaction over its lifetime.

Law 2.7 (Lehman 1997)   *Declining Quality*: E-type programs will be perceived as of declining quality unless rigorously maintained and adapted to a changing operational environment.

Law 2.8 (Lehman 1997)   *Feedback System*: E-type programming processes constitute multi-loop, multi-level feedback systems and must be treated as such to be successfully modified or improved.

2.3.2   Software Reengineering

As an important technology, software reengineering has been paid great attention.

Much progress has been achieved, discussed as follows.

Aversano *et al.* proposed an approach to extracting the requirements for a legacy system evolution from the requirements of the e-Business process evolution. The approach aims to characterise the software system within the whole environment in which its evolution will be performed (Aversano and Tortorella 2003).

Jeyaraman *et al.* presented an experience in reengineering a legacy application into a web based J2EE system with a modified Rational Unified Process. They have demonstrated that the development process could be improved with lessons learnt from the initial iterations (Jeyaraman *et al.* 2003).

Bianchi *et al.* proposed a reengineering process model, which is applied to an in-use legacy system to confirm that the process satisfies previous requirements and to measure its effectiveness. The reengineered system replaced the legacy one to the satisfaction of all the stakeholders; the reengineering process also had a satisfactory impact on the quality of the system (Bianchi *et al.* 2003).

Capilla *et al.* described the process of creation of a product-line using reengineering techniques for evolution and maintenance, from already available products, applied to the web domain (Capilla and Duenas 2003).

Yang and his colleagues have carried out extensive research into software reengineering. Their work is described as follows:

They advocated that extracting formal specifications semantically consistent to the original legacy system will greatly facilitate further redesign and forward engineering. The key approach to the comprehension and production of a formal specification is a notion of abstraction. A unified approach for reverse engineering was described within which the notion of abstraction is classified and precisely defined. Abstraction rules were given and applied to various case studies (Yang *et al.* 2000).

It is widely accepted that reverse engineering has three components: restructuring, comprehension and the production of formal specifications. They advocated that the three components could be achieved using a systematic approach by successfully applying a series of sound rules. A unified approach for reverse engineering was described within which the notion of abstraction is classified and precisely defined (Yang *et al.* 1998).

They proposed an approach through executable stepwise abstraction. A semi-automatic tool environment was built to abstract the target system into higher-level views more quickly to improve the efficiency and to stepwise abstract the subsystems of the target system first and then to further abstract the higher-level view of the subsystems into the full view of the target system. Their approach attempts to maximise the automation with the assistance of abstraction rules and abstraction pattern assertions (Liu *et al.* 2000).

They also considered ontology to be composed of four elements: classes, relations, functions and instances. They showed that these four elements forming the ontology for a legacy system can be extracted from the code of the concerned system using the existing software reengineering tools. They then presented their vision of how the obtained ontology can be applied to understanding and eventual better reengineering of the legacy systems (Yang *et al.* 1999).

They were endeavouring to discover new approaches to developing reverse engineering metrics for software engineers who desperately need them when reverse engineering legacy systems. Their major work is the presentation of a systematic research base and a hierarchical approach to the development of software metrics for reverse engineering (Zhou *et al.* 1999).

They advocated the concept of "simplicity" for program understanding. They proposed a simplified semantic network as domain knowledge representation, and then introduced a linear and domain-oriented program partitioning method, which can partition a huge program into self-contained program modules so that the recovery of domain knowledge can be carried out within a smaller program space. They also introduced a set of rules for recovering domain knowledge from C code followed by a theoretical analysis on these algorithms (Li and Yang 2001).

They matched a software program with a pre-defined domain knowledge base in the representation of a simplified semantic network in order to link the source program with its domain-level interpretation. Moreover, a domain-oriented program partitioning method was also proposed in order to partition a program into self-contained modules of manageable size. In these ways, the computational complexity involved in generating the linkage is significantly reduced, which makes this approach usable (Li *et al.* 2000).

They introduced an approach to recovering domain knowledge with enhanced reliability from source code. In particular, they divided domain knowledge into interconnected knowledge slices and matched these knowledge slices against the source code. Moreover, the knowledge slices were arranged to exchange beliefs with each other through interconnections so that a better evaluation of the authenticity of these knowledge slices can be obtained (Li *et al.* 2001). The recovered ambiguous domain knowledge slices are fused together and an invented dual-way belief propagation method was used to improve the reliability of recovered domain knowledge (Li *et al.* 2001).

An innovative approach was introduced to wrapping semi-structured web pages in order to generate structured data. The approach is based on human design psychology that captures more stable features in web pages. They focused on the product advertisement domain so that a set of design psychology principles for product advertisement was presented and used to design the wrapping rules (Li *et al.* 2002).

They presented an approach to bridging legacy systems to MDA (Model Driven Architecture), which has three contributions: a suitable architecture description language for architecture recovery, the relevant abstraction rules and the integration of reverse engineering with MDA (Qiao *et al.* 2003).

In addition, they also presented a unified software reengineering methodology based on MDA. The methodology consists of a framework, a process and related techniques (Yang 2005).

In summary, software reengineering has played an important role during software evolution. Much effort has been expended in this area. It can be forecast that software reengineering will promote the methodologies, technologies, management and processes of software evolution.

2.3.3   Software Evolution

As an important area, software evolution is related to methodologies, technologies and management. Progress has been made as follows:

In the area of software evolution with component technologies, Mehta *et al.* proposed an evolution methodology that integrates the concepts of features, regression tests and component-based software engineering (Mehta and Heineman 2002).

Casanova *et al.* proposed an approach to supporting evolution in component-based development using component libraries (Casanova *et al.* 2003).

Ye *et al.* presented a UML-based technique that attempts to help resolve difficulties introduced by the implementation transparent characteristics of component-based software systems. For corrective maintenance activities, the technique starts with UML diagrams that represent changes to an evolving component and uses them to support regression testing (Ye and Offutt 2003).

Iida *et al.* analysed software evolution in component-based software developments. They adopted two aspects to characterise software evolution: functional and non-functional. These two aspects construct a two-dimensional evolution space, which can be nicely handled by component-based algebraic specification (Iida and Futatsugi 2000).

Wang *et al.* proposed a component-based approach to online software evolution. An application server is used to evolve the application, without special support from the compiler or operating system (Wang *et al.* 2006).

In the area of concrete techniques, Lavery *et al.* explored the incremental evolution of existing systems by building web-based, value-added services upon foundations derived from analysing and modelling the existing legacy systems (Lavery *et al.* 2004).

Ernst *et al.* focused on dynamic techniques for discovering invariants from execution traces. In program from program derivation, the system rediscovered predefined invariants. In a C program lacking explicit invariants, the system discovered invariants that assisted a software evolution task (Ernst *et al.* 2001).

Fortiz *et al.* proposed the use of two formalisms to manage evolution: a language based on Past Predicate Temporal Logic (PPTL) and Coloured Petri Nets (CPN). Both formalisms allow the structure and behaviour of a system to be specified in the same way and to decide when a system can run or when it can evolve depending on its functioning and structure in the past. A correspondence relationship is established between both formalisms. It allows CPN to be used to reason about the integrity of the systems which evolve (Fortiz and Llorca 2001).

Antonio *et al.* presented a method to build and maintain the traceability links and properties of a set of object-oriented software evolution. The method recovers an "as is" design, compares recovered designs at the class interface level and helps the user to deal with inconsistencies by pointing out regions of code where differences are concentrated (Antonio *et al.* 2001).

Sametinger *et al.* made use of the notation of patterns, aspects and traces for a homogeneous documentation approach to integrate various types of documentation, keep track of traces from requirements to the source code, keep design information in the source code and generate additional design views on software systems so that the evolution can be conducted easily (Sametinger and Riebisch 2002).

Software evolution visualisation is a promising technique for assessing the software development process. Voinea *et al.* studied how complex correlations of software evolution attributes can be made using multivariate visualisation techniques. They proposed two new methods to generate relevant abstraction levels in a hierarchical clustering of software evolution artefacts (Voinea and Telea 2006).

In the area of software evolution based on metrics, Lanza proposed an approach based on a combination of software visualisation and software metrics which have already been successfully applied in the field of software reverse engineering. Using this approach they discussed a simple and effective way to visualise the evolution of software systems that helps to recover the evolution of object-oriented software systems (Lanza 2001).

Subramanian *et al.* proposed a framework called the POMSAE, Process-Oriented Metrics for Software Architecture Evolvability, which will help not only to intuitively develop architectural evolvability metrics but also to trace the metrics back to the evolvability requirements. This will then help analyse the reasons for the strengths/weaknesses in the metrics (Subramanian and Chung 2003).

Aoyama proposed a set of metrics for software architecture evolution and discussed continuous and discontinuous software evolution with the metrics proposed. He claimed that discontinuity arises to reengineer software architecture and is an essential aspect of software evolution. The evolution dynamics with discontinuity reveals the non-homogeneous nature of software evolution over space and time (Aoyama 2002).

Gustafsson *et al.* showed how software metrics and architectural patterns can be used for the management of software evolution. The quality of a software system is assured in the software design phase by computing various kinds of design metrics from the system architecture, by automatically exploring instances of design patterns and anti-patterns from the architecture and by reporting potential quality problems to the designers (Gustafsson *et al.* 2002).

In summary, as more and more successful software systems become legacy systems, software evolution has become an important characteristic in software engineering.

2.4   Summary

Nowadays, software systems change continuously with the changes in techniques and requirements. This promotes software systems from the less-mature to the mature. The research outlined above shows that both software evolution and software process have become the hot spots in software engineering. The research into software evolution and software process is related to methodologies, technologies, tools and management. It can be predicated that a combination of software evolution and software process will promote smooth and effective software evolution.

References

[1] Aaen I (2003) Software process improvement: blueprints versus recipes. IEEE Software 20: 86 – 93

[2] Antonio G, Canfora G, Casazza G, Lucia AD (2001) Maintaining traceability links during object-oriented software evolution. Software-Practice and Experience 31: 331 – 355

[3] Aoyama M (1998) Agile software process and its experience. In: Proceedings of the 20th international conference on software engineering. IEEE Computer Society, Washington DC, pp 3 – 12

[4] Aoyama M (2002) Metrics and analysis of software architecture evolution with discontinuity. In: Proceedings of the international workshop on principles of software evolution. ACM Press, New York, pp 103 – 107

[5] Atkinson DC, Weeks DC, Noll J (2004) The design of evolutionary process modeling languages. In: Proceedings of the 11th Asia-Pacific software engineering conference. IEEE Computer Society, Washington DC, pp 73 – 82

[6] Aversano L, Tortorella M (2003) Evolving legacy system toward e-legacy system in e-business context. In: Proceedings of the 7th European conference on software maintenance and reengineering. IEEE Computer Society, Washington DC, pp 201 – 210

[7] Bandinelli S, Fuggetta A, Grigolli S (1993) Process modeling in-the-large with SLANG. In: Proceedings of the 2nd international conference on software process. IEEE Computer Society Press, Washington DC, pp 75 – 83

[8] Beecham S, Hall T, Rainer A (2005) Defining a requirements process improvement model. Software Quality Control 13: 247 – 279

[9] Bennett K, Rajlich V (2000) Software maintenance and evolution: a roadmap. In: Proceedings of the conference on the future of software engineering. ACM Press, New York, pp 73 – 87

[10] Bianchi A, Caivano D, Marengo V, Visaggio G (2003) Iterative reengineering of legacy systems. IEEE Transactions on Software Engineering 29: 225 – 241

[11] Boehm B (2006) A view of 20th and 21st century software engineering. In: Proceedings of the 28th international conference on software engineering. ACM Press, New York, pp 12 – 29

[12] Cangussu JW, De Carlo RA, Mathur AP (2002) A formal model of the software test process. IEEE Transactions on Software Engineering 28: 782 – 796

[13] Capilla R, Duenas JC (2003) Light-weight product-lines for evolution and maintenance of web sites. In: Proceedings of the 7th European conference on software maintenance and reengineering. IEEE Computer Society, Washington DC, pp 53 – 62

[14] Casanova M, Straeten RV, Jonckers V (2003) Supporting evolution in component-based development using component libraries. In: Proceedings of the 7th European conference on software maintenance and reengineering. IEEE Computer Society, Washington DC, pp 123 – 132

[15] Cass AG, Lerner BS, McCall EK, Osterweil LJ, Sutton SM, Wise A (2000) Little-JIL/Juliette: a process definition language and interpreter. In: Proceedings of the 22nd international conference on software engineering. ACM Press, New York, pp 754 – 757

[16] Chen JYJ (1997) CSPL: An Ada95-like, Unix-based process environment. IEEE Transactions on Software Engineering 23: 171 – 184

[17] Chou S, Chen J (2000) Process program change control in a process environment. Software - Practice and Experience 30: 175 – 197

[18] Chou S, Hsu W, Lo W (2005) DPE/PAC: decentralized process engine with product access control. Journal of Systems and Software 76: 207 – 219

[19] Cobleigh JM, Clarke LA, Osterweil LJ (2000) Verifying properties of process definitions. In: Proceedings of the 2000 ACM SIGSOFT international symposium on software testing and analysis. ACM Press, New York, pp 96 – 101

[20] Conradi R, Fuggetta A (2002) Improving software process improvement. IEEE Software 19: 92 – 99

[21] Cook JE, Wolf AL (1999) Software process validation: quantitatively measuring the correspondence of a process to a model. ACM Transactions on Software Engineering and Methodology 8: 147 – 176

[22] Doppke JC, Heimbigner D, Wolf AL (1998) Software process modeling and execution within virtual environments. ACM Transactions on Software Engineering and Methodology 7: 1 – 40

[23] Ernst MD, Cockrell J, Griswold WG, Notkin D (2001) Dynamically discovering likely program invariants to support program evolution. IEEE Transactions on Software Engineering 27: 99 – 123

[24] Falbo RA, Borges LSM, Valente FFR (2004) Using knowledge management to improve software process performance in a CMM level 3 organization. In: Proceedings of the 4th international conference on quality software. IEEE Computer Society, Washington DC, pp 162 – 169

[25] Fortiz MJR, Llorca JP (2001) Using predicate temporal logic and coloured Petri Nets to specifying integrity restrictions in the structural evolution of temporal active systems. In: Proceedings of international symposium on principles of software evolution. IEEE Computer Society, Washington DC, pp 83 – 87

[26] Fuggetta A (2000) Software process: a roadmap. In: Proceedings of the conference on the future of software engineering. ACM Press, New York, pp 25 – 34

[27] Garcia F, Piattini M, Ruiz F, Visaggio CA (2005) Maintainability of software process

models: an empirical study. In: Proceedings of the 9th European conference on software maintenance and reengineering. IEEE Computer Society, Washington DC, pp 246 – 255

[28] Germain É, Robillard PN (2005) Engineering-based processes and agile methodologies for software development: a comparative case study. Journal of Systems and Software 75: 17 – 27

[29] Gray E, Sampaio A, Benediktsson O (2005) An incremental approach to software process assessment and improvement. Software Quality Control 13: 7 – 16

[30] Grundy JC, Hosking JG (1998) Serendipity: integrated environment support for process modelling, enactment and work coordination. Automated Software Engineering 5: 27 – 60

[31] Gustafsson J, Paakki J, Nenonen L, Verkamo A (2002) Architecture-centric software evolution by software metrics and design patterns. In: Proceedings of the 6th European conference on software maintenance and reengineering. IEEE Computer Society, Washington DC, pp 108 – 115

[32] Henninger S (1998) An environment for reusing software processes. In: Proceedings of the 5th international conference on software reuse. IEEE Computer Society, Washington DC, pp 103 – 112

[33] Iida S, Futatsugi K (2000) Formal approach for handling software evolution in component-based software developments. In: Proceedings of international symposium on principles of software evolution. IEEE Computer Society, Washington DC, pp 252 – 271

[34] ISO, IEC (1998) ISO/IEC 12207 standard for information technology — software life cycle processes

[35] Jaccheri M, Picco GP, Lago P (1998) Eliciting software process models with the E^3 language. ACM Transactions on Software Engineering and Methodology 7: 368 – 410

[36] Jacobson I, Booch G, Rumbaugh J (1999) The unified software development process. Addison-Wesley, London

[37] Jalote P (2000) CMM in practice: process for executing software projects at information systems. Addison-Wesley, Los Angeles

[38] Jalote P, Saxena A (2002) Optimum control limits for employing statistical process control in software process. IEEE Transactions on Software Engineering 28: 1126 – 1134

[39] Jeyaraman G, Krishnamurthy K, Raveendra V (2003) Reengineering legacy application to E-business with modified Rational unified process. In: Proceedings of the 7th European conference on software maintenance and reengineering. IEEE Computer Society, Washington DC, pp143 – 150

[40] Keller MI (1996) Connecting reusable software process elements and components. In: Proceedings of the 10th international software process workshop. IEEE Computer Society, Washington DC, pp 8 – 11

[41] Kirk D (2004) A flexible software process model. In: Proceedings of the 26th international conference on software engineering. IEEE Computer Society, Washington DC, pp 57 – 59

[42] Kornstaedt UB, Reinert R (2002) A concept to support process model maintenance through systematic experience capture. In: Proceedings of the 14th international conference on software engineering and knowledge engineering. ACM Press, New York, pp 465 – 468

[43] Lanza M (2001) The evolution matrix: recovering software evolution using software visualization techniques. In: Proceedings of the 4th international workshop on principles

of software evolution. ACM Press, New York, pp 37 – 42

[44] Lardjane N, Nacer MA (2003) Distributed software process models: an integration methodology. In: Proceedings of ACS/IEEE international conference on computer systems and applications. IEEE Computer Society, Washington DC, p 44

[45] Lavery J, Boldyreff C, Ling B, Allison C (2004) Modelling the evolution of legacy systems to web-based systems. Journal of Software Maintenance and Evolution: Research and Practice 16: 5 – 30

[46] Lehman MM (1997) Laws of software evolution revisited. In: Lecture notes in computer science 1149. Springer, Berlin, pp 108 – 124

[47] Lehman MM, Ramil JF (2000) Towards a theory of software evolution and its practical impact. In: Proceedings of international symposium on the principles of software evolution. IEEE Computer Society, Washington DC, pp 2 – 11

[48] Lehman MM, Ramil JF (2002) Behavioural modelling of long-lived evolution processes: some issues and an example. Journal of Software Maintenance: Research and Practice 14: 335 – 351

[49] Lehman MM, Ramil JF (2002) Software evolution and software evolution processes. Annals of Software Engineering 14: 275 – 309

[50] Lerner BS (2004) Verifying process models built using parameterized state machines. In: Proceedings of the 2004 ACM SIGSOFT international symposium on software testing and analysis. ACM Press, New York, pp 274 – 284

[51] Li Y, Cui Z, Yang H, Jiau HC (2002) Tolerating changes in a design psychology based web page wrapper. In: Proceedings of the 26th international computer software and applications conference. IEEE Computer Society, Washington DC, pp 399 – 404

[52] Li Y, Yang H (2001) Simplicity: a key engineering concept for program understanding. In: Proceeding of the 9th international workshop on program comprehension. IEEE Computer Society, Washington DC, pp 98 – 107

[53] Li Y, Yang H, Chu W (2000) Generating linkage between source code and evolvable domain knowledge for the ease of software evolution. In: Proceedings of international symposium on principles of software evolution. IEEE Computer Society, Washington DC, pp 196 – 205

[54] Li Y, Yang H, Chu W (2001) A concept-oriented belief revision approach to domain knowledge recovery from source code. Journal of Software Maintenance and Evolution: Research and Practice 13: 31 – 52

[55] Li Y, Yang H, Chu W, Cheng X, Cui Z (2001) Improving the reliability of knowledge mining in legacy code by utilising cooperative information. International Journal of Fuzzy Systems 3: 390 – 399

[56] Liu X, Yang H, Zedan H, Cau A (2000) Speed and scale up software reengineering with abstraction patterns and rules. In: Proceedings of international symposium on principles of software evolution. IEEE Computer Society, Washington DC, pp 90 – 99

[57] Manzoni LV, Price RT (2003) Identifying extensions required by RUP (Rational unified process) to comply with CMM levels 2 and 3. IEEE Transactions on Software Engineering 29: 181 – 192

[58] Mehta A, Heineman GT (2002) Evolving legacy system features into fine-grained

components. In: Proceedings of the 24th international conference on software engineering. ACM Press, New York, pp 417 – 427

[59] Mishali O, Katz S (2006) Using aspects to support the software process: XP over eclipse. In: Proceedings of the 5th international conference on aspect-oriented software development. ACM Press, New York, pp 169 – 179

[60] Nikula U, Sajaniemi J (2005) Tackling the complexity of requirements engineering process improvement by partitioning the improvement task. In: Proceedings of the 2005 Australian conference on software engineering. IEEE Computer Society, Washington DC, pp 48 – 57

[61] Nitto ED, Lavazza L, Schiavoni M, Tracanella E, Trombetta M (2002) Deriving executable process descriptions from UML. In: Proceedings of the 24th international conference on software engineering. ACM Press, New York, pp 155 – 165

[62] Oliveira TC, Alencar PSC, Filho IM, Lucena CJPD, Cowan DD (2004) Software process representation and analysis for framework instantiation. IEEE Transactions on Software Engineering 30: 145 – 159

[63] OMG (2002) Software process engineering metamodel specification. Object Management Group

[64] Osterweil LJ (1987) Software processes are software too. In: Proceedings of the 9th international conference on software engineering. ACM Press, New York, pp 2 – 13

[65] Osterweil LJ (1997) Software processes are software too, revisited: an invited talk on the most influential paper of ICSE 9. In: Proceedings of the 19th international conference on software engineering. ACM Press, New York, pp 540 – 548

[66] Osterweil LJ (2003) Understanding process and the quest for deeper questions in software engineering research. ACM SIGSOFT Software Engineering Notes 8: 6 – 14

[67] Padberg F (2003) A software process scheduling simulator. In: Proceedings of the 25th international conference on software engineering. IEEE Computer Society, Washington DC, pp 816 – 817

[68] Pohl K, Weidenhaupt K, Dömges R, Haumer P, Jarke M, Klamma R (1999) PRIME— toward process-integrated modeling environments. ACM Transactions on Software Engineering and Methodology 8: 43 – 410

[69] Pressman RS (2000) Software engineering: a practitioner's approach (ed5). McGraw Hill, New York

[70] Qiao B, Yang H, Chu W, Xu B (2003) Bridging legacy systems to model driven architecture. In: Proceedings of the 27th annual international conference on computer software and applications. IEEE Computer Society, Washington DC, pp 304 – 309

[71] Rajlich V (2006) Changing the paradigm of software engineering. Communications of the ACM 49: 67 – 70

[72] Redwine ST (1991) Software process architecture issues. In: Proceedings of the 7th international software process workshop. IEEE Computer Society, Washington DC, pp 117 – 120

[73] Reis RQ, Reis CAL, Nunes DJ (2001) Automated support for software process reuse: requirements and early experiences with the APSEE model groupware. In: Proceedings of the 7th international workshop on groupware. IEEE Computer Society, Washington DC, pp 50 – 57

[74] Sametinger J, Riebisch M (2002) Evolution support by homogeneously documenting patterns, aspects and traces. In: Proceedings of the 6th European conference on software maintenance and reengineering. IEEE Computer Society, Washington DC, pp 134 – 140

[75] SEI (2004) 2004 Software Engineering Institute annual report. http://www.sei.cmu.edu/annual-report/files/2004_SEI_AnnualReport.pdf

[76] Sliski TJ, Billmers MP, Clarke LA, Osterweil LJ (2001) An architecture for flexible, evolvable process-driven user-guidance environments. In: Proceedings of the 8th European software engineering conference held jointly with 9th ACM SIGSOFT international symposium on foundations of software engineering. ACM Press, New York, pp 33 – 43

[77] Subramanian N, Chung L (2003) Process-oriented metrics for software architecture evolvability. In: Proceedings of the 6th international workshop on principles of software evolution. IEEE Computer Society, Washington DC, pp 65 – 70

[78] Succi G, Benedicenti L, Predonzani P, Vernazza T (1997) Standardizing the reuse of software processes. Standard View 5: 74 – 83

[79] Sutton SM Jr, Heimbigner DM, Osterweil LJ (1990) Language constructs for managing change in process-centered environments. In: Proceedings of the 4th ACM SIGSOFT symposium on software development environments. ACM Press, New York, pp 206 – 217

[80] Sutton SM Jr, Heimbigner DM, Osterweil LJ (1995) APPL/A—a language for software-process programming. ACM Transactions on Software Engineering and Methodology 4: 221 – 286

[81] Tianfield H (2003) An autonomic framework for quantitative software process improvement. In: Proceedings of IEEE international conference on industrial informatics. IEEE Computer Society, Washington DC, pp 446 – 450

[82] Tingey MO (1997) Comparing ISO 9000, Malcolm Baldrige, and the SEI CMM for software. Prentice Hall, New York

[83] Voinea L, Telea A (2006) multiscale and multivariate visualizations of software evolution. In: Proceedings of the 2006 ACM symposium on software visualization. ACM Press, New York, pp115 – 124

[84] Wang Q, Shen J, Wang X, Mei H (2006) A component-based approach to online software evolution. Journal of Software Maintenance and Evolution: Research and Practice 18: 181 – 205

[85] Wang X, Leung HKN (2001) A benchmark-based adaptable software process model. In: Proceedings of the 27th Euromicro conference workshop on software process and product improvement. IEEE Computer Society, Washington DC, pp 216 – 224

[86] Warboys BC, Balasubramaniam D, Greenwood RM, Kirby GNC, Mayes K, Morrison R, Munro DS (1999) Collaboration and composition: issues for a second generation process language. In: Proceedings of the 7th European software engineering conference held jointly with the 7th ACM SIGSOFT international symposium on foundations of software engineering. Springer-Verlag, London, pp 75 – 90

[87] Wu M, Ying J, Yu C (2004) A methodology and its support environment for benchmark-based adaptable software process improvement. In: Proceedings of IEEE international conference on systems, man and cybernetics. IEEE Computer Society, Washington DC, pp 5183 – 5188

[88] Xu P (2005) Knowledge support in software process tailoring. In: Proceedings of the 38th annual Hawaii international conference on system sciences. IEEE Computer Society, Washington DC, pp 87 – 95

[89] Xu R, Qian L (2003) CMM-based software risk control optimization. In: Proceedings of the 2003 IEEE international conference on information reuse and integration. IEEE Computer Society, Washington DC, pp 499 – 503

[90] Yang H (2005) Software evolution with UML and XML. Idea Group Publishing, London

[91] Yang H, Cui Z, O'Brien P (1999) Extracting ontologies from legacy systems for understanding and re-engineering. In: Proceedings of the 23rd annual international computer software and applications conference. IEEE Computer Society, Washington DC, pp 21 – 26

[92] Yang H, Liu X, Zedan H (1998) Tackling the abstraction problem for reverse engineering in a system re-engineering approach. In: Proceedings of conference on software maintenance. IEEE Computer Society, Washington DC, pp 284 – 293

[93] Yang H, Liu X, Zedan H (2000) Abstraction: a key notion for reverse engineering in a system reengineering approach. Journal of Software Maintenance: Research and Practice 12: 197 – 228

[94] Yang H, Ward M (2003) Successful evolution of software system. Artech House, London

[95] Ye W, Offutt J (2003) Maintaining evolving component-based software with UML. In: Proceedings of the 7th European conference on software maintenance and reengineering. IEEE Computer Society, Washington DC, pp 133 – 142

[96] Zhang Y, He Y (2003) Architecture-based software process model. ACM SIGSOFT Software Engineering Notes 28: 1 – 5

[97] Zhao X, Chan K, Li M (2005) Applying agent technology to software process modeling and process-centered software engineering environment. In: Proceedings of the 2005 ACM symposium on applied computing. ACM Press, New York, pp 1529 – 1533

[98] Zhou S, Yang H, Luker P, He X (1999) A useful approach to developing reverse engineering metrics. In: Proceedings of the 23rd international computer software and applications conference. IEEE Computer Society, Washington DC, pp 320 – 321

3   Related Work

Tong Li

School of Software, Yunnan University, Kunming, 650091, China
Software Technology Research Laboratory, De Montfort University, Leicester, LE1 9BH, U.K
tli@ynu.edu.cn

Abstract   Software evolution processes have been receiving more attention recently and much progress has been made. In this chapter, an overview in the inter-disciplinary area both of software process and software evolution is firstly presented. In addition, the work related to this book, including concurrency in the software life cycle, Petri Nets, data dependence analysis and formal functional decomposition, is also discussed. The related work mentioned above indicates that although a variety of methodologies, technologies, tools and managements has been developed, little work has been done on constructing formal process models and the corresponding descriptions to support software evolution. The formal evolution process models are more rigorous and more precise than the informal models and easier to realise in computers. The formal definitions which will be used as the work fundamentals in the following chapters are also presented. This chapter aims to establish the research basis of this book.

Key Words   overview, software evolution process, evolution process model, evolution process description, concurrency, concurrent development, Petri Net, occurrence net, data dependence, dependence analysis, functional decomposition, Hoare Logic, precondition, postcondition.

Objectives

- To discuss the work related to the software evolution process
- To discuss the work related to concurrency in the software life cycle
- To discuss the work related to Petri Nets
- To discuss the work related to data dependence analysis
- To discuss the work related to formal functional decomposition, and
- To establish the research basis from the related work

3.1 Introduction

The area of software evolution process, as the name suggests, has two aspects: software evolution and software process. In this chapter, the related work in the inter-disciplinary area both of software process and software evolution is discussed. After that, the related work on concurrency in the software life cycle, Petri Nets, data dependence analysis and formal functional decomposition is also discussed.

Although a variety of methodologies, technologies, tools and managements has been developed, little work has been done on constructing formal process models and the corresponding descriptions to support software evolution with concurrency and iteration. Formalisms in the software evolution process provide a means to construct precise, abstract models and detailed descriptions which establish the basis of simulation, analysis and improvement.

3.2 Software Evolution Process

The term *software evolution process* denotes the software process under which the corresponding software is evolving. The term *evolution process model* denotes a static and abstract representation of a software evolution process and the term *evolution process description* denotes a static, detailed and concrete representation of a software evolution process. Software evolution processes are a subset of software processes.

The area of software evolution process is related with methodologies, technologies, tools, management and documentation. Different software evolutions require different software evolution processes. The software evolution's work products (programs, documentation and data) are produced as consequences of the activities defined by the software evolution processes. In the recent past, many researchers have paid more attention to and devoted great efforts in this area and have made great progress.

In the aspects of theory and practice of software evolution and evolution process, much progress has been made by Lehman, Ramil and their colleagues. The results that include eight laws of software evolution in project FEAST/1 and FEAST/2 (Feedback, Evolution And Software Technology) (Lehman and Ramil 2000, 2002) have been produced based on more than thirty years of observation and interpretation. There now exists a deeper understanding of the software process and, especially, of the nature and impact of feedback at both management and technical levels. They suggest feedback as a basis for direct relationships between the laws. Their work is summarised as follows:

They explored the phenomenon in depth by modelling the evolution of a number of industrial projects using both black box and system dynamics techniques.

They expected also to demonstrate the impact of feedback on process behaviour and improvement (Lehman and Ramil 1999).

They described a high-level system dynamics model of a real-world software evolution process. The work states that software evolution processes are feedback systems (Chatters *et al*. 2000).

They described a series of system dynamics models developed during the FEAST investigation into software evolution processes. Whereas the earlier models simulated real-world processes with the intention of increasing the understanding of these processes, the work reported is the first step towards simulating the effects of the decisions made by the managers of these processes (Kahen *et al*. 2001).

They described some of the facets of the evolution phenomenon and their implications for the evolution process as identified during many years of active interest in the topic (Lehman and Ramil 2002).

They described a system dynamics model that can serve as the core of a tool to support decision-making regarding the optimal personnel allocation over the system lifetime (Lehman and Ramil 2002).

They argued that quantitative process models can play an important role in seeking sustained improvement of E-type software evolution processes and summarises some of the experiences gained in the FEAST projects to date. They also provided modelling guidelines (Ramil *et al*. 2000).

In addition, they presented a modelling approach. It emphasises simple models that provide a basis for evolution planning and management tools. The results suggest that it is meaningful to search for this kind models (Lehman *et al*. 2001).

Ramil's models aim at capturing the relationship among effort, productivity and a suite of metrics of software evolution extracted from empirical data sets (Ramil 2000).

They presented a case study relating to the evolution of the kernel of a mainframe operating system in which six models based on eight different indicators of evolution activity were proposed (Ramil and Lehman 2000).

They reported on the derivation of qualitative versions from two existing quantitative models of the software evolution process and indicated how this has led to the identification of previously unrecognised behaviours. They showed how qualitative trend abstraction enables a high level of abstraction analysis of empirical data and that, at this level, the empirical patterns observed in several different software systems display similarities (Ramil and Smith 2002).

Wernick *et al*. described a high-level system dynamics model of a real-world software evolution process. The simple feedback-based model demonstrates the influence of the global process on the evolution of the software specification and implementation (Wernick and Lehman 1999).

Their models are then combined into a single simulation model reflecting the effect in a combination of these causes (Wernick and Hall 2002).

Other research in this area is also colourful, discussed as follows:

Rausch presented a model that handles the fundamental structural and behavioural aspects of component-ware and object-orientation. Based on the model, a clear definition of a software evolution step is provided. Each evolution step implies changes of an appropriate set of development documents. Developers are able to track and manage the software evolution process and to recognise and avoid failures due to software evolution (Rausch 2000).

Akkanen *et al.* focused on the major evolution steps, their rationale and their outcomes, hoping that this gives some relevant insight into the issues that are important for software component evolution and maintenance (Akkanen *et al.* 2002).

Tomer *et al.* presented an evolution-oriented three-dimensional model. The model can be used to describe the life cycle of a product line, the evolution of an individual product within that product line and the evolution of an individual artefact (Tomer and Schach 2002).

Harn *et al.* aimed to formalise the software evolution process via a relational hypergraph model with primary-input-driven and secondary-input-driven dependency approaches. Software evolution processes are modelled by a multidimensional architecture containing successive software evolution steps and related software evolution components (Harn *et al.* 1999).

WSL is a wide-spectrum language proposed by Ward (Ward 1989) which covers the whole spectrum from abstract mathematical specifications to executable implementation. Yang *et al.* developed and experimented with a process for software evolution (Yang and Ward 2003). The process has the following stages (Yang and Ward 2003):

(1) To translate source code into EWSL (Extended WSL)

(2) To restructure (including clustering and visualising code)

(3) To abstract

(4) To understand with the support of a cognitive tool

(5) To reuse components

(6) To retarget, and

(7) To measure evolution

In addition, the author of this book and his colleagues also presented an approach to searching for concurrency in a software evolution process according to dependence analysis between activities, to capture activities that can be executed concurrently and then to constructing a software process model defined as a Petri Net. If the concurrency in a software process is local, then an approach to extending the concurrency is presented too (Li *et al.* 2004).

To summarise, increasing attention has been paid to the software evolution process with many achievements concerning the natures, impacts, models, tools and simulations etc, particularly due to the extensive work carried out by Lehman and his colleagues. However, modelling formal software evolution processes based on a meta-model has not been discussed adequately.

3.3 Concurrency in the Software Life Cycle

The user requirements have been increasing remarkably. In order to meet these requirements, a long-term effort to increase the effectiveness of software development and evolution has been needed. If the activities in software processes can be executed concurrently, it is no doubt that the efficiency will be increased. For a long time, much attention has been paid to developing software concurrently.

Concurrency is a widespread characteristic. Most published software development models present software engineering as a series of discrete phases. They often capture the "inevitable intertwining" of pairs of phases and they often capture the need to return to earlier phases when new information is ascertained. However, in fact, software development is a concurrent process. In actual software development projects, activities typically associated with multiple phases are performed concurrently (Aoyama 1993; Davis and Sitaram 1994; Kellner 1991). Concurrent activities exist at any stage in software development processes; for example, the module code, tests, and test execution report all exist concurrently. These activities can be carried out in an unspecified concurrent fashion, such as by interleaving them (Humphrey and Kellner 1989). It is possible that the activities in the software development process overlap and parallel. Not only can the end of the preceding activity overlap the beginning of a latter activity, but also the preceding activities can overlap the latter activities fully as long as the contents of the activities are different (Raccoon 1997; Ronald 1996).

Davis *et al.* presented a software development process model based on state charts that effectively captures the concurrency among activities. Not only does it show the concurrency among the activities performed by software engineers, but also the concurrency among the diverse activities performed by software engineers, managers, and reviewers (Davis and Sitaram 1994).

Aoyama constructed a concurrent development process model based on waterfall model and developed a large communication system based on the concurrent development process model. The model lets a user develop multiple functions concurrently over the entire development process. The model aims to shorten the development cycle and to speed up the development (Aoyama 1993).

Kellner uses state charts to represent the concurrent relationship that existed among activities associated with a specific event, but fails to capture the richness of concurrency that exists across all software development and management activities in any project (Kellner 1991).

In addition, the author of this book and his colleagues combined the object-oriented technology and the evolutionary prototyping approach into concurrent software development and proposed an object-oriented concurrent evolutionary software development model OOCESD. In order to reduce the complexity of concurrent development, we also proposed the concurrent control model CCM and designed a CASE system, CCM-CASE, which supports concurrent development along with computer-aided concurrent control and scheduling (Li and Wang 1998). We also presented a method of modelling and performance analysis for a concurrent development process (Zhao *et al*. 2005).

In summary, concurrency has been widely accepted and applied in software development. As during software development, during software evolution also, many activities can be executed concurrently. This is an important approach to increasing evolution efficiency. Therefore, concurrency must be paid more attention in software evolution processes. This is an important reason why Petri Nets are chosen as the main formalism to model software evolution processes in this book.

3.4 Petri Nets

Petri Nets are graphical formalisms which have gained popularity as tools for the representation of complex logical interactions (like synchronisation, sequentiality, concurrency and conflict) among activities in a system or a process. They have been used to describe a wide range of fields since their invention in 1962 by Petri in his Ph.D. thesis. The fields of application of Petri Nets include (ISO and IEC 2004):

(1) Requirements analysis
(2) Development of specifications, designs and test suites
(3) Descriptions of existing systems prior to reengineering
(4) Modelling business and software processes
(5) Providing the semantics for concurrent languages
(6) Simulation of systems to increase confidence, and
(7) Formal analysis of the behaviour of critical systems

Petri Nets may be applied to the design of a broad range of systems and processes, including air traffic control, avionics, banking, biological and chemical processes, business processes, communication protocols, computer hardware architectures, control systems, databases, defence command and control, distributed computing, electronic commerce, fault tolerant systems, hospital procedures, information systems, Internet protocols and applications, legal processes, logistics, manufacturing systems, metabolic processes, music, nuclear power systems, operating systems, transport systems, security systems, space, telecommunications and workflow (ISO and IEC 2004).

In the areas of software engineering, Petri Nets are used for the specification, documentation and communication of software systems and processes, especially of concurrent systems. When you execute Petri Nets, the behaviour of the systems and processes can be simulated and visualised. Furthermore, the validation, verification and analysis both of systems and processes can also be carried out.

In comparison with other system models, the major characteristics of Petri Nets are as follows (Reisig 1985):

(1) Causal dependencies and independencies in some set of events may be represented explicitly. Events which are independent of each other are not projected onto a linear timescale. Instead, a non-interleaving, partial order relation of concurrency is introduced. This relation is fundamental for the whole conceptual basis of Petri Net theory (Reisig 1985).

(2) Systems may be represented at different levels of abstraction without having to change the description language. These levels of abstraction range from the change of single bits in computer memories to the embedding of a computer system into its environment (Reisig 1985).

(3) Petri Net representations make it possible to verify system properties and to do correctness proofs in a specific way. Once a system has been modelled as a net, properties of the system may be represented by similar means, and correctness proofs may be built using the methods of net theory (Reisig 1985).

Informally, a Petri Net consists of places (or conditions), transitions (or events, activities), flow relation and marking (tokens). Execution of Petri Nets is nondeterministic, since multiple transitions can be enabled at the same time. In general, Petri Nets can be divided into four classes, discussed as follows:

(1) Petri Nets are characterised by places which can represent Boolean values, i.e. a place is marked by at most one unstructured token (Bernardinello and De Cindio 1992).

Typical Petri Nets of this class include the Condition/Event (C/E) Systems proposed by Petri, Elementary Net (EN) Systems and 1-safe systems. The transition rule of 1-safe systems is given according to P/T systems but that a place is restricted to be marked by at most one unstructured token (Bernardinello and De Cindio 1992).

(2) Petri Nets are characterised by places which can represent integer values, i.e. a place is marked by a number of unstructured tokens (Bernardinello and De Cindio 1992).

Typical Petri Nets of this class include Place/Transition (P/T) Systems and Ordinary Petri Nets (PN). P/T Systems allow a place to carry several tokens to flow along the arcs. Ordinary Petri Nets (PN) are a special kind of P/T system which restrict that only one token is allowed to flow along the arcs each time (Bernardinello and De Cindio 1992).

The P/T systems have been one of the more widely used Petri Nets. However, the P/T systems have been questioned because there are some difficulties in interpreting them. For P/T systems, different token games are possible; i.e. different transition occurrence rules can be defined. These differences are considered from the perspective of the distributed software implementations of P/T systems. This leads to more frequent restriction of the P/T systems to 1-safe systems (Bernardinello and De Cindio 1992).

(3) Petri Nets are characterised by places which can represent high-level values, i.e. a place is marked by a multi-set of structured tokens (Bernardinello and De Cindio 1992).

Petri Nets of this class are called high-level Petri Nets. A problem with Petri Nets is the explosion of the number of elements of their graphical form when they are used to describe complex systems. High-level Petri Nets were developed to overcome this problem by introducing higher-level concepts, such as the use of complex structured data as tokens, and using algebraic expressions to annotate net elements (ISO and IEC 2004).

Typical Petri Nets of this class include Predicate-Transition Nets and Coloured Petri Nets. Furthermore, an ISO standard ISO/IEC 15909 is built on Predicate-Transition Nets and Coloured Petri Nets. It also uses some of the notions developed for Algebraic Petri Nets. It is believed that this standard captures the spirit of these earlier developments (ISO and IEC 2004).

(4) Petri Nets are modified and extended (Murata 1989).

Typical Petri Nets of this class include Petri Nets with inhibitor arcs, Timed Nets and Stochastic Nets.

In Petri Nets with inhibitor arcs, an inhibitor arc connects a place to a transition. The inhibitor arc disables the transition when the input place has a token and enables the transition when the input place has no token and other input places have at least one token. The introduction of inhibitor arcs adds the ability to test "zero" (i.e., absence of tokens in a place) and increases the modelling power of Petri Nets to the level of Turing Machines. It has been shown that there are systems that cannot be modelled without introducing inhibitor arcs (Murata 1989).

It is necessary and useful to introduce time delays associated with transitions and/or places in Petri Nets. Such a Petri Net is known as a (deterministic) Timed Net if the delays are deterministically given, or as a Stochastic Net if the delays are probabilistically specified (Murata 1989).

Also there have been many other Petri Nets defined for different purposes in the past decade (Petri Nets World 2005), such as Free Choice Nets S-Systems, State Machines (SM), T-System, Marked Graphs (MG), Structural Free Choice Extensions, High-Level Petri Nets with Abstract Data Types (HL+ADT), OBJSA Nets, Environment Relationship (ER) Nets, Product (Prod) Nets, Well-Formed (Coloured) Nets (WN), Regular Nets (RN) (Petri Nets World 2005), continuous Petri Nets, FIFO nets, place/transactor (PTA) nets, self-modifying nets, a hierarchy of nets (Murata 1989), Dynamic Petri Net, Object Composition Petri Net (OCPN), Extended OCPN (XOCPN), Prioritised Petri Net (P-Net), Distributed OCPN (DOCPN), Enhanced Prioritised Petri Net (EP-Net) (Tan and Guan 2005) and STRPN (Spatial and Temporal Relationship Petri Nets) (Hsu et al. 2003). In general, each of these Petri Nets belongs to one of the classes stated above.

Holloway et al. pointed out that Petri Nets have a greater modelling power than finite state machines. However, computability theory shows that the increase of modelling power often leads to an increase in the computation required to solve problems (Holloway et al. 1997). In general, the simple Petri Nets as compared to complex Petri Nets may prove helpful in modelling. A trade-off between modelling power and formal analysis power is necessary; the more general the model, the less amenable it is to analysis (Murata 1989). Simple Petri Nets often lead to more elegant results and simpler algorithms.

The Petri Nets used in this book are based on class 1. The reasons are as follows:

(1) Petri Nets can accurately describe concurrency and iteration, which are essential to software evolution processes.

(2) Petri Nets are formalisms and can be easily visualised in graphical form compared to communication sequential processes (CSP). Petri Nets are better at describing concurrency than UML, although UML can also be applied to describe software evolution processes.

(3) In contrast to concurrent programs, the granularity of activities in software evolution processes is coarser. The control logic is also simpler than that in concurrent programs. For example, the ISO/IEC 12207 Standard only defines 17 processes and 74 activities. The average activity number of each process is 4.4. Although the ISO/IEC standard is not always obeyed, it provides a clue that it is not necessary to use very complex Petri Nets to model software evolution processes.

(4) The adopted Petri Net can lead to simple models which are easily to be reconstructed. This is carried out more difficultly in complex Petri Nets.

(5) The proposed approach makes use of conflict to simulate the selection in software evolution processes. This is easier to implement for the adopted Petri Net than for a P/T system, which might lead to a selection becoming a concurrency if the tokens in the preset of a transition are more than one.

(6) A ready-made Petri Net is not simply adopted. However, object-oriented technology and Hoare Logic are complemented to the adopted Petri Net to extend its modelling power and convenience. It is believed that the extended Petri Net captures the spirit of Petri Nets. The extended Petri Net is used to model software evolution processes at the process level.

(7) Predicate Nets are a kind of powerful Petri Nets in which predicate formulae are used to describe different tokens representing resources. They also lack the capability of describing functions which are essential to describing tasks. Therefore, Hoare Logic must be added. Specification statements are effective means to define functions which are similar to Hoare Logic but with different notations (Yang and Ward 2003). When Hoare Logic is utilised to describe the functions of tasks, specification statements will not be necessary to be utilised in the proposed approach.

(8) The problem of state space explosion of Petri Nets is coped with by means of hierarchically constructing models (nets) level by level.

The main definitions of Petri Nets applied in this book are as follows:

Definition 3.1 (Reisig 1985)   A triple $N = (C, A; F)$ is called a *net* iff

(1) C and A are disjoint sets;

(2) $F \subseteq (C \times A) \cup (A \times C)$ is a binary relation, the *flow relation* of N.

In this book, the elements in C denote the conditions to fire and the elements in A denote the activities in software evolution processes which will be further discussed in Chapter 4.

Definition 3.2 (Reisig 1985)   Let $N = (C, A; F)$ be a net.

(1) For $x \in N$,

$^{\bullet}x = \{y \mid yFx\}$ is called the *preset* of x;

$x^{\bullet} = \{y \mid xFy\}$ is called the *postset* of x.

(2) For $X \subseteq N$, let

$$^{\bullet}X = \bigcup_{x \in X} {}^{\bullet}x \quad \text{and}$$

$$X^{\bullet} = \bigcup_{x \in X} x^{\bullet}.$$

(3) A pair $(c, a) \in C \times A$ is called a *self-loop* iff $cFa \wedge aFc$. N is called *pure* iff F does not contain any self-loops.

(4) $x \in N$ is called *isolated* iff $^{\bullet}x \cup x^{\bullet} = \emptyset$.

(5) N is called *simple* iff $\forall x, y \in N$: $(^{\bullet}x = {}^{\bullet}y \wedge x^{\bullet} = y^{\bullet}) \Rightarrow x = y$.

Definition 3.3 (Reisig 1985)   Let $N = (C, A; F)$ be a net.

(1) A subset $c \subseteq C$ is called a *case*.

(2) Let $a \in A$ and $c \subseteq C$, a has *concession* in c (is *c-enabled*) iff $^{\bullet}a \subseteq c \wedge a^{\bullet} \cap c = \emptyset$.

(3) Let $a \in A$, let $c \subseteq C$ and let a be c-enabled. $c' = (c - {}^{\bullet}a) \cup a^{\bullet}$ is called the *follower case* of c under a (c' results from the *occurrence* of a in the case c). This is written as $c[a > c'$. Sometimes, for the sake of convenience, $c[a > c'$ is also written as $[a > c'$ or $c[a >$ or $[a >$ for short if some cases are not attended.

Definition 3.4 (Reisig 1985)   Let $N = (C, A; F)$ be a net.

(1) A set $G \subseteq A$ is called *detached* iff $\forall e_1, e_2 \in G$: $(e_1 \neq e_2) \Rightarrow {}^{\bullet}e_1 \cap {}^{\bullet}e_2 = \emptyset = e_1^{\bullet} \cap e_2^{\bullet}$.

(2) Let c and c' be cases of N and let G be detached. G is called a *step* from c to c' (notation: $c[G > c']$) iff each $e \in G$ is c-enabled and $c' = (c - {}^{\bullet}G) \cup G^{\bullet}$. Sometimes, for the sake of convenience, $c[G > c'$ is also written as $[G > c'$ or $c[G >$ or $[G >$ for short if some cases are not attended.

(3) Let c and c' be cases of N. If $c[e_1 > \wedge c[e_2 > \wedge \neg c[\{e_1, e_2\} >$, e_1 and e_2 are called to be in *conflict* with each other.

Definition 3.5 (Reisig 1985)   A net $k = (S, T; F)$ is called an *occurrence net* iff

(1) $\forall a, b \in S \cup T$: $a(F^+)b \Leftrightarrow \neg(bF^+a)$; $(F^+ = F \cup F \circ F \cup F \circ F \circ F \cup \cdots)$

(2) $\forall s \in S$: $|{}^{\bullet}s| \leq 1 \wedge |s^{\bullet}| \leq 1$.

An occurrence net can be used to describe an execution record of a net (Reisig 1985). The execution records are essential to the analysis of software processes. This will be further discussed in Definition 4.6 and Section 4.6.

3.5   Dependence Analysis

In 1966, Bernstein stated a sufficient condition for the independence of two sections of a program. Suppose R_i (W_i) is the set of variables read (written) by a section of code i. *Bernstein's Condition* states that sections i and j may be executed in an arbitrary order, or concurrently if there are no dependences among the statements in the sections, i.e. if $R_i \cap W_j = \emptyset$, $W_i \cap R_j = \emptyset$ and $W_i \cap W_j = \emptyset$. Dependence is the relationship of a calculation B to a calculation A if changes to A, or to the ordering of A and B, could affect B. If A and B are calculations in a program, for example, then B is dependent on A if B uses values calculated by A. There are four types of dependence: *true dependence*, where B uses values calculated by A; *anti dependence*, where A uses values overwritten by B; *output dependence*, where both A and B write to the same variables and *control dependence*, where B's execution is controlled by values set in A (Bernstein 1966; Hawick 2005).

There are also other dependences defined which are similar, but different from those stated above. Program dependences are dependence relationships between statements in a program that are implicitly determined by the control and data flows in the program. Program dependence analysis is an analysis technique to identify various program dependences in program source codes (Ferrante *et al.* 1987). It has been used in various software activities including program understanding (Horwitz and Reps 1992), testing, debugging, maintenance and complexity measurement (Podgurski and Clarke 1990).

The presence of dependence between two entities implies that they cannot be executed concurrently. The fewer the dependencies are, the greater the concurrency is.

In this book, the notion of dependence is used for reference and extended into software processes and the notions of activity dependences and of task dependences are proposed as tools to capture and extend concurrency.

3.6   Formal Functional Decomposition

A formal function specification is a description of what a software system does. The function specification must be clear and accurate. It does not describe how a software system works, but just describes what it does. For a long time, much progress has been made in this area. Attempts have been made to implement the transformation and verification from the function specification to design and from design to coding.

In the logic-based area, logic is used to describe the system's desired properties, including the low-level specification, temporal and probabilistic behaviours. The logic can be augmented with some concrete programming constructs to obtain what is known as wide-spectrum formalism. The transformation is achieved by a set of correctness-preserving refinement steps (Yang and Ward 2003), e.g. FermaT (Ward 1996).

Hoare Logic may be viewed as an extension of first-order predicate calculus that includes inference rules for reasoning about programming language constructs

(Hoare 1969). Hoare Logic provides a means of demonstrating that a program is consistent with its specification. Hoare Logic is not capable of specifying a system at a high level; however, it has distinct advantages for low-level specifications (Yang and Ward 2003). In Hoare Logic, the Hoare triple "$\{P\}$ S $\{Q\}$" is used to describe the semantics of program S, whilst P and Q denote predicates that describe properties of the variables that occur in S. P is called a *precondition* for S and Q is called a *postcondition* for S. The Hoare triple denotes that if P is true before S is executed and the execution of S terminates, then Q is true after the execution of S (Hein 2003). Hoare Logic does not make sure that S terminates. *Partial correctness* is defined as that $\{P\}$ S $\{Q\}$ is true if whenever S terminates after starting in an initial state that satisfies P then the final state will satisfy Q. *Total correctness* is defined as partial correctness with termination (Hein 2003). Therefore, Hoare Logic only handles partial correctness (Hoare 1969).

The similar work in this area includes the "weakest precondition" proposed by Dijkstra (Dijkstra 1976; Dijkstra and Scholten 1990), which is a suitable formalism in software specification and transformation. A weakest precondition describes the initial state of a program and a postcondition describes the final state. By using the semantics of predicate logic and other suitable formal logic, the method can carry out the program transformation (Dijkstra 1976; Dijkstra and Scholten 1990). The weakest precondition method can make sure of the termination of a program.

There are two approaches to proving the total correctness. One is to judge whether the program terminates, such as the method based on a well-ordered set and the method based on counters. These methods prove a program to terminate by means of proving that each loop in the program is only executed a finite number of times. Another approach is to combine the program termination into an axiom system, such as Dijkstra's weakest precondition method. The method defines an axiom system based on Hoare Logic in which the weakest precondition is prescribed to make sure the program terminates.

The WSL (Wide Spectrum Language) transformation theory proposed by Ward (Ward 1989) can handle total correctness. Ward used weakest preconditions, expressed as formulae in infinitary logic, to prove refinement and equivalence between programs. WSL covers the whole range of operations from general specifications to assignments, jumps and labels. He developed theorems for proving the termination of recursive and iterative programs, transforming specifications into recursive programs and transforming recursive procedures into iterative equivalents. He developed a rigorous framework for reasoning about programs with exit statements that terminate nested loops from within; and this forms the basis for many efficiency-improving and restructuring transformations. These are used as a tool for program analysis and to derive algorithms by transforming their specifications (Ward 1989).

The author of this book and his colleagues also presented an approach to decomposing assertions into Java codes (Li *et al.* 2005). We also designed an object-oriented requirements specification language OORSL and proposed a corresponding approach to transforming a formal function specification defined by OORSL into a Java program framework (Li *et al*. 2005).

When modelling software evolution processes, sometimes it is necessary to decompose a formal function into some functions with finer granularity so that these finer functions are easily realised. In such a case, formal transformation and decomposition can be applied. In this book, the precondition and the postcondition based on Hoare Logic are used to describe the function of a task in a software evolution process. Based on functional decomposition, a pair of precondition and postcondition can be transformed into a series of finer pairs of precondition and postcondition that are easily realised.

3.7 Summary

Software evolution processes have been receiving more attention recently and much progress has been made. However, the formal software process models to support software evolution have rarely been discussed. The formal evolution process models are more rigorous and precise than the informal models and easier to be realized in computers.

This book aims to semi-formally construct formal software process models and descriptions to support software evolution. The following conclusions can be drawn which will become the research clues of this book:

(1) The properties of software evolution processes must be analysed in depth.

(2) More attention must be paid to the importance of modelling, description, feedback, dynamics, simulation, improvement, visualisation and model simplicity.

(3) Formalisms must be further adopted.

In order to achieve the goals and establish the research basis for the approach proposed in this book, Petri Nets, decomposition based on Hoare Logic, dependence analysis and concurrency in the software life cycle are used.

References

[1] Akkanen J, Kiss AJ, Nurminen JK (2002) Evolution of a software component-experience with a network editor component. In: Proceedings of the 6th European conference on software maintenance and reengineering. IEEE Computer Society, Washington DC, pp 119 – 125

[2] Aoyama M (1993) Concurrent-development process model. IEEE Software 10: 46 – 55

[3] Bernardinello L, De Cindio F (1992) A survey of basic net models and modular net classes. In: Lecture notes in computer science 609. Springer-Verlag, Berlin, pp 304 – 351

[4] Bernstein AJ (1966) Analysis of programs for parallel processing. IEEE Transactions on Electron Computer 15: 757 – 763

[5] Chatters BW, Lehman MM, Ramil JF, Wernick P (2000) Modelling a software evolution process: a long-term case study. Journal of Software Process: Improvement and Practice 5: 95 – 102

[6] Davis AM, Sitaram PA (1994) A concurrent process model of software development. ACM SIGSOFT Software Engineering Notes 19: 38 – 51

[7] Dijkstra EW (1976) A discipline of programming. Prentice Hall, Engliwood Cliffs

[8] Dijkstra EW, Scholten CS (1990) Predicate calculus and program semantics. Springer-Verlag, Berlin

[9] Ferrante J, Ottenstein KJ, Warren JD (1987) The program dependence graph and its use in optimization. ACM Transactions on Programming Languages and Systems 9: 319 – 349

[10] Harn M, Berzins V, Luqi, Mori A (1999) Software evolution process via a relational hypergraph model. In: Proceedings of 1999 IEEE/IEEJ/JSAI international conference on intelligent transportation systems. IEEE Computer Society, Washington DC pp 599 – 604

[11] Hawick K (2005) High performance computing and communications glossary 2.1. http://wotug.ukc.ac.uk/parallel/acronyms/hpccgloss

[12] Hein JL (2003) Discrete mathematics. Jones and Bartlett Publishers, Boston

[13] Hoare CAR (1969) An axiomatic basis for computer programming. Communications of the ACM 12: 576 – 580

[14] Holloway LE, Krogh BH, Giua A (1997) A survey of Petri Net methods for controlled discrete event systems. Discrete Event Dynamic Systems: Theory and Applications 7: 151 – 190

[15] Horwitz S, Reps T (1992) The use of program dependence graphs in software engineering. In: Proceedings of the 14th international conference on software engineering. ACM Press, New York, pp 392 – 411

[16] Hsu P, Chang Y, Chen Y (2003) STRPN: a Petri-Net approach for modeling spatial-temporal relations between moving multimedia objects. IEEE Transactions on Software Engineering 29: 63 – 76

[17] Humphrey W, Kellner MI (1989) Software process modeling: principles of entity process models. In: Proceedings of the 11th international conference on software engineering. ACM Press, New York, pp 331 – 342

[18] ISO, IEC (2004) ISO/IEC 15909-1 standard for software and system engineering—high-level Petri Nets—part 1: concepts, definitions and graphical notation

[19] Kahen G, Lehman MM, Ramil JF, Wernick PD (2001) System dynamic modelling of software evolution processes for policy investigation: approach and example. Journal of system and software 59: 271 – 281

[20] Kellner MI (1991) Software process modeling support for management planning and control. In: Proceedings of the 1st international conference on the software process. IEEE Computer Society, Washington DC, pp 8 – 28

[21] Lehman MM, Ramil JF (1999) The impact of feedback in the global software process. Journal of Systems and Software 46: 123 – 134

[22] Lehman MM, Ramil JF (2000) Towards a theory of software evolution and its practical impact. In: Proceedings of international symposium on the principles of software evolution. IEEE Computer Society, Washington DC, pp 2 – 11

[23] Lehman MM, Ramil JF (2002) Behavioural modelling of long-lived evolution processes: some issues and an example. Journal of Software Maintenance: Research and Practice 14: 335 – 351

[24] Lehman MM, Ramil JF (2002) Software evolution and software evolution processes. Annals of Software Engineering 14: 275 – 309

[25] Lehman MM, Ramil JF, Sandler U (2001) An approach to modelling long-term growth trends in software systems. In: Proceedings of international conference on software maintenance. IEEE Computer Society, Washington DC, pp 219 – 228

[26] Li T, Wang L (1998) A study on object-oriented software concurrent development technology. In: Proceedings of the 27th international conference and exhibition on technology of object-oriented languages and systems. International Academic Press, Beijing, pp 88 – 93

[27] Li T, Yang H, Jiang J (2004) Mining for concurrency in software process for evolution. In: Proceedings of the 10th joint international computer conference. International Academic Press, Beijing, pp 478 – 483

[28] Li T, Yang H, Xu B, Shi L (2005) An approach to decomposing assertions into Java codes. In: Proceedings of the 2005 international conference on information and knowledge engineering. CSREA Press, Las Vegas, pp 185 – 191

[29] Li T, Yang H, Xu B, Shi L (2005) An approach to transforming parallel function specification into Java program framework. In: Proceedings of the 2005 international conference on software engineering research and practice. CSREA Press, Las Vegas, pp 517 – 523

[30] Murata T (1989) Petri Nets: properties, analysis and applications. Proceedings of the IEEE 77: 541 – 580

[31] Petri Nets World (2005) A classification of Petri Nets. http://www.Informatik.uni-hamburg.de/TGI/PetriNets/classification

[32] Podgurski A, Clarke LA (1990) Formal model of program dependences and its implications for software testing, debugging, and maintenance. IEEE Transactions on Software Engineering 16: 965 – 979

[33] Raccoon LBS (1997) Fifty years of progress in software engineering. ACM SIGSOFT Software Engineering Notes 22: 88 – 104

[34] Ramil JF (2000) Algorithmic cost estimation for software evolution. In: Proceedings of the 22nd international conference on software engineering. ACM Press, New York, pp 701 – 703

[35] Ramil JF, Lehman MM (2000) Metrics of software evolution as effort predictors - a case study. In: Proceedings of the international conference on software maintenance. IEEE Computer Society, Washington DC, pp163 – 172

[36] Ramil JF, Lehman MM, Kahen G (2000) The FEAST approach to quantitative process modelling of software evolution processes. In: Proceedings of the 2nd international conference on product focused software process improvement. Springer-Verlag, London, pp 311 – 325

[37] Ramil JF, Smith N (2002) Qualitative simulation of models of software evolution. Journal of Software Process: Improvement and Practice 7: 95 – 112

[38] Rausch A (2000) Software evolution in component ware using requirements/assurances contracts. In: Proceedings of the 22nd international conference on software engineering. ACM Press, New York, pp 147 – 156

[39] Reisig W (1985) Petri Nets: an introduction. Springer-Verlag, Berlin

[40] Ronald JN (1996) Object-oriented system analysis and design. Prentice Hall, New York

[41] Tan R, Guan S (2005) A dynamic Petri Net model for iterative and interactive distributed multimedia presentation. IEEE Transactions on Multimedia 7: 869 – 879

[42] Tomer A, Schach SR (2002) A three-dimensional model for system design evolution. Systems Engineering 5: 264 – 273

[43] Ward M (1989) Proving program refinements and transformations. D. Phil thesis, Oxford University

[44] Ward M (1996) Program analysis by formal transformation. Computer Journal 39: 596 – 618

[45] Wernick P, Hall T (2002) Simulating global software evolution processes by combining simple models: an initial study. Software Process: Improvement and Practice 7: 113 – 126

[46] Wernick P, Lehman MM (1999) Software process white box modelling. Journal of Systems and Software 46: 193 – 201

[47] Yang H, Ward M (2003) Successful evolution of software system. Artech House, London

[48] Zhao N, Zhao Y, Li T (2005) A method of modelling and performance analysis for concurrent development process of software. In: Proceedings of the 11th joint international computer conference. World Scientific, New Jersey, pp 803 – 809

4 Software Evolution Process Meta-Model EPMM

Tong Li

School of Software, Yunnan University, Kunming, 650091, China
Software Technology Research Laboratory, De Montfort University, Leicester, LE1 9BH, U.K
tli@ynu.edu.cn

Abstract   A software evolution process meta-model is a formal tool used to define software evolution processes. In this chapter, a software evolution process meta-model EPMM is designed. Firstly, five important properties in software evolution processes are discussed. Especially, two properties—iteration and concurrency—are analysed in depth. Furthermore, a Petri Net is extended with object-oriented technology and Hoare Logic. In this case, a formal software evolution process meta-model, EPMM, which is based on the extended Petri Net, is proposed. In EPMM, not only are the structures and behaviours of all important components, e.g. tasks, activities and software processes in software evolution processes, formally defined, but also the important properties of software evolution process are embodied. Therefore, EPMM can model software evolution processes at different abstract levels. Thus, the basis to simulate, control, analyse, measure and improve software evolution processes is established.

Key Words   meta-model, EPMM, property, iteration, concurrency, change, feedback-driven, multi-level framework, Petri Net, Hoare Logic, process, sub-process, activity, task, assertion, object, class, message, execution, global model, cycle.

Objectives

- To discuss the properties of the software evolution process
- To analyse the iteration in the software evolution process
- To analyse the concurrency in the software evolution process
- To design a software evolution process meta-model EPMM
- To define the structures and behaviours of components in the software evolution process, and
- To indicate that EPMM embodies the properties of the software evolution process

4.1   Introduction

A software evolution process model is an abstract and static representation of a software evolution process. A software evolution process can be executed or enacted manually (its activities are executed by human users), semi-automatically (by cooperation between human users and computers) or automatically (by computers or devices). The representation of an evolution process can be informal, semi-formal and formal. A formal model or description establishes the basis of automation process execution.

Software evolution process modelling as an effective abstract approach has been receiving more attention recently. Petri Nets, finite state machines and data flow diagrams as meta-models have been used to model software processes (Bandinelli et al. 1993; Fuggetta 2000). Different types of process models are good for different things. In general, models, by their nature, abstract away details in order to focus on specific narrow issues, which are thereby made correspondingly clearer and more vivid (Osterweil 1997, 2003). Process models require articulate support for some characteristics that are not nearly sufficiently prominent in traditional programming languages. They must be articulate in specifying which activities are to be performed by which kinds of agents (Osterweil 2003). However, software evolution process meta-models are rarely discussed.

A software evolution process meta-model is a formal tool which is used to define software evolution processes. In this chapter, a software evolution process meta-model EPMM is designed.

The goals of EPMM embody how it should capture the important aspects of a software evolution process in order to represent the process properly. In order to fulfil the goals, the following work is accomplished. Firstly, five important properties in software evolution processes are discussed. Especially, two properties—iteration and concurrency—are analysed in depth. Furthermore, a Petri Net is extended; upon the preceding analyses, a formal software evolution process meta-model EPMM based on the extended Petri Net is proposed. In EPMM, the structures and behaviours of all the important components in software evolution processes, such as tasks, activities and software processes are formally defined. Using these definitions, software evolution processes can be modelled. Finally, it is indicated that EPMM embodies the five proposed properties of software evolution processes.

EPMM is based on the extended Petri Net strengthened with object-oriented technology and Hoare Logic. It can represent software evolution processes at different abstract levels. Based on these models, the basis to simulate, control, analyse, measure and improve software evolution processes is established.

4.2 Properties of Software Evolution Processes

During software evolution, the changes at various granularities occur continuously or discontinuously. An evolution process model must embody the properties of evolution and be able to define more dynamic components than with traditional development so that the changes can be described. By observation and analysis, it is found that the following properties exist in software evolution processes:

(1) Iteration. Because of continuous changes in software evolution (Lehman 1997; Yang and Ward 2003), many activities and sets of activities are executed repeatedly with higher frequency than in traditional software development. Iteration becomes an obvious phenomenon in software evolution processes.

(2) Concurrency. There are many concurrent activities at different granularities in software evolution processes. The concurrency is greater than that in traditional software development. The concurrent control and scheduling are necessary during software evolution. Concurrency is also an obvious phenomenon in software evolution processes.

(3) Interleaving of continuous and discontinuous change. Not only continuity but also discontinuity is an essential property in both genetic and scientific evolution. The software evolution processes also possess a similar property. Thus, interleaving of continuity and discontinuity can play an important role in software evolution processes (Aoyama 2001). If a change can be described by a cycle (see Definition 4.8), then the change can be regarded as a continuous change else a discontinuous change. Continuous change and discontinuous change form an essential behaviour during software evolution.

(4) Feedback-driven system. Although the reasons underlying evolution are complex, the motivation of evolution must originate from the dissatisfaction of requirements. Therefore, evolution must be driven by feedback originating from users or environments (Chatters *et al.* 2000; Lehman and Ramil 1999).

(5) Multi-level framework. From different points of view, people can observe evolution process models at different granularities. To reduce the complexity, the models should be refined into several levels. A detailed level is a refinement of an abstract level. Therefore, the evolution process models are complex and multi-level.

In the following sections, iteration and concurrency, two of the five important properties, are further analysed in depth.

4.3 Iteration in Software Evolution Processes

Continuous change is an important phenomenon in software evolution processes. When a change is needed, many activities related to the change in evolution processes have to be executed to realise the change. Therefore, a change might give rise to a series of executions of activities and perhaps these executions might form a cycle to ensure repetitive refinement. From the point of view of a software process, a change can be regarded as a piece of iteration to form a cycle at different abstract levels. Therefore, an evolution can be a process of iteration. Iteration is an important property of software evolution processes.

What components should be included in the iteration? From the perspective of processes, a process includes a set of activities and an activity includes a set of tasks. Therefore, a piece of iteration should include processes, activities and tasks. Because of different perspectives, the same thing might be regarded as a process, an activity or a task. Therefore, the division is not absolute. Abstractly, a piece of iteration can be regarded as a cycle. Depending on different levels of abstract, a cycle can be regarded as a software process, an activity or a task. During software evolution, a piece of iteration can be regarded as a large cycle including many smaller cycles. Each cycle can include some smaller cycles, as shown in Fig. 4.1.

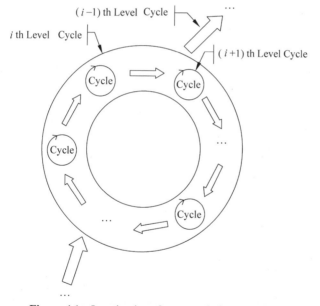

Figure 4.1   Iteration in software evolution processes

In general, the cycle at the higher level can be regarded as a software process. A sub-cycle in the cycle can be regarded as a sub-process or an activity. In order to model software evolution processes level by level, an activity can also be regarded as a software process.

In a cycle, there exist many sub-cycles. These cycles are the abstract descriptions of steps to realise the corresponding changes. They are executed one by one (in fact they can also be executed concurrently, as discussed in the following sections). Depending on projects, these sub-cycles have variations. For example, there are sub-cycles for proposal for changes, risk analysis, reverse engineering, forward engineering, testing, validation, release and feedback in the software life cycle, as shown in Fig. 4.2.

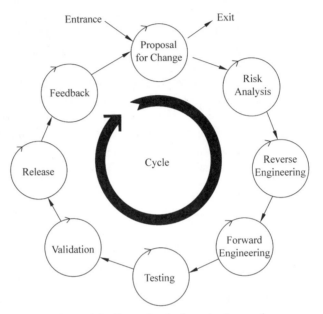

Figure 4.2   Example of sub-cycles in a cycle

It should be pointed out that a software evolution process can include several cycles, but not only cycles. Depending on projects, the structure of a software evolution process might be more complex than that of a cycle. Iteration is one of the structures of software evolution processes. Nevertheless, iteration might be a framework of software evolution processes.

4.4   Concurrency in Software Evolution Processes

Concurrency is a broad kind of phenomenon in software processes, especially in software evolution processes. There exist a number of concurrent components during software evolution. According to different granularities, the concurrency in software evolution processes can be divided into six classes from the coarse to the fine, discussed in the following subsections.

4.4.1   Version Concurrency

In the software life cycle, there are many versions of a software system. Version concurrency is the concurrency among these versions. When a version is being evolved, other versions of the same software system are perhaps also being developed or evolved, as shown in Fig. 4.3. The version concurrency is the coarsest-grained concurrency in software evolution processes. Version concurrency rarely happens in traditional software processes.

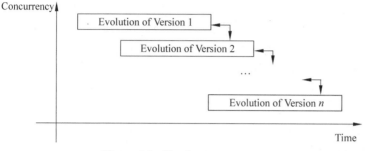

Figure 4.3 Version concurrency

4.4.2 Process Concurrency

During software evolution, there are many software processes. Process concurrency is the concurrency among these software processes. Software processes can be executed concurrently or sequentially, as shown in Fig. 4.4. Sometimes, there is synchronisation relation among software processes. The synchronisation is controlled by software evolution process models.

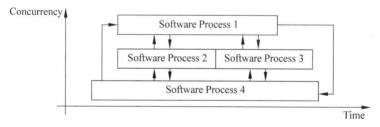

Figure 4.4 Process concurrency

4.4.3 Sub-Process Concurrency

A software process can be divided into several sub-processes, which can be executed concurrently. Sub-process concurrency is the concurrency among these sub-processes. It is the global concurrency within a software process, as shown in Fig. 4.5.

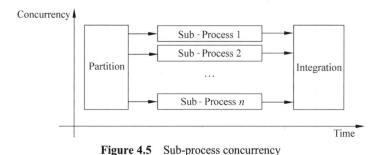

Figure 4.5   Sub-process concurrency

4.4.4   Phase Concurrency

In general, the software life cycle is divided into several phases. In the traditional software life cycle model, these phases are executed sequentially. In fact, these phases might be executed concurrently. Phase concurrency is the concurrency among these phases within a software process. For example, a software process can be divided into several phases in its life cycle, as shown in Fig. 4.6. Phase concurrency rarely happens in traditional software processes.

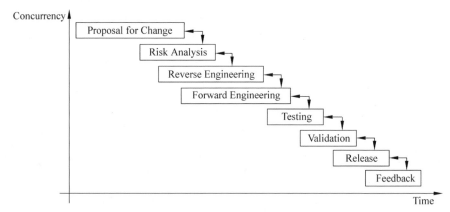

Figure 4.6   Phase concurrency

4.4.5   Activity Concurrency

In the software life cycle, there are a variety of activities. A software process consists of activities. Activity concurrency is the concurrency among these activities. Activities can be executed concurrently. An example of activity concurrency is that many programmers are coding at the same time, as shown in Fig. 4.7.

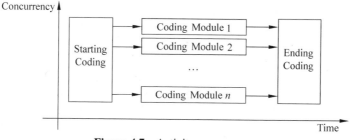

Figure 4.7   Activity concurrency

4.4.6   Task Concurrency

An activity consists of tasks. Tasks can also be executed concurrently if the resources are sufficient to meet their needs. Task concurrency is the concurrency among tasks. Task concurrency is the finest-grained concurrency in software evolution processes.

4.5   Static Component Definitions of EPMM

The software evolution process meta-model (EPMM) is a tool used to define software evolution process models. When EPMM is designed, the following factors are considered:

(1) The meta-model should embody the important properties of software evolution processes discussed above.

(2) The meta-model should accord with the ISO/IEC 12207 Standard in which each process includes a three-level framework. Furthermore, a whole-view level should be included in a software evolution process at a highest abstract level. Therefore, a four-level framework is designed in EPMM. In addition, each level can be regarded as a view which shows a model with different granularity for a specific role.

(3) During software evolution, roles cooperate with each other to evolve the legacy software system. The integration of development, management and evolution are strengthened. Therefore, the interactions between activities in software evolution processes occur with higher frequency. A software evolution process model sets up a framework to integrate different components in the software evolution process. Therefore, the meta-model should support the definition of the interaction and integration.

(4) According to the preceding property analysis and the characteristics of Petri Nets, Petri Nets are suitable to model software evolution processes. Therefore, a Petri Net is chosen as the main formalism to define the software evolution process meta-model.

(5) The Petri Net defined in the previous chapter is extended with object-oriented technology and Hoare Logic in order to meet the modelling requirements. Abstract data types and inheritance are added in order to define activities; Hoare Logic is added in order to define tasks. These extensions have been embodied in the formal definitions of EPMM.

(6) In general, software evolution processes are more complex than traditional software processes. Therefore, the meta-model is powerful so that it can also define traditional software processes.

Based on the considerations stated above, EPMM is designed. A model defined by EPMM is called an *evolution process model* or an EPM for short. Both EPMM and EPM are formal. The formal definitions of EPMM are given in the following subsections.

4.5.1   Task

Definition 4.1   A *task* is a 4-tuple $t = (\{Q_1\}, \{Q_2\}, Mi, Mo)$ where

(1) Q_1 and Q_2 are first-order predicate formulae. $\{Q_1\}$ is called the *precondition* that defines the state before task t is executed; $\{Q_2\}$ is called the *postcondition* that defines the state after task t is executed.

(2) $A(F) = (\{Q_1\}, \{Q_2\})$ is called a *2-assertion*, which defines the function of task t.

(3) Mi is a set of messages which will be received by task t. When task t receives one or several of these messages, task t is executed.

(4) Mo is a set of messages which will be sent out by task t. $\forall m \in Mo, m = (r, b)$, which denotes that t sends a message m to r when task t is executed. r is called the *receiver* of message m. b, called the *message body*, is a set of parameters.

A task is shown in Fig. 4.8. A task is a component at the finest granularity in software evolution processes.

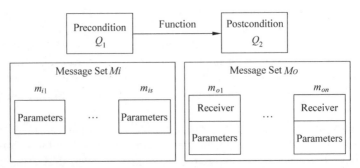

Figure 4.8   A task

The receivers can be processes, activities, tasks, conditions (see Definition 4.3) or roles. When the message body *true* is sent to conditions in a process, the conditions hold and the process might be driven to be executed. When all tasks of an activity send the message *Finish* to the activity, the activity terminates and becomes inactive (see Definition 4.7). When the receiver of a message is a process or an activity, all of their tasks will receive the message; this is a method of broadcasting messaging, which provides an efficient mechanism of message passing.

4.5.2   Activity

Definition 4.2   An *activity* is a 4-tuple $a = (I, O, L, B)$ where

(1) I, O and L are called the *input data structure*, the *output data structure* and the *local data structure* respectively;

(2) B, called the *activity body*, is either a software process p or a set of tasks *Main*, $t_1, t_2, \cdots, t_n$. These tasks or the software process operate on data structure I, O and L. Task *Main* is a special task which is executed firstly by receiving the message *Execution*;

(3) The definition of an activity is a class called the *activity class*. When the activity is executed, an object called the *activity object* is created.

An activity can be seen as a class (the description of the activity) and an object (the execution of the activity) because its tasks operate on the data structures I, O and L; each task can be regarded as an operation on the activity object, as shown in Fig. 4.9. When an activity is executed, an activity object is created.

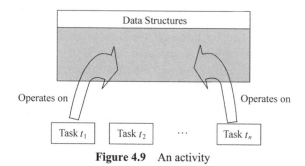

Figure 4.9   An activity

Tasks in an activity object can send and receive messages. When it receives a message, the task is executed if it is active (see Definition 4.7). When it is executed, the task operates on the data structures I, O and L.

If an activity is defined as a software process, the new software process at a lower level must be defined. The software process at the lower level refines the software process at the higher level which the activity belongs to, as shown in Fig. 4.10.

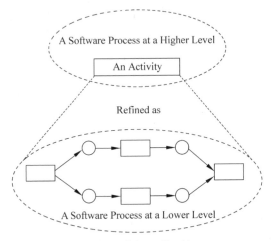

Figure 4.10 An activity refined by a process

Resources are essential elements in software processes. Software processes are very sensitive to the scarcity or abundance of resources. Therefore, a process should accurately describe the resource requirements and resource product of activities. In EPMM, data structures are regarded as the abstraction of resources; or resources can be abstracted as data structures. An activity is allowed to apply resources (input data structure) and provide resources (output data structure). The flow of input and output data in software processes forms the resource flow. Activities are the consumers of input resources and the producers of output resources. The attributes of an activity are described in the local data structure.

During software evolution, all the data, cost, time, human resources, software, hardware and other objects supporting software evolution can be regarded as resources. Resources can be classified as abstract resources (such as time), data resources (such as cost), tangible resources (such as computers) and human resources (such as available programmers). They can be described by data structures. When a software evolution process applies a resource, the application is implemented as the access to the corresponding data structure. Time is critical to software evolution. If time is not sufficient, an activity cannot be enacted smoothly. Therefore, time is also regarded as a kind of resource and described in data structures.

4.5.3 Software Process

Definition 4.3 A 4-tuple $\Sigma = (C, A; F, M)$ is called a *software process system* where

(1) $(C, A; F)$ is a net without isolated elements, $A \cup C \neq \emptyset$;

(2) C is a finite set of conditions; $\forall c \in C$ is called a *condition*;

(3) A is a finite set of activities; $\forall a \in A$ is called an *activity*; the occurrence of a is called that *a is executed* or that *a fires*;

(4) $M \subseteq 2^C$ is called the *case set* of Σ. 2^C denotes the power set of C;

(5) $\forall a \in A$, $\exists m \in M$, such that a has concession in m.

Definition 4.4 Let $\Sigma = (C, A; F, M)$ be a software process system. Let $M_0 \in M$ ($M_0 \subseteq C$) be a case of Σ and $p = (C, A; F, M_0)$. M_0 is called the *initial marking* of p; $d \in M_0$ is called a *token*; p is called a *software process*.

If confusion might arise, then C, A, F and M_0 are denoted as $p.C$, $p.A$, $p.F$ and $p.M_0$ respectively.

In fact, a software process is an extended Petri Net. In the process, an activity can also be refined as another software process. Thus, software processes can be constructed level by level so that the finer-grained process can be obtained continuously with the increase of depth until the modellers are satisfied with the granularity of the software process. When a software process refines an activity, the consistency must be preserved. Namely, both the syntax and semantics between the higher-level model and the lower-level model must be consistent.

A software process can be executed according to Definition 3.3. Graphically, an activity is represented respectively as a rectangle, a condition as a circle and a token as a black dot in the graph. A software process is shown in Fig. 4.11, $i = 1$, $2, \cdots, n$.

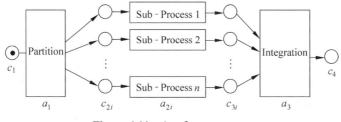

Figure 4.11 A software process

The software process shown in Fig. 4.11 is defined by EPMM as follows:

$p = (C, A; F, M_0)$;

$C = \{c_1, c_{21}, \cdots, c_{2n}, c_{31}, \cdots, c_{3n}, c_4\}$;

$A = \{a_1, a_{21}, \cdots, a_{2n}, a_3\}$;

$F = \{(c_1, a_1), (a_1, c_{21}), (a_1, c_{22}), \cdots, (a_1, c_{2n}), (c_{21}, a_{21}), (c_{22}, a_{22}), \cdots, (c_{2n}, a_{2n}), (a_{21}, c_{31}), (a_{22}, c_{32}), \cdots, (a_{2n}, c_{3n}), (c_{31}, a_3), (c_{32}, a_3), \cdots, (c_{3n}, a_3), (a_3, c_4)\}$;

$M_0 = \{c_1\}$;

$a_1 = $ Partition;

$a_{2i} = $ Sub-process i; ($i = 1, 2, \cdots, n$)

$a_3 = $ Integration.

4.5.4　Example: Prototype Evolution Process Model

The example in Fig. 4.11 is a traditional software process. In the following, a workflow of a prototype evolution is shown in Fig. 4.12. The software process to describe the prototype evolution is shown in Fig. 4.13. $VA_i (i = 0,1,\cdots,6)$ denotes the virtual activities which do nothing except for passing tokens from one condition to another condition.

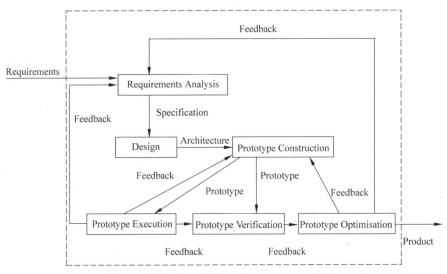

Figure 4.12 A workflow of prototype evolution

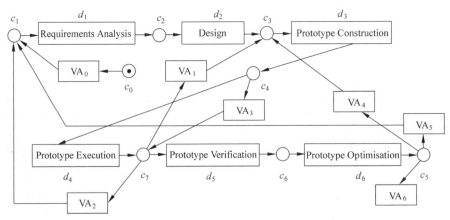

Figure 4.13 A prototype evolution process model

In this example, the activities are executed sequentially. However, they can also be executed concurrently if they are defined as being executed concurrently. The information in workflow, such as requirements, architecture, feedback and prototype, is defined as the data structures of corresponding activities.

A prototype provides a communication tool for requirements elicitation among all respects involved in the evolution activities, especially between users and developers. It is not only used as a tool in the context of a single project, but also describes a continuous evolution process of a rapidly changing software system. It is not only a model or experimental tool, but also the kernel of the goal system. It has been widely used and has been proved to be an effective software evolution approach.

4.5.5   Global Model

Definition 4.5   A *global model* is a 2-tuple $g = (P, E)$ where

(1) P is a set of software processes;

(2) $E \subseteq P \times P$ is a binary relation and a partial order, called the *embedded relation* of P. $E = \{(p, p') \mid p, p' \in P \land p'$ is embedded in $p\}$. p' is called a *sub-process* of p.

During software evolution, there exist many software processes. Therefore, a global model is defined to list all software processes involved in the evolution. A sub-process is used to refine an activity, i.e. it will be embedded in a super process. A global model shown in Fig. 4.14 (enclosed in dotted lines) is defined as follows:

$g = \{P, E\}$.

$P = \{$Software process 1, Software process 2, Software process 3, $\cdots$, Software process n, Software process 2.1, Software process 2.2, $\cdots$, Software process 2.$m\}$;

$E = \{($Software process 2, Software process 2.1$)$, $($Software process 2, Software process 2.2$)$, $\cdots$, $($Software process 2, Software process 2.$m)\}$.

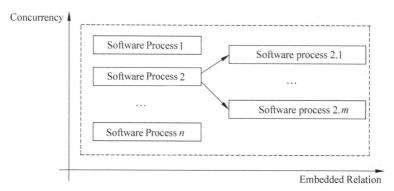

Figure 4.14   A global model

4.6 Dynamic Component Definitions of EPMM

Definition 4.6   Let $k = (S, T; \ F')$ be an occurrence net; let $m = (C, A; F, M_0)$ be a software process. A mapping $p: k \rightarrow m$ is called an *execution of m* if

(1) $p(S) \subseteq C \wedge p(T) \subseteq A \wedge \forall (x, y) \in F' : p(x, y) = (p(x), p(y)) \in F$;

(2) $\forall t \in T: p(^{\bullet}t) = {}^{\bullet}p(t) \wedge p(t^{\bullet}) = p(t)^{\bullet}$;

(3) $\forall s_1, s_2 \in S: s_1 \neq s_2 \wedge p(s_1) = p(s_2) \Rightarrow {}^{\bullet}s_1 \neq {}^{\bullet}s_2 \wedge s_1^{\bullet} \neq s_2^{\bullet}$;

(4) $\forall c \in C: p(s) = c \wedge {}^{\bullet}s = \varnothing \Rightarrow c \in M_0$.

In Definition 4.6, an occurrence net is used to describe an execution of a software process. In fact, it is an execution record of the software process. The execution record dynamically describes an execution of the software process. Each execution may result in a step sequence different from others. During software evolution, an execution record is essential for analysing and improving a software evolution process. A simulated execution record is good for obtaining critical information so as to improve the process before execution. A real execution record is good for analysing critical information so as to obtain experiences for the future.

Definition 4.7   From being created to being finished, an activity and its tasks are called *active*, else *inactive*.

The execution of a software process and its activities is controlled by the firing rules of Petri Nets defined in the previous chapter. When an activity is executed, it creates an activity object (an instance of the activity). After the activity object sends a message *Execution* to its task *Main*, task *Main* is executed. Then it sends messages to other tasks to drive them to be executed. A task can send messages to the tasks belonging to other activities, even other software processes. But the messages do not always cause the receivers to be executed immediately. When a task receives a message, if it is active, then the task is executed; else the execution will be delayed until the task becomes active. A task can send a message *Finish* to its activity. After all tasks send message *Finish* to their activity, the activity object finishes; the activity and its tasks become inactive. Whether a new activity will be executed is determined by the software process. The interaction between software processes is illustrated in Fig. 4.15.

Definition 4.8   Let $m = (C, A; F, M_0)$ be a software process. For $M_1, M_2, \cdots, M_n \subseteq C$, if $\exists$ a step sequence $G_1 G_2 \cdots G_{n-1} (G_1, G_2, \cdots, G_{n-1} \subseteq A)$ such that $M_1[G_1 > M_2, M_2[G_2 > M_3, \cdots, M_{n-1}[G_{n-1} > M_n,$ and $M_1 = M_n$, the step sequence is called a *cycle*.

A cycle can describe iteration, an important property of software evolution processes.

The example of a software process with cycles is shown in Fig. 4.16. When it is executed, the corresponding execution record is shown in Fig. 4.17. In this example, the software process includes cycles because it records three step

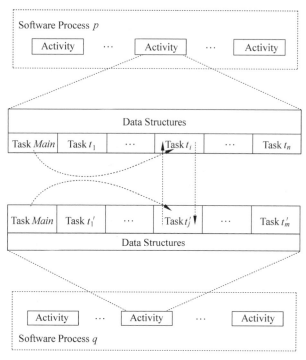

Message Flows

Figure 4.15 Interaction between software processes

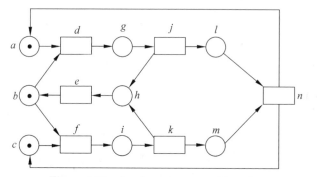

Figure 4.16 A software process with cycles

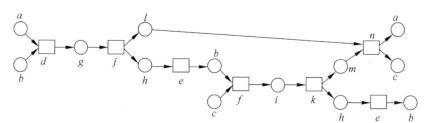

Figure 4.17 An execution record of a software process

sequences which transfer marking M_0 to marking M_0. These three step sequences are described as follows:

Sequence 1: $M_0 = \{a, b, c\}$ $[\{d\}>$ $\{g, c\}$ $[\{j\}>$ $\{l, h, c\}$ $[\{e\}>$ $\{l, b, c\}$ $[\{f\}>$ $\{l, i\}$ $[\{k\}>$ $\{l, m, h\}$ $[\{e, n\}>$ $\{a, b, c\} = M_0$;

Sequence 2: $M_0 = \{a, b, c\}$ $[\{d\}>$ $\{g, c\}$ $[\{j\}>$ $\{l, h, c\}$ $[\{e\}>$ $\{l, b, c\}$ $[\{f\}>$ $\{l, i\}$ $[\{k\}>$ $\{l, m, h\}$ $[\{n\}>$ $\{a, c, h\}$ $[\{e\}>$ $\{a, b, c\} = M_0$;

Sequence 3: $M_0 = \{a, b, c\}$ $[\{d\}>$ $\{g, c\}$ $[\{j\}>$ $\{l, h, c\}$ $[\{e\}>$ $\{l, b, c\}$ $[\{f\}>$ $\{l, i\}$ $[\{k\}>$ $\{l, m, h\}$ $[\{e\}>$ $\{l, m, b\}$ $[\{n\}>$ $\{a, b, c\} = M_0$.

In Fig. 4.17, for the sake of simplicity, the alphabets do not denote the names of conditions and activities in the occurrence net; they denote the names of conditions and activities which originate from the software process.

4.7 Supports for Software Evolution Processes

EPMM effectively supports the properties of software evolution processes discussed in Section 4.2. The reasons are discussed as follows:

(1) Iteration: A cycle is an effective implementation approach to a piece of iteration. In EPMM, a step sequence $G_1 G_2 \cdots G_{n-1}$ with $M_1[G_1 > M_2, M_2[G_2 > M_3, \cdots,$ $M_{n-1}[G_{n-1} > M_1$ is called a cycle. This indicates that a new piece of iteration can be executed because the case has returned to the original state. An execution of the cycle realises a piece of iteration and many executions of the cycle realise many pieces of iteration and a gradual evolution of a corresponding part of the software. Because the cycle is dynamic, it embodies the property of iteration, which is also dynamic.

(2) Concurrency: Concurrency is an important property of software evolution processes. As discussed before, Petri Nets possess an excellent descriptive power for the concurrent semantics. EPMM makes full use of the concurrent power of Petri Nets. Using EPMM based on Petri Nets, the concurrent phenomena in software evolution processes, such as version concurrency, process concurrency, sub-process concurrency, phase concurrency and activity concurrency, can be described precisely. These concurrent components can be processed and treated equally from the different points of view. Although there are no the concepts of versions and phases, they can be regarded as activities or software processes. The finer-grained concurrent components can be obtained from the coarser-grained concurrent components by stepwise refinement.

(3) Interleaving of continuous and discontinuous change: As stated before, on the one hand, continuous change can be effectively described by cycles of EPMM. On the other hand, discontinuous change can also be described by the activities which are not in a cycle of EPMM. By means of combining both cycle and non-cycle in EPMM, the interleaving of continuous change and discontinuous change can also be effectively described.

(4) Feedback-driven system: Software evolution processes, apart from the most primitive, are complex multi-loop, multi-agent, multi-level feedback systems (Lehman and Ramil 2002). The cycles in EPMM can also effectively describe the feedback-driven systems. In fact, a cycle denotes a feedback-driven process and also a feedback-driven system because any activity in a cycle can be regarded as the operation which transfers input, i.e. the feedback of the previous iteration, into output, i.e. the result which can be submitted as a new feedback to the next iteration. In this way, an effective feedback control mechanism is constructed. Another feedback-driven method of EPMM is to send a message body *true* to conditions of specified software processes. The message will set these conditions to hold. If these conditions can enable some activities to fire, these activities are driven by the feedback from the message sender. Detailed feedback information can also be sent by messages with parameters. The nested cycles of EPMM at different granularities with different roles in tasks form a multi-loop, multi-role, multi-level feedback system.

(5) Multi-level framework: EPMs described by EPMM have a four-level framework: the global level, the process level, the activity level and the task level. Each level embodies a specified point of view. Different roles might only be concerned with different levels. Furthermore, because an activity can be defined as a software process, an EPM can be constructed level by level so that it also forms a multi-level framework at the process level in the framework. Namely, the four-level framework nests another multi-level framework at the process level. The nested multi-level framework provides the modellers with the abundant semantics to describe the evolution processes and leads to modularity.

In summary, EPMM embodies the preceding properties of software evolution processes.

4.8   Summary

In this chapter, five important properties of software evolution processes are analysed. Firstly, iteration describes the continuous changes and the processes to realise these changes. It is the framework of software evolution processes. The continuous changes in evolution processes can be described by iteration at different levels of abstraction. Secondly, concurrency is another important property in software evolution processes. In fact, a lot of process components, such as processes and activities, are executed concurrently so that the evolution efficiency can be increased. Thirdly, interleaving of continuous and discontinuous changes needs to be considered during software evolution. Fourthly, a software evolution process is a feedback-driven system. It is impossible that evolution can occur with no feedback from users or environments. Finally, the framework of evolution process models must be multi-level. This leads to a modelling approach of successive refinement.

Evolutionary behaviours vary significantly from application to application, organisation to organisation, system to system, time to time and release to release. Therefore, there is no all-purpose software evolution process model. An evolution process meta-model used to model software evolution processes becomes very important. For embodying the properties of software evolution processes stated above, a Petri Net is extended and a formal evolution process meta-model EPMM based on the extended Petri Net is proposed. EPMM can be used to define software evolution processes with preceding properties embodied. EPMM possesses the following characteristics:

(1) It is a meta-model characterised to define software evolution processes.

(2) It is based on Petri Nets and embodies the properties of iteration, concurrency, continuous and discontinuous changes, feedback-driven and multi-level frameworks.

(3) It includes static components and dynamic components. The former includes tasks, activities, software processes and global models; the latter includes execution records of software processes.

(4) It is modularised to support abstract and step-refinement.

(5) It possesses object-oriented characteristics.

Making use of EPMM, modellers can construct software evolution process models according to real-world requirements. Based on these models, the basis to simulate, control, analyse, measure and improve the software evolution process is established.

References

[1] Aoyama M (2001) Continuous and discontinuous software evolution: aspects of software evolution across multiple product lines. In: Proceedings of the 4th international workshop on principles of software evolution. ACM Press, New York, pp 87 – 90

[2] Bandinelli S, Fuggetta A, Grigolli S (1993) Process modeling in-the-large with SLANG. In: Proceedings of the 2nd international conference on software process. IEEE Computer Society Press, Washington DC, pp 75 – 83

[3] Chatters BW, Lehman MM, Ramil JF, Wernick P (2000) Modelling a software evolution process: a long-term case study. Journal of Software Process: Improvement and Practice 5: 95 – 102

[4] Fuggetta A (2000) Software process: a roadmap. In: Proceedings of the conference on the future of software engineering. ACM Press, New York, pp 25 – 34

[5] Lehman MM (1997) Laws of software evolution revisited. In: Lecture notes in computer science 1149. Springer, Berlin, pp 108 – 124

[6] Lehman MM, Ramil JF (1999) The impact of feedback in the global software process. Journal of Systems and Software 46: 123 – 134

[7] Lehman MM, Ramil JF (2002) Software evolution and software evolution processes. Annals of Software Engineering 14: 275 – 309

[8] Osterweil LJ (1997) Software processes are software too, revisited: an invited talk on the most influential paper of ICSE 9. In: Proceedings of the 19th international conference on software engineering. ACM Press, New York, pp 540 – 548

[9] Osterweil LJ (2003) Understanding process and the quest for deeper questions in software engineering research. ACM SIGSOFT Software Engineering Notes 8: 6 – 14

[10] Yang H, Ward M (2003) Successful evolution of software system. Artech House, London

5 Software Evolution Process Description Language EPDL

Tong Li

School of Software, Yunnan University, Kunming, 650091, China
Software Technology Research Laboratory, De Montfort University, Leicester, LE1 9BH, U.K
tli@ynu.edu.cn

Abstract   A software evolution process description language is a computer language that is used to describe software evolution processes. In this chapter, according to the requirements of software evolution and based on EPMM, an object-oriented software evolution process description language EPDL is designed. EPDL extends the descriptive power of EPMM. All of the static components in EPMM are defined in EPDL and the dynamic components in EPMM are embodied when EPDL programs are executed. An EPDL program can be regarded as a detailed and extended description of a software evolution process model. In this chapter, firstly, the design goals of EPDL are presented. Secondly, the characteristics and the program structure of EPDL are discussed. Thirdly, the syntax of EPDL is formally defined with Extended Backus-Naur Form. Fourthly, the semantics of EPDL are informally described. Finally, an example of an EPDL program is given. EPDL supports the description of software evolution processes and can be implemented in computers. In contrast to EPMM, EPDL is more powerful and more convenient for use. Normally, after a software evolution process model is constructed, EPDL is used to describe and extend the details of the model.

Key Words   software evolution process description language, EPDL, EPMM, syntax, semantics, design goal, object-orientation, Backus-Naur Form, Petri Net, Hoare Logic, process, sub-process, activity, task, assertion, object, class, message, code segment, program.

Objectives

- To propose the design goals of EPDL
- To discuss the characteristics and the program structure of EPDL
- To define the syntax of EPDL, and
- To describe the semantics of EPDL

5.1   Introduction

Software process modelling languages and process description languages are important tools for defining software processes. Humans must employ some powerful process abstractions (Osterweil 2003). Because software processes are complex entities, researchers have created a number of languages (Sutton *et al.* 1990, 1995; Cass *et al.* 2000; Cobleigh *et al.* 2000; Lerner 2004; Warboys *et al.* 1999; Jaccheri *et al.* 1998; Nitto *et al.* 2002; Atkinson *et al.*2004; Chen 1997; Cook and Wolf 1999; Bandinelli *et al.* 1993; Sliski *et al.* 2001) that make it possible to represent in a precise and comprehensive way a number of software process features and facets. These languages must be tolerant and allow for incomplete, informal, and partial specification (Fuggetta 2000). However, software evolution process description languages are rarely discussed. A software evolution process description language is a computer language that is used to describe software evolution processes.

Because it is much abstract, an EPM defined by EPMM is difficult to enact directly. It should be supplemented with some necessary information so that it can be enacted, i.e. executed. Therefore, a software evolution process description language should be designed to describe these processes in detail. A program of a software evolution process description language is a detailed representation of a software evolution process. Software evolution process modelling typically starts with abstract concepts and is iteratively refined into detailed descriptions. Therefore, the language not only needs to reflect this evolutionary characteristic but also needs to provide valuable information at every abstraction level.

According to the requirements of software evolution, based on EPMM, an object-oriented software evolution process description language EPDL is designed. EPDL extends the descriptive power of EPMM. All of the static components of EPMM are defined in EPDL. The dynamic components of EPMM are not defined in EPDL because they describe the execution of EPMM and they are embodied when EPDL programs are executed. An EPDL program, called an EPD (Evolution Process Description), can be regarded as a detailed and extended description of a software evolution process model.

In this chapter, firstly, the design goals of EPDL are presented. Secondly, the characteristics and the program structure of EPDL are discussed. Thirdly, the syntax of EPDL is formally defined. Fourthly, the semantics of EPDL are informally described. Finally, an example of an EPDL program is given.

5.2   Survey of EPDL

5.2.1   Design Goals

The design goals of EPDL embody how a language should capture the aspects of software evolution processes in order to describe a process properly. In order to support software evolution effectively, the design goals are considered as follows:

(1) Simplicity: The language should omit unnecessary notions and use intuitive and simple syntax and semantics. This leads to ease of study and use.

(2) Flexibility: The language can be applied to a variety of software evolutions and software developments. It should not be confined to a certain kind of specific software, such as management information systems.

(3) Expressiveness: The language can accurately reflect the details of software evolution processes in order to enact them smoothly.

(4) Consistency: The language must be consistent with static components of EPMM. The dynamic components of EPMM are embodied when EPDL programs are executed. EPMM is a subset of EPML with different notations. Generally, EPDL is more concrete than EPMM.

5.2.2 Characteristics

Based on the goals stated above and in order to support software evolution effectively, EPDL is designed to possess the following characteristics:

(1) Dynamics: Because a software evolution process is dynamic, EPDL has the syntax components to define tasks, activities, processes and other components during software evolution. When an EPDL program is executed, the dynamics are embodied.

(2) Concurrency: There are many concurrent components during software evolution. Therefore, EPDL can define concurrency at different granularities.

(3) Iteration: EPDL possesses the power to describe iteration during software evolution to support continuous changes.

(4) Integration: Because there are many roles during software evolution, EPDL can describe the behaviours of these roles and the cooperation between them, and can integrate all of the components and information into a unified software evolution process.

(5) Modularity: It is accepted as a common view that software processes are software and the descriptions of software processes are programs. As a language, the modularity is a fundamental characteristic to ensure well-structured evolution processes.

(6) Abstraction and refinement: EPDL supports the abstract and detailed descriptions to achieve an ideal granularity. A detailed process representation can be used to replace an abstract activity to refine the granularity of the process to which the activity belongs.

(7) Object-oriented computer language: EPDL has object-oriented features and is more powerful than EPMM.

(8) The description is a program: The description of a software evolution process is an EPDL program, and vice versa.

5.2.3   Program Structure

According to EPMM, EPDL syntax components are mapped into four levels: the global model, the software process, the activity and the task. The structure of EPDL is the same as EPMM.

The global model level lists the software processes involved in software evolution. The relations between sub-processes and their super processes are defined. In this way, an overview of the software evolution is described.

The process level is based on an extended Petri Net to define the behaviours of a software process and the relations between activities involved in the software process. The properties of software evolution processes, i.e. iteration, concurrency, feedback-driven and the interleaving of continuous and discontinuous change are focused on.

The activity level describes the inner structure of an activity. An activity description is a class in an object-oriented system. A software process can be regarded as an object-oriented system.

The task level describes the function and messages of a task. A task is a method (or operation) of an activity.

These levels form a multi-level program structure of EPDL. The structure of an EPDL program is shown in Fig. 5.1.

EPDL main syntax components are defined as follows by Extended Backus-Naur Form (EBNF). In these definitions, the component bracketed by "<>" denotes the syntax component; the component bracketed by "[ ]" denotes that it can occur 0 time to 1 time. For the sake of conciseness, the unimportant syntax components are omitted. The semantics of syntax components are described informally.

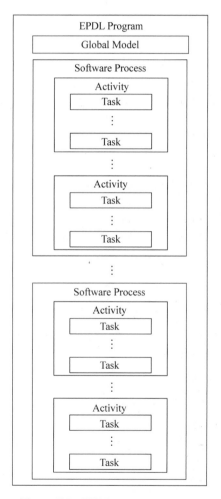

Figure 5.1   EPDL program structure

5.3 Task

```
<Task>::=TASK <Task Name> ROLE: <Role Name List>; ON MESSAGES
<Message Name List> BEGIN <Code Segment> END;
```

After an activity to which the task belongs has been executed, i.e. the activity object has been created, when a task assigned a name receives one or several messages indicated by <Message Name List>, the code segment is executed. If <Task Name> is *Main*, when its activity is executed, *Main* will receive a message *Execution*(0), such that *Main* is executed firstly.

```
<Code Segment>::=<2-Assertion>|<Message Sending>|<Code Segment>;
<Code Segment>|IF <Predicate Formula> THEN <Code Segment> [ELSE <Code Segment>]
FI|WHILE <Predicate Formula> DO <Code Segment> OD
```

In EPMM, the function of a task is described as a 2-assertion. If the 2-assertion is course-grained, it should be decomposed repeatedly into one of sequence, selection and repetition structures. This will be discussed in detail in Chapter 8. A code segment describes the results of the functional decomposition of a task. The <Message Sending> clause sends messages to receivers.

```
<2-Assertion>::={<Precondition>; <Postcondition>}
```

A 2-assertion defines the function of a task. It consists of a precondition and a postcondition. Whenever the execution of a task begins in a state satisfying <Precondition> and the execution of the task terminates, the resulting state satisfies <Postcondition>. When a 2-assertion is executed, if its precondition does not hold, i.e. the execution conditions are not sufficiently provided, the 2-assertion waits until its precondition holds. The concept of execution of a 2-assertion will be defined in Chapter 8.

```
<Precondition>::=PRECONDITION <Predicate Formula>
```

A precondition is a first-order predicate formula which defines the state before a task is executed.

```
<Postcondition>::=POSTCONDITION <Predicate Formula>
```

A postcondition is a first-order predicate formula which defines the state after a task is executed.

```
<Predicate Formula>::=<Atom>|(<Predicate Formula>)|not <Predicate Formula>|
<Predicate Formula> and <Predicate Formula>|<Predicate Formula> or <Predicate
Formula> |<Predicate Formula> imply <Predicate Formula>| <Predicate Formula> iff
<Predicate Formula>|all(<Variable List>) (<Predicate Formula>)| exists (<Variable
List>)(<Predicate Formula>)
```

<Predicate Formula> defines a first-order predicate formula. "not" denotes "¬"; "and" denotes "∧"; "or" denotes "∨"; "imply" denotes "⇒"; "iff" denotes

" $\Leftrightarrow$ "; "all" denotes " $\forall$ " and "exists" denotes " $\exists$ ".

```
<Atom>::=<Simple Boolean Expression>
```

An atom is a simple Boolean expression.

```
<Simple Boolean Expression>::=<Arithmetic Expression> <Relational Operator>
<Arithmetic Expression>
```

A simple Boolean expression defines the relation to compare the values of two arithmetic expressions.

```
<Message Name List>::=<Message Name>[(<Variable List>)]|<Message Name>
[(<Variable List>)], <Message Name List>
```

<Message Name List> is a set of message names which will be processed by the task. When a task receives one of these messages, the task is executed if it is active or, if it is inactive, the task will be executed after it becomes active.

```
<Variable List>::=<Variable Name>|<Variable Name>, <Variable List>
```

<Variable List> is a set of variable names.

```
<Message Sending>::=SEND <Message Name> TO <Receiver List> (<Message Body>)
```

A message assigned a name includes the receiver list and message body. If the receiver is a task, the message will be processed by the task; if the receiver is a condition and the message body is a predicate formula which holds, a token is set to the condition.

```
<Receiver List>::=<Receiver>|<Receiver>,<Receiver List>
```

A receiver list is a set of message receivers.

```
<Receiver>::=[<Software Process Name>.] [<Activity Name>.] [<Task Name>]
|[<Software Process Name>.]<Condition Name>|<Role Name List>
```

Receivers might be processes, activities, tasks, conditions or roles. When message body *true* is sent to conditions in a process, the conditions hold and the process might be driven to be executed. When all tasks of an activity send the message *Finish* to the activity, the activity terminates and become inactive. When the receiver of a message is a process or an activity, all of their tasks will receive the message. If the receiver is in the same software process as the sender, ⟨Software Process Name⟩ may be omitted. If the receiver is in the same activity as the sender, ⟨Activity Name⟩ may also be omitted.

```
<Software Process Name>::=<Identifier>(<Level Number>)
```

<Software Process Name> is an identifier with a level number (integer) so that the software process model can be constructed level by level.

```
<Message Body>::=<Parameter Set>
```

<Message Body> consists of parameters.

`<Parameter Set>::=<Expression>|<Expression>, <Parameter Set>`

A parameter set is a set of expressions.

`<Expression>::=<Arithmetic Expression>|<Simple Boolean Expression>`

An expression is either an arithmetic expression or a simple Boolean expression.

`<Role Name>::=PRM|PM|SA|DR|PR|CP|MA|GL|OP|USER|ALL|<User_Defined Role Name>`

A role name is one of PRM(Process Manager), PM(Project Manager), SA(System Analyst), DR(Designer), PR(Programmer), CP(Code Programmer), MA(Maintenance Analyst), GL(Group Leader), OP(Operator), USER(User), ALL(all the roles involved in the software evolution process) and other roles defined by modellers.

`<Role Name List>::=<Role Name>|<Role Name>,<Role Name List>`

<Role Name List> is a set of <Role Name>.

5.4   Activity

`<Activity>::=ACTIVITY <Activity Name> [FROM [<Software Process Name>.]`
`<Activity Name>] [IMPORTS <Variable Declaration List>;] [EXPORTS <Variable`
`Declaration List>;] [LOCALS <Variable Declaration List>;] BEGIN <Activity`
`Body> END;`

An activity is an abstract data type that defines the data structures and the operations (the tasks) on the data structures. When an activity is executed, i.e. it fires, an activity object is created and its task *Main* (one of the tasks in the activity) is executed firstly on receiving the message *Execution*. When it receives the message *Finish* from all of its tasks or its refined software process terminates (if the activity is refined as a software process), the activity object terminates.

An activity called the *sub-activity* can inherit characteristics from another activity called the *super activity*. A sub-activity is also a class and can be defined by FROM clause that denotes that the sub-activity inherits the characteristics from <Software Process Name>. <Activity Name>. The <Software Process Name> may be omitted if the super activity is in the same software process. A sub-activity can refuse to inherit the characteristics of its super activity. New characteristics can also be added to it or the inherited characteristics changed. If a syntax component which occurs in the super activity does not occur in the sub-activity, the characteristics of the syntax component are inherited by the sub-activity. If a syntax component which occurs in the super activity occurs in the sub-activity with some change, the characteristics of the old syntax component are replaced with the new one. If a syntax component which does not occur in the super activity occurs in the sub-activity, the new characteristics of the new syntax component are created in the sub-activity.

IMPORTS clause, EXPORTS clause and LOCALS clause define respectively the input, output and local data structures.

`<Variable Declaration List>`::=`<Variable Declaration>` | `<Variable Declaration>`; `<Variable Declaration List>`

`<Variable Declaration List>` is a set of variable declarations.

`<Variable Declaration>`::=`<Variable List>`: `<Variable Type>`

`<Variable Declaration>` declares variables used by an activity.

`<Task List>`::=`<Task>`|`<Task>` `<Task List>`

`<Task List>` is a set of task definitions in which the tasks of the activity are defined.

`<Activity Body>`::=`<Task List>`|`<Software Process Name>`

If an activity is a set of tasks, `<Activity Body>` defines these tasks; if an activity is defined as a software process, `<Activity Body>` indicates the process name.

An activity is either a set of tasks or a software process. The latter denotes that a detailed representation (a software process) replaces an abstract representation (an activity). Based on this characteristic, the stepwise refinement approach can be used to construct the software process. Thus, a software process can be constructed level by level. When a detailed process replaces an abstract activity, the consistency of semantics between the processes at two levels must be preserved.

5.5   Software Process

`<Software Process>`::=**PROCESS** `<Software Process Name>` [**FROM** `<Software Process Name>`] [**TYPE** `<Type Definition List>`;] [**PACKAGE IMPORTS** `<Variable Declaration List>`; **EXPORTS** `<Variable Declaration List>`; **LOCALS** `<Variable Declaration List>`; **ENTRANCE** `<Activity name>`; **EXIT** `<Activity name>`; **MINI SPECIFICATION** `<Mini Specification>`; **KEY WORDS** `<Key Words>`] [`<Activity List>`] **BEGIN** [**CONDITION SET** `<Condition Assignment Statement List>`;] [**ACTIVITY SET** `<Activity Assignment Statement List>`;] [**ARC SET** `<Arc Assignment Statement List>`;] [`<Initial Marking>`] **END;**

A software process based on Petri Nets is composed of a condition set, an activity set, an arc set (flow relation) and an initial marking. It is executed according to Definition 3.3.

A software process called the *inherited sub-software process* can inherit characteristics from another software process called the *super software process*.

In order to avoid the confusion with the sub-process as defined in Definition 4.5, this process is called the *inherited sub-software process*. An inherited sub-software process is also a software process and can be defined by the FROM clause that denotes that the inherited sub-software process inherits the characteristics from <Software Process Name>. The semantics of the FROM clause are the same as those of the FROM clause of an activity. When using the FROM clause, if a condition or an activity is removed (using the "–" operation) in an inherited sub-software process, all the arcs attached to the condition and the activity are also removed in the sub-software process.

TYPE clause defines new data types used in activities. New data types are constructed by means of system data types. System data types include INTEGER, STRING, REAL, BOOLEAN, STRUCTURE, UNION, "{}" (enumerated type), ROLE, MESSAGE and SEQ.

The reserved word PACKAGE indicates that the software process is a process package. IMPORTS clause, EXPORTS clause and LOCALS clause have the same semantics as the corresponding clauses in <Activity>. ENTRANCE clause and EXIT clause indicate the entrance activity and the exit activity of the software process package respectively. MINI SPECIFICATION clause indicates a set of strings which is used to describe the software process package briefly. KEY WORDS clause indicates a set of key words of the mini specification. These clauses are used to define the process package. When a process package is used to refine an activity, the arcs which point at the activity are changed to pointing at the entrance activity and the arcs which point from the activity are changed to pointing from the exit activity.

```
<Type Definition List>::=<Type Definition> | <Type Definition>;
<Type Definition List>
```

<Type Definition List> is a set of type definitions.

```
<Type Definition>::=STRUCTURE <Type Name> BEGIN <Variable Declaration
List> END
```

<Type Definition> defines a new data type.

```
<Activity List>::=<Activity>|<Activity> <Activity List>
```

<Activity List> is a set of activity definitions in which the activities of the software process are defined.

```
<Condition Assignment Statement List>::=<Condition Assignment Statement>|
<Condition Assignment Statement>; <Condition Assignment Statement List>
```

<Condition Assignment Statement List> is a set of <Condition Assignment Statement>.

```
<Condition Assignment Statement>::=<Condition Set Name>:=<Condition
Expression>
```

The value of <Condition Expression> is assigned to <Condition Set Name>.

<Condition Expression>::=<Condition Set Name>∪<Condition Set>|<Condition Set Name>-<Condition Set>|<Condition Set>

<Condition Expression> is either a condition set; or a union set or a difference set of two condition sets.

<Condition Set>::={<Condition Name List>}

<Condition Set> is a set of condition names defined by <Condition Name List>.

<Condition Name List>::=<Condition Name>|<Condition Name>, <Condition Name List>

<Condition Name List> is a list of condition names separated by commas.

<Activity Assignment Statement List>::=<Activity Assignment Statement>|<Activity Assignment Statement>; <Activity Assignment Statement List>

<Activity Assignment Statement List> is a set of <Activity Assignment Statement>.

<Activity Assignment Statement>::=<Activity Set Name>:=<Activity Expression>

The value of <Activity Expression> is assigned to <Activity Set Name>.

<Activity Expression>::=<Activity Set Name>∪<Activity Set>|<Activity Set Name>-<Activity Set> |<Activity Set>

<Activity Expression> is either an activity set; or a union set or a difference set of two activity sets.

<Activity Set>::={<Activity Name List>}

<Activity Set> is a set of activity names defined by <Activity Name List>.

<Activity Name List>::=<Activity Name>|<Activity Name>, <Activity Name List>

<Activity Name List> is a list of activity names separated by commas.

<Arc Assignment Statement List> ::=<Arc Assignment Statement> | <Arc Assignment Statement>; <Arc Assignment Statement List>

<Arc Assignment Statement List> is a set of <Arc Assignment Statement>.

<Arc Assignment Statement>::=<Arc Set Name>:=<Arc Expression>

The value of <Arc Expression> is assigned to <Arc Set Name>.

<Arc Expression>::=<Arc Set Name>∪<Arc Set>|<Arc Set Name>-<Arc Set>|<Arc Set>

<Arc Expression> is either an arc set; or a union set or a difference set of two arc sets.

<Arc Set>::={<Arc Element List>}

<Arc Set> is a set of arc elements.

`<Arc Element List>::=<Arc Element>|<Arc Element>, <Arc Element List>`

<Arc Element List> is a list of arc elements separated by commas.

`<Arc Element>::=(<Condition Name>, <Activity Name>)|(<Activity Name>, <Condition Name>)`

<Arc Element> is an arc in which either a condition name points at an activity name or an activity name points at a condition name.

`<Initial Marking>::=MARKING <Condition Set>`

<Initial Marking> defines the initial marking of a software process.

5.6 Global Model

`<Global Model>::=GLOBAL MODEL <Global Model Name> BEGIN [<Software Process Name List>;] [EMBEDDED RELATION <Embedded Relation>] END;`

The global model indicates the software process names involved in the software evolution and the embedded relation between these processes. An EPDL program must include a global model. The software processes, which have not been defined in the embedded relation, can be executed concurrently. The synchronisation control is realised by means of message passing.

`<Software Process Name List>::=<Software Process Name>|<Software Process Name>; <Software Process Name List>`

<Software Process Name List> indicates the software process names involved in the software evolution.

`<Embedded Relation>::=<Refinement>|<Refinement>;<Embedded Relation>`

<Embedded Relation> is a set of refinements.

`<Refinement>::=(<Super Software Process Name>, <Sub Software Process Name>)`

<Refinement> defines the relation between two software processes. It indicates that an activity in a super software process will be refined as a sub-software process, i.e. the sub-software process must be embedded in the super software process.

5.7 EPDL Program

`<EPDL Program>::=PROGRAM <Program Name> [<Glossary>;] BEGIN <Global Model> <Software Process List> END.`

An EPDL program assigned a name is a software evolution process description. It includes a glossary list, a global model and a set of software processes.

```
<Glossary>::=<Term>|<Term>; <Glossary>
```

In software evolution processes, there exist many meaningful terms. <Glossary> formalises these terms.

```
<Term>::=#define <Term Name>: <Term Explanation>
```

#define clause is used to define and to symbolise a term. The modellers can refer to the symbolised term name to replace the term explanation in an EPDL program.

```
<Software Process List>::=<Software Process>|<Software Process> <Software
Process List>
```

<Software Process List> is a set of software processes.

5.8 Example

Figure 4.16 shows an example of a software process which includes iteration shown in Fig. 4.17. For the sake of conciseness, only PROCESS is given. The corresponding EPDL program is as follows:

```
PROCESS Iteration
 BEGIN
   CONDITION SET
     C:={a, b, c, g, h, i, l, m};
   ACTIVITY SET
     A:={d, e, f, j, k, n};
   ARC SET
     F:={(a, d), (d, g), (g, j), (j, l), (l, n), (j, h), (b, d), (b, f), (e, b),
(h, e), (c, f), (f, i), (i, k), (k, h), (k, m), (m, n), (n, c), (n, a)};
   MARKING {a, b, c}
 END;
```

It is convenient to modify a software process in EPDL. For example, if modellers need to add a condition vertex p and an arc which points to p from n into the process in Fig. 4.16, the new process shown in Fig. 5.2 can be obtained by means of modifying the old process using the inheritance method, described as follows:

```
PROCESS Iteration FROM Iteration
 BEGIN
   CONDITION SET
     C:=C∪{p};
   ARC SET
     F:=F∪{(n, p)};
 END;
```

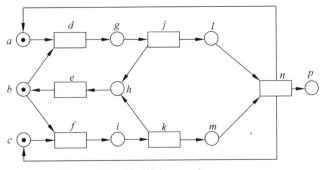

Figure 5.2 Modifying a software process

In this example, the inheritance mechanism is adopted to modify the software process. The inheritance mechanism can even be adopted to create a new inherited sub-software process. The sub-software process is very useful when developing large-scale software processes. For example, by changing the following statement

"PROCESS Iteration FROM Iteration" into

"PROCESS Sub-Iteration FROM Iteration",

an inherited sub-software process called Sub-Iteration is defined.

5.9   Summary

A software evolution process description language is a computer language that is used to describe formal software evolution processes. In this chapter, according to the requirements of software evolution and based on EPMM, an object-oriented software evolution process description language EPDL is designed. The syntax of EPDL is formally defined and the semantics of EPDL are informally described in this chapter.

EPDL supports the description of software evolution processes and can be implemented in computers. In contrast to EPMM, EPDL is more powerful and more convenient for use by non-professional modellers. However, EPMM is more abstract and is more suitable for the description of the important aspects of software evolution processes. Normally, after a software evolution process model is constructed, EPDL is used to describe and extend the details of the model. EPDL is an object-oriented language. A new software process or a new activity can be generated by means of inheriting the characteristics from the old one using the FROM clause. They can inherit all the characteristics from the corresponding super process or super activity; they can refuse to inherit some characteristics; they can also add some new characteristics and change some inherited characteristics.

References

[1] Atkinson DC, Weeks DC, Noll J (2004) The design of evolutionary process modeling languages. In: Proceedings of the 11th Asia-Pacific software engineering conference. IEEE Computer Society, Washington DC, pp 73 – 82

[2] Bandinelli S, Fuggetta A, Grigolli S (1993) Process modeling in-the-large with SLANG. In: Proceedings of the 2nd international conference on software process. IEEE Computer Society Press, Washington DC, pp 75 – 83

[3] Cass AG, Lerner BS, McCall EK, Osterweil LJ, Sutton SM, Wise A (2000) Little-JIL/ Juliette: a process definition language and interpreter. In: Proceedings of the 22nd international conference on software engineering. ACM Press, New York, pp 754 – 757

[4] Chen JYJ (1997) CSPL: An Ada95-like, Unix-based process environment. IEEE Transactions on Software Engineering 23: 171 – 184

[5] Cobleigh JM, Clarke LA, Osterweil LJ (2000) Verifying properties of process definitions. In: Proceedings of the 2000 ACM SIGSOFT international symposium on software testing and analysis. ACM Press, New York, pp 96 – 101

[6] Cook JE, Wolf AL (1999) Software process validation: quantitatively measuring the correspondence of a process to a model. ACM Transactions on Software Engineering and Methodology 8: 147 – 176

[7] Fuggetta A (2000) Software process: a roadmap. In: Proceedings of the conference on the future of software engineering. ACM Press, New York, pp 25 – 34

[8] Jaccheri M, Picco GP, Lago P (1998) Eliciting software process models with the E^3 language. ACM Transactions on Software Engineering and Methodology 7: 368 – 410

[9] Lerner BS (2004) Verifying process models built using parameterized state machines. In: Proceedings of the 2004 ACM SIGSOFT international symposium on software testing and analysis. ACM Press, New York, pp 274 – 284

[10] Nitto ED, Lavazza L, Schiavoni M, Tracanella E, Trombetta M (2002) Deriving executable process descriptions from UML. In: Proceedings of the 24th international conference on software engineering. ACM Press, New York, pp 155 – 165

[11] Osterweil LJ (2003) Understanding process and the quest for deeper questions in software engineering research. ACM SIGSOFT Software Engineering Notes 8: 6 – 14

[12] Sliski TJ, Billmers MP, Clarke LA, Osterweil LJ (2001) An architecture for flexible, evolvable process-driven user-guidance environments. In: Proceedings of the 8th European software engineering conference held jointly with 9th ACM SIGSOFT international symposium on foundations of software engineering. ACM Press, New York, pp 33 – 43

[13] Sutton SM Jr, Heimbigner DM, Osterweil LJ (1990) Language constructs for managing change in process-centered environments. In: Proceedings of the 4th ACM SIGSOFT symposium on software development environments. ACM Press, New York, pp 206 – 217

[14] Sutton SM Jr, Heimbigner DM, Osterweil LJ (1995) APPL/A—a language for software-process programming. ACM Transactions on Software Engineering and Methodology 4: 221 – 286

[15] Warboys BC, Balasubramaniam D, Greenwood RM, Kirby GNC, Mayes K, Morrison R, Munro DS (1999) Collaboration and composition: issues for a second generation process language. In: Proceedings of the 7th European software engineering conference held jointly with the 7th ACM SIGSOFT international symposium on foundations of software engineering. Springer-Verlag, London, pp 75 – 90

6 Framework of Software Evolution Processes

Tong Li

School of Software, Yunnan University, Kunming, 650091, China
Software Technology Research Laboratory, De Montfort University, Leicester, LE1 9BH, U.K
tli@ynu.edu.cn

Abstract   Both EPMM and EPDL support modelling and describing software evolution processes. In this chapter, the framework of software evolution processes defined by EPMM and EPDL is discussed. The framework is a combination of both hierarchical and an object-oriented frameworks. Firstly, a software evolution process forms a four-level framework: the global level, the process level, the activity level and the task level. Each level possesses specific structures and needs different modelling methods. In addition, according to the characteristics of models at different levels, a top-down spiral meta-process with six steps for modelling software evolution processes is proposed. In order to effectively support the meta-process, several guidelines for constructing evolution process models are presented. Furthermore, a procedure for modelling software evolution processes at the global level is developed. Finally, the relationship between descriptions and models of software evolution processes is also discussed.

Key Words   EPMM, EPDL, framework, architecture, hierarchical framework, object-oriented framework, global level, process level, activity level, task level, initial block, meta-process, procedure, global model, refinement, granularity, role, recursion.

Objectives

- To discuss the framework of software evolution processes
- To propose the steps for modelling software evolution processes
- To propose an approach to modelling software evolution processes at the global level, and
- To discuss the relationship between descriptions and models of software evolution processes

6.1 Introduction

Software processes denote a set of interrelated processes in the software life cycle. A software process provides a framework for managing activities. The ISO/IEC 12207 Standard for Information Technology—Software Life Cycle Processes defines a software process as a set of interrelated activities. An activity under a process is a set of cohesive tasks (ISO and IEC 1998). In his pioneering paper, Osterweil presented a widely accepted view that software process is software too (Osterweil 1987, 1997). The phrase "software process is software too" suggests that the processes by which software is created are a particular type of software, and presumably this type is some sort of subtype of the larger universe of software (Osterweil 2003). Architecture must allow the provision of the needed functionality and performance (Redwine 1991). Software process architecture integrates concurrent and asynchronous processes, incremental and iterative process enaction, distributed multi-site processes and people-centred processes (Aoyama 1998). The Object Management Group (OMG) presented a four—layered architecture of modelling. The definition of the corresponding process is at level M1. The meta-model stands at level M2 and serves as a template for level M1 (OMG 2002). These denote that the framework and the architecture are important research areas on software processes. However, the framework of software evolution processes is rarely discussed.

Both EPMM and EPDL support modelling and describing software evolution processes respectively. The models and descriptions of software evolution processes are structured. In these models and descriptions, different components demonstrate different views of the processes. From the whole viewpoints, the framework discussed here is the architecture of software evolution processes. In this chapter, at first, the framework with a four-level structure of software evolution processes is discussed. According to the framework, six steps and several guidelines for modelling software evolution processes are proposed. Furthermore, a semi-formal procedure is developed to model software evolution processes at the global level. Finally, the relationship between descriptions and models of software evolution processes is also discussed.

6.2 Framework of Software Evolution Processes

The framework of software evolution processes is a combination of both a hierarchical and an object-oriented frameworks. When a software process refines an activity at a higher level, a hierarchical structure of frameworks is formed. Because an activity is a class, the activities in software processes form an object-oriented framework. The combined framework has the advantages of both these two kinds of frameworks. In general, the framework includes four levels, as shown in Fig. 6.1.

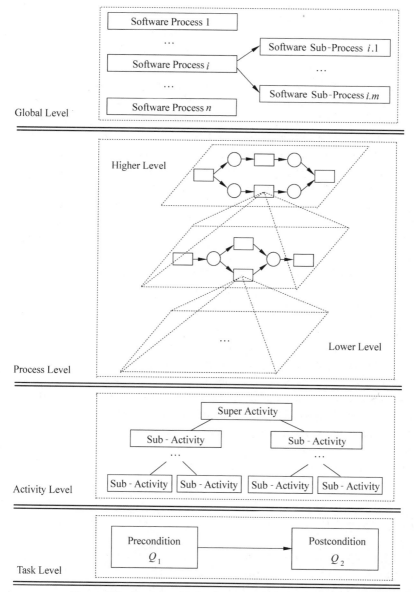

Figure 6.1   Framework of software evolution processes

(1) Global level: This level describes an overview of the software evolution processes. At this level, an EPM mainly lists the software processes involved in the software evolution. Specially, this level also indicates the sub-processes which will be embedded in the specified software processes. Also at this level, an EPM represents the global process framework from a strategic view. From the point of view of the software process, modellers can observe and control the whole of the software evolution process to avoid tunnel vision. However, this

level does not define the concurrency between software processes; the concurrent semantics can be defined at the process level by means of Petri Nets.

(2) Process level: This level consists of a set of software processes from coarse granularity to fine granularity and from the abstract to the concrete. These processes are distributed at different abstract levels. These software processes at different levels are obtained continuously by means of stepwise refinement. The process at a higher level is an abstract description of the process at a lower level, and the process at a lower level is a refinement to the process at a higher level. Both the higher level and the lower level are consistent in syntax and semantics. In addition, the concurrency between activities is defined by Petri Nets. Not losing the universality, a software process might be as well regarded as an activity. By means of describing the concurrency between activities, the concurrency between software processes can also be defined at the process level.

(3) Activity level: In EPM, the description of an activity is a class. A sub-class can inherit the characteristics of its super class. When an activity is executed, it is instantiated as an object. Therefore, an EPM at the activity level forms an object-oriented framework. The framework possesses the properties of object-oriented systems, including inheritance, abstract data type, encapsulation and information hiding etc.

(4) Task level: A task is an operation which transfers the input of an activity into the output. It is also the operation on an activity object. This level is located at the bottom of the framework. The function of a task is described by a 2-assertion consisting of a precondition and a postcondition. Based on Hoare Logic, both the precondition and the postcondition can precisely define the function of a task. By means of repeatedly decomposing a task's function into one of three basic control structures, the function is decomposed into a series of finer functions which can be realised easily.

6.3 Steps for Modelling Software Evolution Processes

The approach to modelling software evolution processes is tied up with the framework of software evolution processes. The framework decides that the workflow of the proposed modelling approach is a top-down spiral process called the *meta-process*. The meta-process is divided into six steps: communication, modelling at the global level, modelling at the process level, modelling at the activity level, modelling at the task level and efficiency improvement, as shown in Fig. 6.2.

The process combines elements of the linear sequential philosophy applied repetitively with the iterative philosophy. Each cycle produces a working version of an EPM with increasing functionality and improvement.

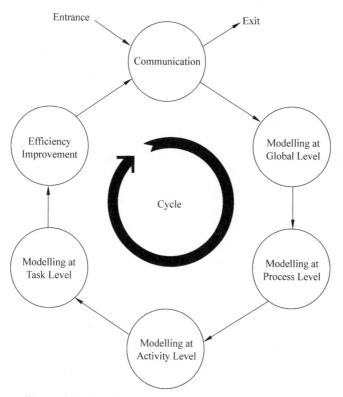

Figure 6.2   Steps for modelling software evolution processes

Step 1: Communication.

This step carries out communications between users and modellers. The main activities include elicitation, analysis and negotiation, feedback and validation. Elicitation determines what the customer requires. Analysis and negotiation understand the relationships among various customer requirements and shape those relationships to achieve a successful result. For the products of modelling software evolution processes at the end of a cycle, the users provide a feedback. According to the feedback, validation determines where the next step is.

Step 2: Modelling at the global level.

This step identifies all the software processes and determines their embedded relations. These processes and their relations constitute the global model. The model at this level aims to provide users with a global evolution roadmap. Perhaps the model is not operational; but it gives the users a bird's eye view of the software evolution process.

Step 3: Modelling at the process level.

This step defines software processes. The models at this level aim to provide users with a roadmap which identifies the relationship between activities in a software evolution process. The model is at the tactical level and medium-grained.

Step 4: Modelling at the activity level.

This step defines details of activities. The models at this level aim to provide users with a detailed roadmap which indicates what activities do. In general, the models at this level are fine-grained.

Step 5: Modelling at the task level.

This step defines the details of tasks, including defining the function of each task using preconditions, postconditions and messages. After this step, all the classes (activities) and their operations (tasks) have been defined. Furthermore, if a function is coarse-grained, it should be decomposed into a series of finer functions so that these finer functions can be carried out smoothly. In general, the models at this level are finest-grained.

Step 6: Efficiency improvement.

After modelling at the task level, an EPM has been constructed. However, can it be executed at a higher speed? Is the efficiency satisfactory? Perhaps they are not. This step captures and extends the concurrency in a software evolution process and reconstructs the corresponding EPM so as to improve the efficiency of the software evolution process.

The following guidelines are suggested to be applied for modelling software evolution processes:

(1) Communications with humans are necessary so that timely feedbacks from users can be obtained. On the other hand, the modelling process should be conducted by the users. Therefore, completely formal modelling is difficult. On the other hand, human users are easily out of control; therefore, completely informal modelling is imprecise. Combining the informal and the formal modelling, a semi-formal modelling approach is necessary. However, all the models produced by the proposed approach are fully formal.

(2) Refinement is a fundamental philosophy in modelling. The level numbers of refinement should not be too deep using the white box approach (see Chapter 7). Too many levels will increase the complexity of the processes. Although the numbers of refinement depends on modellers, according to requirements, a large process should be divided into smaller processes.

(3) The division of the model granularity is relative. The granularities of different projects and between different users are inconsistent. For example, from the point of view of a programmer, a model might be coarser-grained; but from the point of view of a manager, it might be fine-grained. Therefore, the granularity of a model should be determined by modellers depending on the real-world requirements.

(4) Roles are very important. When defining activities and tasks, appropriate roles should be identified.

(5) It is very important to ensure interface consistency between models at higher level and lower level.

(6) When a project is very big and complex, the black box approach is preferred. The black box approach decomposes a process into two. Therefore, it

can effectively reduce the complexity of a model.

(7) When recursively modelling, it is necessary to ensure the existence of an exit in the process of modelling.

(8) The object-oriented modelling technology can be used to model activity classes (the descriptions of activities) and activity objects (the instances of activities).

(9) After modelling, the modellers should optimise these models, such as removing redundant components and merging similar components.

6.4   Designing Global Models

Designing global models refers to modelling software evolution processes at the global level. EPMM is strictly formal and can describe software evolution processes exactly. The modelling approach is top-down. For each software process in the global model, an initial block is firstly modelled, as shown in Fig. 6.3. By modelling software evolution processes level by level, modellers can obtain a series of models at different abstract levels. Procedure 6.1 constructs EPM at the global level.

Figure 6.3   Initial block

Procedure 6.1   (Procedure for Modelling Evolution Processes at the Global Level)

```
PROCEDURE Modelling_Global_Model;
VAR i: integer; /* i is the level number of a software process. */
   p, p(0), .., p(MAX): software process;
/* p(0), …, p(MAX) denote software processes from level 0 to level
MAX respectively. MAX is the maximum level number. */
BEGIN
   Identify all the software processes which constitute set P;
   E:=Ø; /* E denotes the embedded relation. */
   FOR each p∈P DO /* loop for every p */
      BEGIN
         Define p(0) as an initial block;
         IF modellers consider that the start of p must be determined by other processes
            THEN p(0).M₀:=Ø /* p(0).M₀ denotes the initial marking of p(0). */
            ELSE p(0).M₀:={start};
         Replace p with p(0) in P
      END;
   FOR each p(0)∈P DO
      BEGIN
         i:=0;
```

```
    Call Modelling_Process(i, p(i)); /* Call Procedure 7.1 */
    Replace p(0) with p(i+1) in P;
    Replace p(0) with p(i+1) in E
  END;
  Define global model g=(P, E)
END. /*End of Modelling_Global_Model */
```

6.5   Evolution Process Descriptions

Though similar to certain ways, an evolution process description (EPD) differs much from an evolution process model (EPM). An EPM is abstract, which is an abstract and static representation of a software evolution process; an EPD is concrete, which defines all details of a software evolution process so that it can be enacted. However, both them can be used to specify software evolution processes. Therefore, an EPD can be regarded as a detailed description of an EPM.

In comparison with software development, modelling can be compared to design and describing to coding. In fact, modelling a software evolution process is to design the process to produce an EPM; describing a software evolution process is to code the process in detail to produce an EPD using EPDL, as shown in Table 6.1. After an EPM is constructed, it should be described by EPDL.

Table 6.1   Comparison with software development

Process Modelling and Description		Software Development	
Phase	**Product**	**Phase**	**Product**
1. Modelling Evolution Process	**EPM**	**1. Software Design**	**Design Product**
1.1 At the Global Level	Global Model	1.1 System Design	System Architecture
1.2 At the Process Level	Processes	1.2 Subsystem Design	Subsystems
1.3 At the Activity Level	Activities	1.3 Object Design	Classes/Objects
1.4 At the Task Level	Tasks	1.4 Method Design	Methods
2. Describing Evolution Process	**EPDL Program**	**2. Software Coding**	**Source Codes**

Because EPMM is more abstract than EPDL, much information in software evolution processes, such as code segment and role, can be described by EPDL but cannot be described by EPMM. From the point of view of modelling, the preceding information should also not be described in EPM because the model should be abstract. If all the information has been described, the model is too concrete so that it becomes the description of a software evolution process. A description is the refinement of an EPM and can be defined by EPDL.

As stated before, EPDL has the same framework and structure as EPMM. Therefore, it is not difficult to transform an EPM defined by EPMM into a process description EPD, i.e. an EPDL program. The advantages of separating a model from a description are the same as that of separating design from coding. Keeping the model abstract is in favour of defining important aspects and omitting minor aspects.

6.6   Summary

In this chapter, the framework of software evolution processes is discussed.

Firstly, a software evolution process described by EPMM forms a multi-level framework: the global level, the process level, the activity level and the task level. Each level possesses specified structures and different modelling requirements.

Secondly, according to the characteristics of models at different levels, a top-down spiral meta-process for modelling software evolution processes is proposed. The meta-process includes six steps: communications, modelling at the global level, modelling at the process level, modelling at the activity level, modelling at the task level and efficiency improvement. In order to effectively support the meta-process, some guidelines to construct EPMs are also presented.

Thirdly, a procedure for modelling software evolution processes at the global level is developed.

Finally, after an EPM is constructed, an EPDL program can be constructed using EPDL. A program is a detailed description of an EPM.

The approach proposed in this chapter also needs further discussions and refinements in the later chapters.

References

[1] Aoyama M (1998) Agile software process and its experience. In: Proceedings of the 20th international conference on software engineering. IEEE Computer Society, Washington DC, pp 3 – 12

[2] ISO, IEC (1998) ISO/IEC 12207 standard for information technology—software life cycle processes

[3] OMG (2002) Software process engineering metamodel specification. Object Management Group

[4] Osterweil LJ (1987) Software processes are software too. In: Proceedings of the 9th international conference on software engineering. ACM Press, New York, pp 2 – 13

[5] Osterweil LJ (1997) Software processes are software too, revisited: an invited talk on the most influential paper of ICSE 9. In: Proceedings of the 19th international conference on software engineering. ACM Press, New York, pp 540 – 548

[6] Osterweil LJ (2003) Understanding process and the quest for deeper questions in software engineering research. ACM SIGSOFT Software Engineering Notes 8: 6 – 14

[7] Redwine ST (1991) Software process architecture issues. In: Proceedings of the 7th international software process workshop. IEEE Computer Society, Washington DC, pp 117 – 120

7 Designing Processes and Activities

Tong Li

School of Software, Yunnan University, Kunming, 650091, China
Software Technology Research Laboratory, De Montfort University, Leicester, LE1 9BH, U.K
tli@ynu.edu.cn

Abstract   Modelling software evolution processes at the process level (designing process) and at the activity level (designing activity) are two important steps. In this chapter, based on EPMM and EPDL, the approaches to modelling software evolution processes at these two levels are proposed. The concepts of the process package and the basic block are presented. The modelling procedures are top-down refinement and stepwise refinement; they produce software evolution processes at different abstract levels. Furthermore, three different process reuse methods are presented: reuse by inheritances, reuse of process package (the black box approach) and reuse of basic blocks (the white box approach). In addition, it is proved that the interface consistency of software processes over hierarchies constructed by the black box approach and the white box approach is preserved.

Key Words   process, activity, basic block, process package, sequence block, concurrency block, selection block, iteration block, input flow, output flow, procedure, white box approach, black box approach, refinement, reuse, object-orientation, inheritance, interface consistency, consistency preservation, proof.

Objectives

- To propose the semi-formal procedures to model software evolution processes at the process level and at the activity level
- To propose the white box approach and the black box approach of activity refinement
- To propose the methods for the reuse of EPMs, and
- To prove the interface consistency of software processes over hierarchies

7.1 Introduction

Designing processes and activities is respectively called as modelling software evolution processes at the process level and at the activity level. The approaches to modelling software processes are various, but mainly include top-down and bottom-up approaches. Software process modelling as an effective abstract approach has been receiving more attention recently. There have been a great number of studies in this area (Bandinelli *et al.* 1993; Fuggetta 2000; Osterweil 1997, 2003; Lehman and Ramil 2002). However, the approaches to modelling software evolution processes are rarely discussed.

In this chapter, at first, two semi-formal procedures are proposed to model software evolution processes at the process level and at the activity level respectively. These procedures are top-down refinement and stepwise refinement. The refinements utilise both the white box approach and the black box approach. The notions of the process package and the basic block are presented to support refinement. Furthermore, these procedures also support the reuse of EPMs. Three different reuse approaches are presented. The reuse of software processes is carried out by means of refinements which produce software processes at different levels. It is proved that the interface consistency of software processes over different hierarchies is preserved.

7.2 Designing Processes

Designing processes refers to modelling software evolution processes at the process level. The definitions of software processes are based on Petri Nets. A software process is composed of many finer Petri Net models called *blocks*. Blocks include basic blocks and process packages. *Basic blocks* describe some kinds of basic behaviours in evolution processes. *Process packages* are reusable software processes. Modelling evolution processes at the process level is to refine activities repeatedly as these blocks until there are no activities which should be further refined.

At this level, modelling approaches include the white box approach and the black box approach. When an activity is refined as a basic block, because the inner structures are open to the outside, the white box approach is applied. When an activity is refined as a process package, because the inner structures are hidden from the outside, the black box approach is applied. Procedure 7.1 describes the refinement approach.

7.2.1 Basic Blocks

Definition 7.1 The sequence block, concurrency block, selection block and iteration block are called *basic blocks*. A basic block can be described as a 5-tuple $b = (C, A; F, A_e, A_x)$ where

(1) C, A and F are called the *condition set*, the *activity set* and the *arc set*, respectively;

(2) A_e, $A_x \subseteq A$ are called the *entrance* and the *exit* of b, respectively.

Basic blocks, which are enclosed by dotted lines in figures, are described as follows where each e_i ($i = 1, 2, \cdots$) denotes an activity.

(1) Sequence block: This describes that activities e_i and e_j are executed sequentially, as shown in Fig. 7.1. Formally, $C = \{c\}$, $A = \{e_i, e_j\}$, $F = \{(e_i, c), (c, e_j)\}$, $A_e = \{e_i\}$, $A_x = \{e_j\}$.

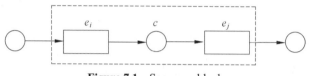

Figure 7.1   Sequence block

(2) Concurrency block: This describes that activities e_i and e_j are executed concurrently, as shown in Fig. 7.2. Formally, $C = \{c_1, c_2, c_3, c_4\}$, $A = \{e_0, e_i, e_j, e_n\}$, $F = \{(e_0, c_1), (e_0, c_2), (c_1, e_i), (c_2, e_j), (e_i, c_3), (e_j, c_4), (c_3, e_n), (c_4, e_n)\}$, $A_e = \{e_0\}$, $A_x = \{e_n\}$.

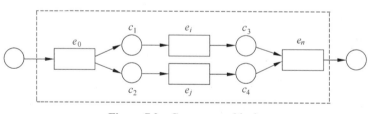

Figure 7.2   Concurrency block

(3) Selection block: This describes that activities e_i and e_j are executed selectively, as shown in Fig. 7.3. Formally, $C = \{\ \}$, $A = \{e_i, e_j\}$, $F = \{\ \}$, $A_e = \{e_i, e_j\}$, $A_x = \{e_i, e_j\}$.

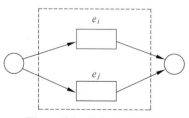

Figure 7.3   Selection block

(4) Iteration block: This describes that activities e_i and e_j are executed repeatedly, as shown in Fig. 7.4. Formally, $C = \{c_1, c_2\}$, $A = \{e_0, e_i, e_j, e_n\}$, $F = \{(e_0, c_1), (c_1, e_i), (e_i, c_2), (c_2, e_j), (e_j, c_1), (c_2, e_n)\}$, $A_e = \{e_0\}$, $A_x = \{e_n\}$.

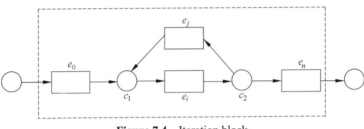

Figure 7.4   Iteration block

The approach to modelling software processes is top-down. First, an initial block is modelled. Furthermore, the initial block is repeatedly refined by basic blocks using a recursive procedure until modellers consider the granularity of the model to be satisfactory.

7.2.2   Software Process Package

A software process package is used to refine an activity, i.e. an activity is replaced with a software process.

Definition 7.2   Let $p = (C, A; F, M_0)$ be a software process. For activity $a \in A$, inflow$(a) = \{(x, a) \mid (x, a) \in F, x \in C\}$ is called the *input flow* of a; outflow$(a) = \{(a, y) \mid (a, y) \in F, y \in C\}$ is called the *output flow* of a. For set $G \subseteq A$, inflow $(G) = \bigcup_{a \in G}$ inflow(a), outflow$(G) = \bigcup_{a \in G}$ outflow(a).

Definition 7.3   A *software process package* is a 11-tuple $c = (C, A; F, M_0, I, L, O, a_e, a_x, S, W)$ or a 2-tuple $c = (f, p)$ where

(1) $p = (C, A; F, M_0)$, called the *body* of software process package c, is a software process and $M_0 = \varnothing$;

(2) $f = (I, L, O, a_e, a_x, S, W)$ is called the *interface* of software process package c;

(3) $I \subseteq A.I$, $L \subseteq A.L$ and $O \subseteq A.O$ are respectively called the *input data structure*, the *local data structure* and the *output data structure* of software process package c; $A.I = \bigcup_{a_i \in A} a_i.I$, $A.L = \bigcup_{a_i \in A} a_i.L$, $A.O = \bigcup_{a_i \in A} a_i.O.a_i.I, a_i.L$ and $a_i.O$ denote the input data structure, the local data structure and the output data structure of $a_i (a_i \in A)$, respectively;

(4) a_e, $a_x \in A$ are called the *entrance* and the *exit* of c respectively if $\exists$ a step sequence $G_1 G_2 \cdots G_{n-1}$ ($G_1, G_2, \cdots, G_{n-1} \subseteq A$) and $\exists$ cases $M_1, M_2, \cdots, M_n \subseteq C$, such that $[a_e > M_1, M_1[G_1 > M_2, \cdots, M_{n-1}[G_{n-1} > M_n, M_n[a_x > \text{ and } (M_n - {}^{\bullet}a_x) = \varnothing$;

(5) When c refines an activity a, inflow$(a_e) = \{(x, a_e)|(x, a)\in\text{inflow}(a)\}$, outflow$(a_x) = \{(a_x, y)| (a, y)\in\text{outflow}(a)\}$;

(6) S, called the *mini specification*, is a set of strings which is used to describe the software process package c concisely;

(7) W is a set of *key words* of the mini specification.

7.2.3 Procedure for Modelling Processes

Modelling software evolution processes at the process level, i.e. designing processes, is described by Procedure 7.1, which is called by Procedure 6.1.

Procedure 7.1 (Procedure for Modelling Evolution Processes at the Process Level)

```
PROCEDURE Modelling_Process(VAR i: integer, p(i): software process);
VAR p(i+1): software process;
BEGIN
 p(i+1):=p(i);
 FOR each a∈p(i).A DO /* p(i).A denotes the set of activities in p(i). */
   BEGIN
     Analyse a;
     IF modeller wants to apply the white box approach THEN
       BEGIN /* the white box refinement */
         Determine a basic block b=(C, A; F, Ae, Ax);
         p(i+1).C:= p(i+1).C∪b.C;
         p(i+1).A:= p(i+1).A-{a}∪b.A;
         p(i+1).F:=p(i+1).F-inflow(a)-outflow(a) ∪{(x, y) | (x, a)∈inflow(a)∧y∈
b.Ae}∪{(x, y)|x∈b.Ax∧(a, y)∈outflow(a)}
       END ELSE
     IF modeller wants to apply the black box approach THEN
       BEGIN /* the black box refinement */
         Search for a process package p' which can be used to refine a;
         IF p' is not found
           THEN construct process package p';
         Let p'=(C, A; F, M0, I, L, O, ae, ax, S, W);
         a.I:=p'.I; /* a.I denotes the input data structure of a. */
         a.L:=p'.L; /* a.L denotes the local data structure of a. */
         a.O:=p'.O; /* a.O denotes the output data structure of a. */
         a.B:=p'; /* a.B denotes the body of activity a. */
         P:=P∪{p'}; /* p' is added into set P in global model. */
         E:=E∪{(p(0), p')} /* The embedded relation is added into set E in global
model. */
       END
   END; /*end of FOR loop */
 IF modeller wants to continue refining THEN Call Modelling_Process(i+1, p(i+1))
END. /*End of Modelling_Process*/
```

By Procedure 7.1, the modellers can get a series of software processes at different granularities. These processes can be selected for use according to the different requirements. After modelling, because EPDL is an object-oriented language, it is not difficult to describe these processes by means of inheritance. Therefore, modellers can make full use of the advantages of software reuse to decrease the modelling costs and increase the modelling speed.

Procedure 7.1 supports both the white box and the black box modelling approach. The *white box approach* means that the details of lower processes (basic blocks) are open to its higher model. The *black box approach* means that the details of lower processes are hidden from its higher model. The white box approach and the black box approach are shown in Fig. 7.5. When modelling an evolution process, both the white box approach and the black box approach can be used interchangeably.

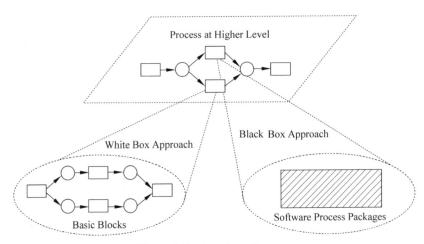

Figure 7.5   Activity refinement

Theoretically, Procedure 7.1 can refine software processes infinite times by means of calling itself recursively. However, too many refinement times are not suitable for real-world projects. The most suitable number of refinement times depends on the projects and modellers involved.

7.3   Designing Activities

Designing activities refers to modelling software evolution processes at the activity level, as described by Procedure 7.2.

Procedure 7.2   (Procedure for Modelling Evolution Processes at the Activity Level)

```
PROCEDURE Modelling_Activity(VAR p: software process);
  BEGIN
    FOR each a∈p.A DO /* p.A denotes the set of activities in p. */
      BEGIN
```

```
Analyse a;
IF there is another activity b from which a can inherit its characteristics
   THEN
      BEGIN
         Define a as b;
         Adjust a according to requirements
      END ELSE
      BEGIN
         Define input, output and local data structures;
         Determine the paths of message passing;
         Define the task set T of a;
         Call Modelling_Task(T); /* Call Procedure 8.1 to model tasks. */
         Define a with data structures and tasks
      END
   END /* End of FOR loop */
END. /* End of Modelling_Activity */
```

Because an activity is a class, all the activities form an object-oriented architecture and constitute an object-oriented system. Therefore, object-oriented modelling technologies can be used to model activities.

7.4 Reuse of Software Evolution Processes

Software reuse is a popular method of developing software. Process reuse is a special type of software reuse. It emphasises the composition from pre-packaged software processes or ready-made activities rather than by constructing them directly. The reuse methods of software evolution processes include the reuse by inheritance, the reuse of process packages and the reuse of basic blocks.

7.4.1 Reuse by Inheritance

An important characteristic of object-oriented technology is inheritance. Inheritance is one of the most successful reuses in the history of software.

The reuse by inheritance is described by the FROM clause in EPDL. This method includes reuse at the process level and at the activity level. The basic reuse statements of EPDL are as follows:

(1) ACTIVITY <Sub-Activity Name> FROM <Super Activity Name> [<Other Definitions>];

(2) PROCESS <Inherited Sub-Software Process Name> FROM <Super Software Process Name> [<Other Definitions>].

At the activity level, if <Other Definitions> is omitted, the sub-activity will completely inherit all the characteristics of its super activity. Similarly, at the process level, if <Other Definitions> is omitted, the sub-process will completely inherit all the characteristics of its super process. These rarely happen because a completely identical activity or process is meaningless. Therefore, <Other Definitions> always occurs to modify the characteristics which the process or activity have inherited. In <Other Definitions>, there are three situations in occurrences of definitions D_1, D_2 and D_3, as shown in Fig. 7.6.

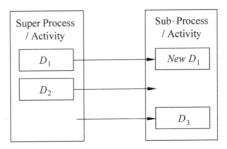

Figure 7.6 Situations of inheritance

In Fig. 7.6, D_1 is inherited by a sub-process or a sub-activity; but D_1 is replaced with a new D_1 in the sub-process or the sub-activity. D_2 occurs in the super process or the super activity but it does not occur in the sub-process or the sub-activity, which denotes that D_2 is completely inherited by the sub-process or the sub-activity. D_3 does not occur in the super process or the super activity but it occurs in the sub-process or the sub-activity, which denotes that the sub-process or the sub-activity adds a new characteristic, D_3, which does not belong to the super process or the super activity.

When an inherited sub-process inherits a super process, if a " – " operation is applied to a set (condition set, activity set or arc set), the corresponding elements in these sets are removed. The inheritance relations between super process/super activity and sub-process/sub-activity constitute a hierarchical architecture which possesses the characteristics of object-oriented systems.

It should be pointed out that there are two kinds of sub-processes. The first is derived by means of inheritance as discussed in this section. The second is derived by means of refining an activity. These two kinds of sub-processes are different from each other. Therefore, if confusion might be possible, the former is called the *inherited sub-process*.

7.4.2 Reuse of Basic Blocks

When a basic block is used to replace an activity, the basic block is reused. The basic blocks are the finest-grained reusable components of software processes. When a basic block replaces an activity (the white box approach), it is of importance to preserve the interface consistency between before replacement and after replacement.

Definition 7.4 Let $p = (C, A; F, M_0)$ be a software process. For $a \in p.A$, a software process $p' = (C, A; F, M_0)$ is obtained by means of refining a as $b = (C, A; F)$. If $\exists M$, $M' \subseteq p.C$ such that $M[a > M'$, then $\exists$ a step sequence $G_0 G_1 G_2 \cdots G_{n-1} G_n$ ($G_0, G_1, \cdots, G_n \subseteq b.A \subseteq p'.A$) and $\exists$ cases $M_1, M_2, \cdots, M_n \subseteq b.C \subseteq p'.C$ such that $M[G_0 > M_1, M_1[G_1 > M_2, M_2[G_2 > M_3, \cdots, M_{n-1}[G_{n-1} > M_n$, and $M_n[G_n > M'$, p is *interface consistent* with p', or p' is *interface consistent* with p, or p and p' preserve the *interface consistency*.

Theorem 7.1 Let $p = (C, A; F, M_0)$ be a software process; let $b = (C, A; F, A_e, A_x)$ be a basic block. For $a \in p.A$, a software process $p' = (C, A; F, M_0)$ is defined as follows:

(1) $p'.C = p.C \cup b.C$;

(2) $p'.A = p.A - \{a\} \cup b.A$;

(3) $p'.F = p.F -$ inflow(a) $-$ outflow(a) $\cup \{(x, y)|(x, a) \in$ inflow(a) $\wedge y \in b.A_e\} \cup \{(x, y)| x \in b.A_x \wedge (a, y) \in$ outflow(a)$\}$;

(4) $p'.M_0 = p.M_0$.

If $\exists M$, $M' \subseteq p.C$ (of course M, $M' \subseteq p'.C$) such that $M[a > M'$, then $\exists$ a step sequence $G_1 G_2 \cdots G_{n-1}$ ($G_1, G_2, \cdots, G_{n-1} \subseteq p'.A$) and $\exists$ cases $M_1, M_2, \cdots, M_n \subseteq p'.C$ such that $M[A_e > M_1, M_1[G_1 > M_2, M_2[G_2 > M_3, \cdots, M_{n-1}[G_{n-1} > M_n$, and $M_n[A_x > M'$.

Proof In software process p:

Suppose a is M-enabled in p. Namely, before a is executed, ${}^{\cdot}a \subseteq M \wedge a^{\cdot} \cap M = \emptyset$; after a is executed, $M' = (M - {}^{\cdot}a) \cup a^{\cdot}$.

Let $R = M - {}^{\cdot}a$. The conditions in R are not used by a and b.

(1) Suppose b is a sequence block. $b = (\{c\}, \{e_i, e_j\}; \{(e_i, c), (c, e_j)\}, \{e_i\}, \{e_j\})$. The corresponding parts of software process p (dotted line) and p' is shown in Fig. 7.7.

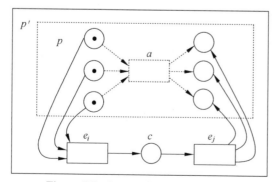

Figure 7.7 Reuse of a sequence block

If a is M-enabled in p, e_i is M-enabled in p'. It follows that $M[\{e_i\}>\{c\}\cup R$, $\{c\}\cup R[\{e_j\}> M'$.

(2) Suppose b is a concurrency block. $b = (\{c_1, c_2, c_3, c_4\}, \{e_0, e_i, e_j, e_n\}; \{(e_0, c_1),$ $(e_0, c_2), (c_1, e_i), (c_2, e_j), (e_i, c_3), (e_j, c_4), (c_3, e_n), (c_4, e_n)\}, \{e_0\}, \{e_n\})$. The corresponding parts of software process p (enclosed by dotted lines) and p' are shown in Fig. 7.8.

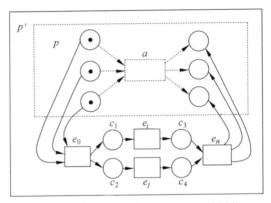

Figure 7.8   Reuse of a concurrency block

If a is M-enabled in p, e_0 is M-enabled in p'. It follows that
$$M[\{e_0\}>\{c_1, c_2\}\cup R, \{c_1, c_2\}\cup R[\{e_i, e_j\}>\{c_3, c_4\}\cup R, \{c_3, c_4\}\cup R[\{e_n\}> M';$$
or
$$M[\{e_0\}>\{c_1, c_2\}\cup R, \{c_1, c_2\}\cup R[\{e_i\}>\{c_3, c_2\}\cup R, \{c_3, c_2\}\cup R[\{e_j\}>\{c_3, c_4\}$$
$$\cup R, \{c_3, c_4\}\cup R[\{e_n\}> M';$$
or
$$M[\{e_0\}>\{c_1, c_2\}\cup R, \{c_1, c_2\}\cup R[\{e_j\}>\{c_1, c_4\}\cup R, \{c_1, c_4\}\cup R[\{e_i\}>\{c_3, c_4\}$$
$$\cup R, \{c_3, c_4\}\cup R[\{e_n\}> M'.$$

(3) Suppose b is a selection block. $b = (\{\ \}, \{e_i, e_j\}; \{\ \}, \{e_i, e_j\}, \{e_i, e_j\})$. The corresponding parts of software process p (dotted line) and p' are shown in Fig. 7.9.

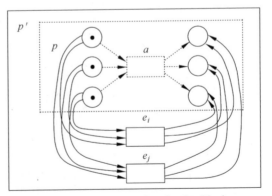

Figure 7.9   Reuse of a selection block

If a is M-enabled in p, e_i and e_j are M-enabled in p'. However, they cannot fire concurrently. If e_i fires, $M[\{e_i\}>M'$. If e_j fires, $M[\{e_j\}>M'$. In this case, the step sequence $G_1G_2\cdots G_{n-1}$ ($G_1, G_2, \cdots, G_{n-1} \subseteq p'. A$) is empty, i.e. $n = 1$.

(4) Suppose b is an iteration block. $b = (\{c_1, c_2\}, \{e_0, e_i, e_j, e_n\}; \{(e_0, c_1), (c_1, e_i), (e_i, c_2), (c_2, e_j), (e_j, c_1), (c_2, e_n)\}, \{e_0\}, \{e_n\})$. The corresponding parts of software process p (enclosed by dotted lines) and p' are shown in Fig. 7.10.

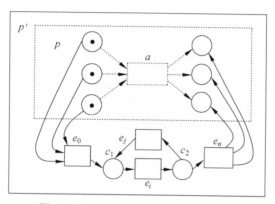

Figure 7.10   Reuse of an iteration block

If a is M-enabled in p, e_0 is M-enabled in p'. It follows that $M[\{e_0\}>\{c_1\} \cup R$, $\{c_1\} \cup R\,[\{e_i\}>\{c_2\} \cup R$, $\{c_2\} \cup R[\{e_j\}>\{c_1\} \cup R,\cdots$, $\{c_1\} \cup R[\{e_i\}>\{c_2\} \cup R$, $\{c_2\} \cup R\,[\{e_n\}>M'.\ \square$

Theorem 7.1 indicates that when a basic block replaces an activity, the interface consistency is preserved between before the replacement and after the replacement. Namely the white box approach preserves the interface consistency.

Obviously, Fig. 7.11(a), which describes the iteration of e_i and e_j, can be simplified as Fig. 7.11(b) which also describes the same iteration. This leads to a

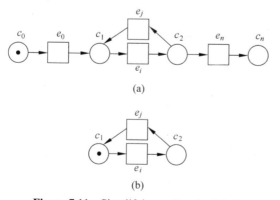

Figure 7.11   Simplifying an iteration block

simple and clear software process. When modelling, Fig. 7.11(b) can replace Fig. 7.11(a) to describe the iteration of e_i and e_j.

7.4.3 Reuse of Process Packages

A software process package is an encapsulated software process. In black box modelling, a software process package is often used to refine an activity. When a refinement happens, the process package is a sub-process of the process to which the activity belongs. The sub-process and its super process are at different levels. In this way, a hierarchical framework of software processes is constructed. A hierarchical separation of the software processes in a consistent way can effectively reduce the complexity of modelling and cope with the state space explosion of Petri Nets. Therefore, it is of importance to preserve the interface consistency over hierarchical software processes.

In EPDL, a software process package can be described as a software process. Namely, both software process and software process package can be described in the same way. The reuse of a software process package is shown in Fig. 7.12.

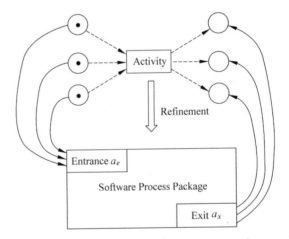

Figure 7.12 Reuse of a software process package

Theorem 7.2 Let $p = (C, A; F, M_0)$ be a software process, $c = (C, A; F, M_0, I, L, O, a_e, a_x, S, W)$ a software process package. For $a \in p.A$, a is refined as c. If $\exists$ $M, M' \subseteq p.C$ such that $M[a > M'$, then $\exists$ a step sequence $G_1 G_2 \cdots G_{n-1}$ ($G_1, G_2, \cdots, G_{n-1} \subseteq c.A$) and $\exists$ cases $M_1, M_2, \cdots, M_n \subseteq c.C$, such that $M[a_e > M_1, M_1[G_1 > M_2, M_2[G_2 > M_3, \cdots, M_{n-1}[G_{n-1} > M_n,$ and $M_n[a_x > M'$.

Proof Suppose a is M-enabled in p. Namely, before a is executed, $\dot{}a \subseteq M \land a\dot{} \cap M = \emptyset$; after a is executed, $M' = (M - \dot{}a) \cup a\dot{}$.

Let $R = M - {}^{\bullet}a$. The conditions in R are not used by a and c. The following properties refer to the properties of software process package in Definition 7.3.

Since inflow$(a_e) = \{(x, a_e)|(x, a) \in \text{inflow}(a)\}$ (Property (5)), ${}^{\bullet}a = {}^{\bullet}a_e$.

Since $c.M_0 = \emptyset$ (Property (1)), if a is M-enabled, a_e is M-enabled.

It follows that $M[a_e>$.

Therefore, in c, $\exists$ a step sequence $G_1 G_2 \cdots G_{n-1}$ $(G_1, G_2, \cdots, G_{n-1} \subseteq c.A)$ and $\exists$ cases $M_1, M_2, \cdots, M_n \subseteq c.C$, such that $M[a_e > M_1, M_1[G_1 > M_2, \cdots, M_{n-1}[G_{n-1} > M_n,$ and $M_n[a_x>$ (Property (4))

Since outflow$(a_x) = \{(a_x, y)|(a, y) \in \text{outflow}(a)\}$ (Property (5)), $a^{\bullet} = a_x^{\bullet}$.

Therefore, if $M_n[a_x > M'', M'' = (M_n - {}^{\bullet}a_x) \cup a_x^{\bullet} = (M_n - {}^{\bullet}a_x) \cup a^{\bullet}$.

Since $(M_n - {}^{\bullet}a_x) = \emptyset$ (Property (1)), $M'' = a^{\bullet}$.

Therefore, after a_x is executed, in software process p, only the conditions in $a^{\bullet}$ and the conditions in R hold, i.e. $[a_x > a^{\bullet} \cup R = a^{\bullet} \cup (M - {}^{\bullet}a) = M' \subseteq p.C$.

It follows that $[a_x > M'. \square$

Theorem 7.2 indicates that when a software process package refines an activity, the interface consistency is preserved between before the replacement and after the replacement. Namely, the black box approach preserves the semantic consistency and interface consistency.

7.5 Summary

In this chapter, based on EPMM and EPDL, firstly, two procedures of modelling software evolution processes at the process level and at the activity level are proposed. The notions of both process packages and basic blocks are also presented. These procedures are top-down refinement and stepwise refinement. They produce some software processes at different levels.

Secondly, three different reuse methods are presented: reuse by inheritances, reuse of process package (the black box approach) and reuse of basic blocks (the white box approach).

Thirdly, it is proved that the interface consistency of software processes over hierarchies constructed by the black box approach and the white box approach is preserved.

Finally, it should be pointed out that an EPDL program can be coded after an EPM is constructed. The program is a detailed and refined description of a software evolution process.

References

[1] Bandinelli S, Fuggetta A, Grigolli S (1993) Process modeling in-the-large with SLANG. In: Proceedings of the 2nd international conference on software process. IEEE Computer Society Press, Washington DC, pp 75 – 83

[2] Fuggetta A (2000) Software process: a roadmap. In: Proceedings of the conference on the future of software engineering. ACM Press, New York, pp 25 – 34

[3] Lehman MM, Ramil JF (2002) Behavioural modelling of long-lived evolution processes: some issues and an example. Journal of Software Maintenance: Research and Practice 14: 335 – 351

[4] Lehman MM, Ramil JF (2002) Software evolution and software evolution processes. Annals of Software Engineering 14: 275 – 309

[5] Osterweil LJ (1997) Software processes are software too, revisited: an invited talk on the most influential paper of ICSE 9. In: Proceedings of the 19th international conference on software engineering. ACM Press, New York, pp 540 – 548

[6] Osterweil LJ (2003) Understanding process and the quest for deeper questions in software engineering research. ACM SIGSOFT Software Engineering Notes 8: 6 – 14

8 Designing Tasks

Tong Li

School of Software, Yunnan University, Kunming, 650091, China

Software Technology Research Laboratory, De Montfort University, Leicester, LE1 9BH, U.K

tli@ynu.edu.cn

Abstract After an activity is designed (modelling software evolution processes at the activity level), its tasks should be designed (modelling software evolution processes at the task level). The kernel objective of designing a task is functional decomposition. The function of a task is defined by both a precondition and a postcondition, which are first order predicate formulae. They define a function which transfers inputs into outputs. Although a task is the finest-grained component in software evolution processes, the function of a task might be more complex and coarse-grained when a task is first defined. In this chapter, an approach is proposed to decompose a function into finer functions that are easy to carry out. By means of matching the code segments in the segment base, matching the decomposition case in the case base and executing the decomposition rules in the rule base, functional decomposition is carried out. The decomposition process is described by a decomposition tree and executed until the granularity of the functions is appropriate. By synthesising the data in the decomposition tree, a framework composed of finer functions is generated. Three decomposition rules including sequence, selection and repetition decomposition rules are proposed and proved to be correct. The decomposed work products can be described by EPDL.

Key Words task, function, precondition, postcondition, functional decomposition, code segment, 2-assertion, input vector, output vector, basic control structure, sequence decomposition, selection decomposition, repetition decomposition, correctness, decomposition rule, predicate formula, termination, antecedent, case base, segment base, rule base, decomposition tree, match.

Objectives

- To propose a procedure to model tasks

- To present three decomposition rules to decompose a 2-assertion into one of three basic control structures
- To construct the case base, the segment base and the rule base to support decomposition, and
- To propose an approach that transforms a 2-assertion into a code segment composed of finer 2-assertions

8.1 Introduction

After an activity is designed, its tasks should be designed. *Designing tasks* refers to modelling software evolution processes at the task level, which is rarely discussed.

The kernel objective of designing a task is functional decomposition. Functional decomposition is a method for designing the detailed structure of individual programs or modules. It is also a method for designing the large-scale (architecture) structure of software. As its name suggests, functional decomposition is a method that focuses on the functions or actions that the software has to carry out (Bell 2000).

Hoare Logic may be viewed as an extension of first-order predicate calculus that includes inference rules for reasoning about programming language constructs (Hoare 1969). Hoare Logic provides a means of demonstrating that a program is consistent with its specification. In Hoare Logic, the Hoare triple "$\{P\}$ S $\{Q\}$" is used to describe the semantics of program S (Hein 2003). Hoare Logic does not make sure that S terminates. Therefore, Hoare Logic only handles partial correctness (Hoare 1969). The similar work in this area includes the "weakest precondition" proposed by Dijkstra (Dijkstra 1976; Dijkstra and Scholten 1990), which is a suitable formalism in software specification and transformation. The weakest precondition method can make sure of the termination of a program.

The function of a task is defined by both a precondition and a postcondition based on Hoare Logic, which are first order predicate formulae. The precondition defines the state before a task is executed; the postcondition defines the state after a task is executed. They define a function which transfers inputs into outputs. Tasks are the finest-grained components in software evolution processes from the points of view of EPMM and EPDL. However, the function of a task might be more complex and coarse-grained when a task is first defined from the points of view of modellers. Under these circumstances, the task might be too complex to be enacted. Its function needs to be decomposed into some finer and simpler functions.

In this chapter, an approach is proposed to decompose a function into finer functions that are easy to carry out. By means of matching the code segments in the segment base, matching the decomposition case in the case base and executing the decomposition rules in the rule base, functional decomposition is carried out. The decomposition process is described by a decomposition tree and executed until modellers consider that the granularity of the functions is appropriate. By synthesising the information in the decomposition tree, a framework composed of finer functions is generated. The framework is called a *code segment* which is combined into an integrated function by sequence, selection and repetition control structures. Accordingly, sequence, selection and repetition decomposition rules are proposed and are proved to be partially correct. If these decomposition results terminate, the corresponding decompositions are totally correct. The proposed approach emphasises that human modellers should participate in decomposition so that the insufficient knowledge base can draw on their knowledge and experience.

8.2   Procedure of Designing Tasks

Procedure 8.1 shows how to model software evolution processes at the task level, which is called by Procedure 7.2.

Procedure 8.1   (Procedure for Modelling Evolution Processes at the Task Level)

```
PROCEDURE Modelling_Task(VAR T: set of tasks);
  BEGIN
    Identify roles who execute the tasks in T;
    FOR each t∈T DO
      BEGIN
        Analyse t;
        Determine the roles that execute t;
        Determine messages to be received and their parameters;
        Define messages to be sent;
        Define the function of t as A(F)=(PR(X), PO(X, Y)); /* PR(X) denotes the
        precondition; PO(X, Y) denotes the postcondition. */
        IF A(F) is coarse-grained THEN
          Call Decomposing_2-Assertion(A(F)); /* Call Procedure 8.5 */
      END /* End of FOR loop */
  END. /* End of Modelling_Task */
```

Procedure 8.1 is role-centred. The role is an abstract concept. A role might be a person, a group of persons, a device, a tool or an agent in a computer. A person may play many roles and different persons may also play the same role. According to the different abstract levels, roles can also be divided into many levels. Roles at a higher level execute abstract and global tasks, and roles at a lower level execute concrete and local tasks. In EPM, a software process is executed by many roles. A task is executed by one to several roles.

8.3   Structures of Functional Decomposition

In order to decompose the function of a task, the structures of functional decomposition must be discussed. For the further discussion of tasks, a detailed definition of a function is presented as follows:

Definition 8.1　A *function F* is a 4-tuple $F = (D, R, PR(X), PO(X, Y))$ where

(1) $X = (x_1, x_2, \cdots, x_m)$ is the *input vector* and $Y = (y_1, y_2, \cdots, y_n)$ is the *output vector*. The elements in X and Y are called *variables*. $\{X\} = \{x_1, x_2, \cdots, x_m\}$, $\{Y\} = \{y_1, y_2, \cdots, y_n\}$ denote the set of input variables and the set of output variables respectively.

(2) $D = D_1 \times \cdots \times D_m$, is the *domain* of input vector, where $x_i \in D_i$ $(1 \leqslant i \leqslant m)$. $R = R_1 \times \cdots \times R_n$ is the *range* of output vector, where $y_j \in R_j (1 \leqslant j \leqslant n)$. D_i and R_j are data structures.

(3) $PR(X)$ is called the *precondition* and $PO(X, Y)$ is called the *postcondition*. They are first-order predicate formulae.

(4) The input vector X which satisfies $PR(X)$ is called a *legal input*. For legal input X, the output vector Y which satisfies $PO(X, Y)$ is called a *legal output*.

(5) $A(F) = (PR(X), PO(X, Y))$ is called the *2-assertion* of function F. The execution of $A(F)$ denotes that for a legal input X which satisfies $PR(X)$, if $A(F)$ terminates, a legal output Y which satisfies $PO(X, Y)$ is generated. $A(F)$ has no side effect, i.e. after $A(F)$ terminates, it does not change any variables' value except for the variables in Y.

The main part of a function is the 2-assertion $A(F) = (PR(X), PO(X, Y))$. $A(F)$ will be the focus in this chapter. $A(F)$ describes the function of a task as it describes the function of a program. However, the granularity of a task is generally much coarser than a program. The description of $A(F)$ in a task is more abstract than that in a program.

It should be pointed out that the execution of $A(F)$ can be carried out by computers, human users or both. For executing $A(F)$ in a computer, a section of executable code must be related to $A(F)$ so that the section of executable code implements the function described by $A(F)$.

In 1966, Bohm and Jacopini proposed that sequence, selection and repetition are basic control structures (Bohm and Jacopini 1966). Making use of their ideas, basic control structures of 2-assertions are proposed, as shown in Fig. 8.1. In some cases, $A(F)$ can be decomposed into one of the basic control structures. With repeated decomposition, the granularity of $A(F)$ might become appropriate.

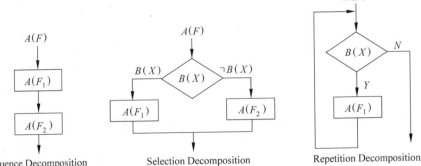

Sequence Decomposition　　　Selection Decomposition　　　Repetition Decomposition

Figure 8.1　Basic control structures of 2-assertions

Definition 8.2 To decompose a 2-assertion $A(F)$ into two 2-assertions $A(F_1)$ and $A(F_2)$ which are executed sequentially is called a *sequence decomposition*, denoted by $A(F) \models A(F_1) : A(F_2)$; $A(F_1) : A(F_2)$ is called a *sequence decomposition structure*.

Definition 8.3 To decompose a 2-assertion $A(F)$ into two 2-assertions $A(F_1)$ or $A(F_2)$, of which one can be executed according to a Boolean condition $B(X)$, is called a *selection decomposition*, denoted by $A(F) \models A(F_1) | B(X) | A(F_2)$; $A(F_1) | B(X) | A(F_2)$ is called a *selection decomposition structure*.

Definition 8.4 To decompose a 2-assertion $A(F)$ into a 2-assertion $A(F_1)$, which is executed repeatedly while Boolean condition $B(X)$ is true and exited while $B(X)$ is false, is called a *repetition decomposition*, denoted by $A(F) \models B(X)^* A(F_1)$; $B(X)^* A(F_1)$ is called a *repetition decomposition structure*.

Definition 8.5 Sequence decomposition, selection decomposition and repetition decomposition are called *decomposition*, denoted by $A(F) \models STR(F)$. $STR(F)$ is called a *decomposition structure*. The execution of $STR(F)$ means the 2-assertions in $STR(F)$ are executed according to the semantics of the corresponding control structure.

Definition 8.6 Let $F = (D, R, PR(X), PO(X, Y))$ and $A(F) \models STR(F)$. $STR(F)(X)$ denotes the output vector of $STR(F)$ when X is the input vector.

(1) A decomposition is called *partially correct* iff $\forall X \in D$, $PR(X)$ is true, if $STR(F)$ is executed and $STR(F)$ terminates, then $PO(X, STR(F)(X))$ is true.

(2) A decomposition is called *totally correct* iff $\forall X \in D$, $PR(X)$ is true, if $STR(F)$ is executed, then $STR(F)$ terminates and $PO(X, STR(F)(X))$ is true.

Generally, if human users execute $STR(F)$, they can make sure that $STR(F)$ terminates; if a computer executes $STR(F)$, it cannot make sure that $STR(F)$ terminates.

8.4 Decomposition Rules

Definition 8.7 A decomposition rule is a 2-tuple $RULE = (STR(F), P(F))$. $STR(F)$ is a decomposition structure. $P(F)$ is called a *decomposition procedure* which decomposes $A(F)$ into $STR(F)$.

Decomposition rules describe how to decompose $A(F)$. They play important roles in the knowledge base supporting task decomposition. The more rules there are, the more smoothly the decomposition is realised. Because it is difficult to decompose $STR(F)$ automatically, the rules and the procedures need to interact with human modellers.

To describe the decomposition procedures, $\{X\}$-antecedent must be firstly discussed. The concept of $\{X\}$-antecedent was presented and a formal system, RAINBOW, was developed for deriving antecedents by Smith. RAINBOW uses a problem-reduction approach to deriving antecedents (Smith 1985).

Definition 8.8 (Smith 1985)   Let $(\forall x_1 \cdots \forall x_i \forall x_{i+1} \cdots \forall x_n)G$ be a closed formula. A $\{x_1, \cdots, x_i\}$-*antecedent* of $(\forall x_1 \cdots \forall x_n)G$ is a formula P whose free variables are a subset of $\{x_1, \cdots, x_i\}$ such that $(\forall x_1 \cdots \forall x_i)(P \Rightarrow (\forall x_{i+1} \cdots \forall x_n)G)$ is true.

In the following, for the sake of simplicity, $\{x_1, \cdots, x_n\}$-antecedent is called $\{X\}$-*antecedent*, i.e. an $\{X\}$-*antecedent* of $(\forall x_1 \cdots \forall x_n)G$ is a formula P whose free variables are set $\{X\} = \{x_1, \cdots, x_n\}$ such that $\forall X(P \Rightarrow G)$ is true.

Definition 8.9   Let P be a predicate formula. $P(a/b)$ denotes the formula obtained from P by replacing all occurrences of a with b.

When executing the following procedures, the variables in X and Y should be renamed so that different variables have distinct names in $PR(X)$ and $PO(X, Y)$ if necessary.

8.4.1   Sequence Decomposition

The sequence decomposition decomposes $A(F)$ into $A(F_1)$ and $A(F_2)$ which are executed sequentially.

Let $A(F_1) = (PR_1(X), PO_1(X, Y))$, $A(F_2) = (PR_2(X), PO_2(X, Y))$. Procedure 8.2 describes how to derive $PR_1(X)$, $PR_2(X)$, $PO_1(X, Y)$ and $PO_2(X, Y)$.

Procedure 8.2   (Procedure of Sequence Decomposition)

```
PROCEDURE Sequence_Decomposition(PR(X), PO(X, Y): first-order predicate
formula);
BEGIN
    Transform PO(X, Y) so that PO(X, Y)≡PO₁(X, Y₁)∧PO₂(X, Y₂) and {X}∩{Y}=Ø and
{Y₁}∩{Y₂}=Ø; /* Y₁, Y₂ are two sub-vectors that consist of the elements in Y. */
    Let A(F₁)=(PR(X), PO₁(X, Y₁));
    Let A(F₂)=(PR(X), PO₂(X, Y₂))
END.
```

Theorem 8.1   The decomposition $A(F) \models A(F_1):A(F_2)$ of Procedure 8.2 is partially correct. If both $A(F_1)$ and $A(F_2)$ terminate, then $A(F) \models A(F_1):A(F_2)$ is totally correct.

Proof   Suppose $A(F) = (PR(X), PO_1(X, Y_1) \wedge PO_2(X, Y_2))$, $A(F_1) = (PR(X), PO_1(X, Y_1))$, $A(F_2) = (PR(X), PO_2(X, Y_2))$ and $\forall X \in D, PR(X)$ is true.

Firstly, $A(F_1)$ is executed. If it terminates, $PO_1(X, Y_1)$ is true.

Since $A(F_1)$ just changes the variable values of Y_1 and $\{X\} \cap \{Y\} = \emptyset$ and $\{Y_1\} \subseteq \{Y\}$, $PR(X)$ is still true.

Next, $A(F_2)$ is executed. If it terminates, $PO_2(X, Y_2)$ is true.

Since $A(F_2)$ just changes the variable values of Y_2 and $\{X\} \cap \{Y\} = \emptyset$ and $\{Y_2\} \subseteq \{Y\}$ and $\{Y_1\} \cap \{Y_2\} = \emptyset$, $PO_1(X, Y_1)$ is still true.

Therefore $PO_1(X, Y_1) \wedge PO_2(X, Y_2)$ is true. It follows that $PO(X, Y)$ is true.

Hence $A(F) \models A(F_1):A(F_2)$.

Because $A(F_1)$ and $A(F_2)$ is supposed to terminate, the decomposition of

Procedure 8.2 is partially correct. If both of them terminate, the decomposition of Procedure 8.2 is totally correct. $\square$

8.4.2 Selection Decomposition

The selection decomposition decomposes $A(F)$ into $A(F_1)$ when $B(X)$ is true and $A(F_2)$ when $B(X)$ is false.

Let $A(F_1) = (PR_1(X_1), PO_1(X_1, Y))$, $A(F_2) = (PR_2(X_2), PO_2(X_2, Y))$, such that $(\forall X \in D)(PR(X) \wedge B(X) \Rightarrow PR_1(X_1))$, $(\forall X \in D)(PR(X) \wedge \neg B(X) \Rightarrow PR_2(X_2))$, $(\forall X \in D)$ $(\forall Y \in R)(PO_1(X_1, Y) \wedge B(X) \Rightarrow PO(X, Y))$ and $(\forall X \in D)(\forall Y \in R)(PO_2(X_2, Y) \wedge \neg B(X) \Rightarrow PO(X, Y))$ hold. X_1, X_2 are the sub-vectors that consist of the elements in X. Procedure 8.3 describes how to derive $B(X)$, $PR_1(X_1)$, $PR_2(X_2)$, $PO_1(X_1, Y)$ and $PO_2(X_2, Y)$.

Procedure 8.3　(Procedure of Selection Decomposition)

```
PROCEDURE Selection_Decomposition(PR(X), PO(X, Y): first-order predicate
formula);
BEGIN
  Transform PR(X) and PO(X, Y) so that {X}∩{Y}=∅;
  REPEAT
    Transform PO(X, Y) so that PO(X, Y)≡PO₁(X₁, Y)∨PO₂(X₂, Y);
    FOR each atom a in PR(X)∧(∃variable x in a∧x∉{X₁}) DO
      Let PR₁(X₁)=PR(X)(a/true);
    FOR each atom a in PR(X)∧(∃variables x in a∧x∉{X₂}) DO
      Let PR₂(X₂)=PR(X)(a/true);
    Derive {X}-antecedent J'(X) of (∀X∈D)(PR(X)⇒PR₁(X₁));
    Derive {X}-antecedent J"(X) of (∀X∈D)(PR(X)⇒PR₂(X₂));
    Derive {X}-antecedent K'(X) of (∀X∈D)(∀Y∈R)(PO₁(X₁, Y)⇒PO(X, Y));
    Derive {X}-antecedent K"(X) of (∀X∈D)(∀Y∈R)(PO₂(X₂, Y)⇒PO(X, Y));
    Let B'(X)≡J'(X)∧K'(X);
    Let B"(X)≡J"(X)∧K"(X)
  UNTIL (∀X∈D)(PR(X)⇒B'(X)∨B"(X)) is true;
  Let A(F₁)=(PR₁(X₁), PO₁(X₁, Y));
  Let A(F₂)=(PR₂(X₂), PO₂(X₂, Y));
  Let B(X)≡B'(X)
END.
```

Theorem 8.2　The decomposition $A(F) \models A(F_1)|B(X)|A(F_2)$ of Procedure 8.3 is partially correct. If both $A(F_1)$ and $A(F_2)$ terminate, then $A(F) \models A(F_1)|B(X)| A(F_2)$ is totally correct.

Proof　Since $J'(X)$ is $\{X\}$-antecedent of $(\forall X \in D)(PR(X) \Rightarrow PR_1(X_1))$, $(\forall X \in D)$ $(J'(X) \Rightarrow (PR(X) \Rightarrow PR_1(X_1))) \equiv (\forall X \in D)(PR(X) \wedge J'(X) \Rightarrow PR_1(X_1))$ is true.

Since $J"(X)$ is $\{X\}$-antecedent of $(\forall X \in D)(PR(X) \Rightarrow PR_2(X_2))$, $(\forall X \in D)$ $(J"(X) \Rightarrow (PR(X) \Rightarrow PR_2(X_2))) \equiv (\forall X \in D)(PR(X) \wedge J"(X) \Rightarrow PR_2(X_2))$ is true.

Since $K'(X)$ is $\{X\}$-antecedent of $(\forall X \in D)(\forall Y \in R)(PO_1(X_1, Y) \Rightarrow PO(X,$

115

$Y))\wedge\{X\}\cap\{Y\} = \varnothing$, $(\forall X\in D)(K'(X) \Rightarrow (\forall Y\in R)(PO_1(X_1, Y) \Rightarrow PO(X, Y)))\equiv$ $(\forall X\in D)(\forall Y\in R)(PO_1(X_1, Y)\wedge K'(X)\Rightarrow PO(X, Y))$ is true.

Since $K''(X)$ is $\{X\}$-antecedent of $(\forall X\in D)(\forall Y\in R)(PO_2(X_2, Y)\Rightarrow PO(X, Y))\wedge$ $\{X\}\cap\{Y\} = \varnothing$, $(\forall X\in D)(K''(X)\Rightarrow(\forall Y\in R)(PO_2(X_2, Y)\Rightarrow PO(X, Y)))\equiv(\forall X\in D)$ $(\forall Y\in R)(PO_2(X_2, Y)\wedge K''(X)\Rightarrow PO(X, Y))$ is true.

Since $(\forall X\in D)(PR(X)\wedge J'(X) \Rightarrow PR_1(X_1))$, $(\forall X\in D)(\forall Y\in R)(PO_1(X_1, Y)\wedge$ $K'(X)\Rightarrow PO(X, Y))$ and $B'(X)\equiv J'(X)\wedge K'(X)$, $(\forall X\in D)(PR(X)\wedge B'(X) \Rightarrow$ $PR_1(X_1))$ are true, $(\forall X\in D)(\forall Y\in R)(PO_1(X_1, Y)\wedge B'(X)\Rightarrow PO(X, Y))$ is true.

For the same reason,

$(\forall X\in D)(PR(X)\wedge B''(X)\Rightarrow PR_2(X_2))$ is true,

$(\forall X\in D)(\forall Y\in R)(PO_2(X_2, Y)\wedge B''(X)\Rightarrow PO(X, Y))$ is true.

In the following, it will be proved that if $\forall X\in D$, $PR(X)$ is true, after $A(F_1)$ or $A(F_2)$ are executed according to $B(X)$ and terminate, then $PO(X, Y)$ is true.

(1) Suppose $\forall X\in D$, $PR(X)$ is true and $B(X)$, i.e. $B'(X)$ is true.

Since $(\forall X\in D)(PR(X)\wedge B'(X)\Rightarrow PR_1(X_1))$ is true, $PR_1(X_1)$ is true.

After $A(F_1)$ is executed, if it terminates, $PO_1(X_1, Y)$ is true.

Since $A(F_1)$ just changes the variable values of Y and $\{X\}\cap\{Y\} = \varnothing$, $B'(X)$ is still true.

Since $PO_1(X_1, Y)\wedge B'(X)\Rightarrow PO(X, Y)$ is true, $PO(X, Y)$ is true.

(2) Suppose $\forall X\in D$, $PR(X)$ is true and $\neg B(X)$, i.e. $\neg B'(X)$ is true.

Since $(\forall X\in D)(PR(X)\Rightarrow B'(X)\vee B''(X))$, $B'(X)\vee B''(X)$ is true.

Since $\neg B'(X)$ is true, $B''(X)$ is true.

Similarly to (1), after $A(F_2)$ is executed and terminates, $PO(X, Y)$ is true.

It follows that $A(F)\models A(F_1)|B(X)|A(F_2)$.

Because $A(F_1)$ and $A(F_2)$ is supposed to terminate, the decomposition of Procedure 8.3 is partially correct. If both $A(F_1)$ and $A(F_2)$ terminate, the decomposition of Procedure 8.3 is totally correct. $\square$

8.4.3   Repetition Decomposition

The repetition decomposition decomposes $A(F)$ into $A(F_1)$ which is executed repeatedly when $B(X)$ is true until $B(X)$ is false.

Let $A(F)=(PR(X), PO(X, Y))$, $A(F_1)=(PR_1(X), PO_1(X, Y))$. Procedure 8.4 describes how to derive $B(X)$ and $A(F_1)$.

Procedure 8.4   (Procedure of Repetition Decomposition)

```
PROCEDURE Repetition_Decomposition(PR(X), PO(X, Y): first-order predicate
formula);
BEGIN
  REPEAT
    Transform PO(X, Y) so that PO(X, Y)≡I(X, Y)∧D(X);
```

```
Let B(X)≡¬D(X)
UNTIL (∀X∈D)(PR(X)⇒B(X)) is true;
Let PR₁(X)≡B(X);
Let PO₁(X, Y)≡I(X, Y)
END.
```

$I(X, Y)$ is called a *loop invariant*. Procedure 8.4 tries to search for $B(X)$ and $PR(X) \Rightarrow B(X)$. If such a $B(X)$ cannot be found, the procedure cannot be applied.

Theorem 8.3 The decomposition $A(F) \models B(X)*A(F_1)$ of Procedure 8.4 is partially correct. If $B(X)*A(F_1)$ terminates, then $A(F) \models B(X)*A(F_1)$ is totally correct.

Proof Suppose $A(F_1) = (B(X), I(X, Y))$, $PO(X, Y) \equiv I(X, Y) \wedge D(X)$, $B(X) \equiv \neg D(X)$ and $(\forall X \in D)(PR(X) \Rightarrow B(X))$ is true.

Firstly, $\forall X \in D$, if $PR(X)$ is true, then $B(X)$ is true. After $A(F_1)$ is executed, if it terminates, $I(X, Y)$ is true.

Secondly, if $B(X)$ is true repeatedly, then $A(F_1)$ is executed repeatedly and after $A(F_1)$ is executed, if it terminates, $I(X, Y)$ is still true.

Finally, suppose $\neg B(X)$ is true, the repetition exits and $\neg B(X) \wedge I(X, Y)$ is true.

It is possible that $\neg B(X)$ is true when $\{X\} \cap \{Y\} \neq \varnothing$ and the values of variables in $\{X\} \cap \{Y\}$ is changed.

Since $\neg B(X) \wedge I(X, Y) \equiv D(X) \wedge I(X, Y) \equiv PO(X, Y)$, $PO(X, Y)$ is true.

Namely, $A(F) \models B(X)*A(F_1)$.

Because $A(F_1)$ is supposed to terminate, the decomposition of Procedure 8.4 is partially correct. If $B(X)*A(F_1)$ terminates, then the decomposition of Procedure 8.4 is totally correct. □

These decomposition procedures above-mentioned are sightless. They depend on a lot of knowledge. The execution of these procedures to realise completely automatic decomposition is difficult. Furthermore, the execution conditions of these procedures are rigorous. If a predicate formula cannot be transformed into an appropriate form, the corresponding procedure cannot be applied. Therefore, interactions with human modeller are very necessary to reduce the difficulty and blindness. With the help of modellers, some temporary variables can be added and some variable names can be changed so that a suitable form can be derived and these procedures can be applied.

In addition, modellers can also develop new procedures so that more flexibility can be supplied.

8.5 Structure of the Knowledge Base

The approach to decomposing a 2-assertion of a task refines repeatedly an abstract 2-assertion and obtains gradually a series of finer 2-assertions. Because the decomposition is a creative work, a knowledge base is necessary.

The knowledge base consists of a case base, a segment base and a rule base. The case base stores decomposed cases which decompose a 2-assertion into one of sequence, selection and repetition control structures. The segment base stores code segments which are decomposed from 2-assertions. A code segment refines a 2-assertion and carries out the function of the 2-assertion. The rule base stores the decomposition rules proposed before. New rules can also be supplemented into the rule base by human modellers.

8.5.1 The Case Base

The case base consists of a sequence case base, a selection case base and a repetition case base. The sequence case base stores the decomposition cases that decompose a 2-assertion $A(F)$ into two sequential 2-assertions $A(F_1) = (PR(X), PO_1(X, Y_1))$ and $A(F_2) = (PR(X), PO_2(X, Y_2))$. The selection case base stores the decomposition cases which decompose a 2-assertion $A(F)$ into two 2-assertions $A(F_1) = (PR_1(X_1), PO_1(X_1, Y))$ or $A(F_2) = (PR_2(X_2), PO_2(X_2, Y))$ according to a Boolean condition $B(X)$. The repetition case base stores the decomposition cases that decompose a 2-assertion $A(F)$ into a repeatedly executing 2-assertion $A(F_1) = (PR_1(X), PO_1(X, Y))$ when a Boolean condition $B(X)$ is true.

The structures of the case base are shown in Table 8.1—Table 8.3 respectively. The case base also stores the decomposition cases which are added by modellers. There might be many cases in the case base; this is the reason why the case base is called a "*base*".

Table 8.1 Structure of the sequence case base

Precondition	Postcondition	Sub-Postcondition	Sub-Postcondition
$PR(X)$	$PO(X, Y)$	$PO_1(X, Y_1)$	$PO_2(X, Y_2)$

Table 8.2 Structure of the selection case base

Precondition	Postcondition	Condition	Sub-Precondition1	Sub-Postcondition1	Sub-Precondition2	Sub-Postcondition2
$PR(X)$	$PO(X, Y)$	$B(X)$	$PR_1(X_1)$	$PO_1(X_1, Y)$	$PR_2(X_2)$	$PO_2(X_2, Y)$

Table 8.3 Structure of the repetition case base

Precondition	Postcondition	Condition	Sub-Precondition	Sub-Postcondition
$PR(X)$	$PO(X, Y)$	$B(X)$	$PR_1(X)$	$PO_1(X, Y)$

8.5.2   The Segment Base

If a 2-assertion $A(F) = (PR(X), PO(X,Y))$ is successfully decomposed into a code segment which consists of finer 2-assertions, the code segment can be stored in the segment base. The segment base stores the 2-assertion $A(F) = (PR(X), PO(X, Y))$ and the corresponding address of the code segment. The structure of the segment base is shown in Table 8.4.

Table 8.4   Structure of the segment base

Precondition	Postcondition	Address of Code Segment
$PR(X)$	$PO(X, Y)$	SEG_ADDR

8.5.3   The Rule Base

The rule base stores decomposition rules which consist of the decomposition structure $STR(F)$ and the address of the corresponding decomposition procedure which implements the decomposition. The structure of the rule base is shown in Table 8.5.

Table 8.5   Structure of the rule base

Decomposition Structure	Address of Procedure
$STR(F)$	PRO_ADDR

8.6   Decomposition

Functional decomposition is a repeated process which decomposes a 2-assertion into a series of 2-assertions which consists of the sequence, the selection and the repetition control structures. The process can be described by a decomposition tree.

8.6.1   The Decomposition Tree

Definition 8.10   A decomposition tree is a 2-tuple $T = (V, E)$ where
(1) V is a set of vertices; $E \subseteq V \times V$ is a set of edges and T is a tree.
(2) $\forall v \in V$, $v = (v_n, v_t, B(X), A(F), p)$. v_n is the name of vertex v. When v is not a leaf, v_t is the vertex type whose value is one of "$\wedge$", "$\vee$" and "$*$", which denote

the sequence decomposition, the selection decomposition and the repetition decomposition respectively.

(3) $B(X)$ is the condition of the selection structure or repetition structure.

(4) $A(F)$ is a 2-assertion which describes the function of vertex v.

(5) If $A(F)$ matches a 2-assertion in the segment base, p is the address of the corresponding code segment.

A decomposition tree is gradually growing up with the decomposition process. Human modellers determine what time the decomposition will terminate. A simple example of a decomposition tree is shown in Fig. 8.2.

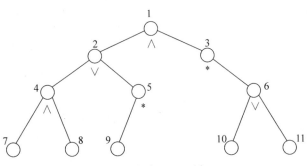

Figure 8.2   A decomposition tree

8.6.2   Match Between Two 2-Assertions

In decomposition, it is necessary to detect whether a 2-assertion $A(F)$ matches another 2-assertion in the segment base or in the case base.

Definition 8.11   Let $A(F) = (PR(X), PO(X, Y))$ and $A(F') = (PR'(X), PO'(X, Y))$ be two 2-assertions. $A(F)$ is called to *match* $A(F')$ iff $PR(X) \Rightarrow PR'(X)$ and $PO'(X, Y) \Rightarrow PO(X, Y)$.

Theorem 8.4   Let $A(F) = (PR(X), PO(X, Y))$, $A(F') = (PR'(X), PO'(X, Y))$ and their executions terminate. If $A(F)$ matches $A(F')$, the execution of $A(F)$ can be replaced by the execution of $A(F')$ in a code segment.

Proof   Suppose $\forall X \in D$, D is the domain of X, $PR(X)$ is true.

(1) If $A(F)$ is executed and terminates, then $PO(X, Y)$ is true.

(2) Suppose $A(F)$ is replaced by $A(F')$ and then $A(F')$ is executed.

Since $PR(X)$ is true and $PR(X) \Rightarrow PR'(X)$, $PR'(X)$ is true.

It follows that $A(F')$ is executed and terminates, $PO'(X, Y)$ is true.

Since $PO'(X, Y) \Rightarrow PO(X, Y)$, $PO(X, Y)$ is true.

Namely, after $A(F)$ is replaced by $A(F')$ in a process segment, the result is the same.

It follows that the execution of $A(F)$ can be replaced by the execution of $A(F')$. □

8.6.3   The Decomposition Process

The functional decomposition is a process of top-down and step refinement, described in Procedure 8.5 and shown in Fig. 8.3. Procedure 8.5 is called by Procedure 8.1.

Procedure 8.5   (Decomposition Procedure)

```
PROCEDURE Decomposing_2-Assertion(A(F): 2-assertion);
VAR T: decomposition tree;
  BEGIN
    T:=∅;
    REPEAT
      IF A(F) matches code segments in the segment base THEN
        /* Maybe A(F) matches many code segments. */
        BEGIN
          Modellers choose a suitable code segment;
          IF a suitable code segment is found THEN
            BEGIN
              Grow T according to the structure of the code segment;
              Get a new 2-assertion A(F) from T
            END
        END ELSE
      IF A(F) matches decomposition cases in the case base THEN
        /* Maybe A(F) matches many cases. */
        BEGIN
          Modellers choose a suitable case;
          IF a suitable case is found THEN
            BEGIN
              Grow T according to the structure of the case;
              Get a new 2-assertion A(F) from T
            END
        END ELSE
      BEGIN
        Modellers choose a suitable rule in the rule base;
        IF a suitable rule is found THEN
          BEGIN
            Decompose A(F) according to the rule;
            Store the result to the case base;
            Grow T according to the structure of the rule;
            Get a new 2-assertion A(F) from T
          END ELSE Design a new decomposition rule
      END
    UNTIL modellers determine to exit;
    Synthesise the information of T to generate a code segment;
    Store the code segment to the segment base
  END.
```

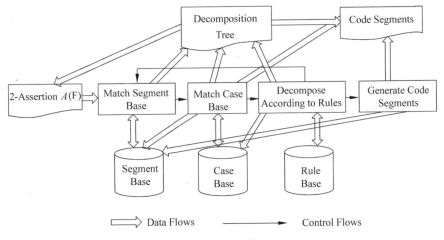

Figure 8.3 Decomposition process

Procedure 8.5 adds decomposition results into the case base and the segment base. Therefore, the knowledge base will be becoming abundant continuously. In the process of decomposition, Procedure 8.5 needs a lot of knowledge. With the continuous decomposition, many new decomposition cases are produced. These decomposition cases are stored into the case base. After the function described by a 2-assertion is decomposed into a code segment, the code segments are stored into the segment base. New decomposition rules can also be developed and stored in the rule base.

With the application of Procedure 8.5, the knowledge in the knowledge base becomes more and more abundant. The more knowledge the knowledge base stores, the more effectively a 2-assertion decomposes.

8.6.4   Supports by Modellers

Because the knowledge in the knowledge base is insufficient in the decomposition process, it is necessary for modellers to provide help and guide the decomposition. When the knowledge base provides multiple choices to decompose, it is also necessary that modellers determine which one will be applied.

To be more specific, the human modellers will accomplish the following work:

(1) When a 2-assertion matches multiple decomposition cases in the case base or multiple code segments in the segment base, modellers must determine which one is applied.

(2) When multiple rules may be applied to realise the decomposition, modellers must determine which rule is applied.

(3) In Hoare Logic, any specification can be "correctly" refined to an infinite loop. However, this is not suitable for decomposing a 2-assertion. Therefore,

modellers must avoid this situation when choosing a suitable decomposition.

(4) In the process of interactive decomposition, modellers may transform a predicate formula into another equivalent predicate formula so that the decomposition can be carried out successfully and smoothly according to the expertise of modellers.

(5) Modellers may add, delete and modify the contents in the segment base, the rule base and the case base when necessary.

(6) When a decomposition cannot be performed, modellers must determine whether or not a backtracking is executed. When backtracking, modellers must determine the step to which the backtracking will go and how to decompose in the next step.

(7) Modellers may evaluate the results of decomposition and determine whether the decomposition should be executed once again and how it will be executed.

(8) Modellers may determine whether the decomposition cases and segments derived in the decomposition process will be added into the knowledge base.

8.7 Summary

Designing tasks is the last step of modelling a software evolution process. The kernel work in this step is to refine a 2-assertion at coarser granularity as a code segment composed of several 2-assertions at finer granularity. These finer-grained 2-assertions are expected to be easy to carry out.

A 2-assertion consists of a precondition and a postcondition; they define the function of a task. In this chapter, an approach is proposed to decompose 2-assertions. By means of matching the code segments in the segment base, matching the decomposition cases in the case base and executing the decomposition rules in the rule base, a 2-assertion is decomposed repeatedly until the modellers are satisfied with the software evolution process model at the task level. The decomposition tree is used to describe the process of decomposition. By synthesising the information in the decomposition tree, a code segment is generated. The approach emphasises the involvement of modellers in the decomposition so as to supply the knowledge necessary to support the decomposition.

Decomposition rules are at the core of the proposed approach. Three decomposition rules are proposed to respectively realise sequence, selection and repetition decomposition. The decompositions are proved to be partially correct. If all the 2-assertions terminate, the decompositions are proved to be totally correct.

The decomposed work products cannot be described by EPMM because EPMM can only define abstract functions. However, EPDL can describe all of the decomposed work products.

References

[1] Bell D (2000) Software engineering: a programming approach (ed3). Addison-Wesley, London

[2] Bohm C, Jacopini G (1966) flow diagram, Turing Machine and language with two formation rules. Communications of the ACM 9: 179 – 191

[3] Dijkstra EW (1976) A discipline of programming. Prentice Hall, Engliwood Cliffs

[4] Dijkstra EW, Scholten CS (1990) Predicate calculus and program semantics. Springer-Verlag, Berlin

[5] Hein JL (2003) Discrete mathematics. Jones and Bartlett Publishers, Boston

[6] Hoare CAR (1969) An axiomatic basis for computer programming. Communications of the ACM 12: 576 – 580

[7] Smith DR (1985) Top-down synthesis of divide-and-conquer algorithms. Artificial Intelligence 27: 43 – 96

9 Efficiency Improvement of the Software Evolution Processes

Tong Li

School of Software, Yunnan University, Kunming, 650091, China
Software Technology Research Laboratory, De Montfort University, Leicester, LE1 9BH, U.K
tli@ynu.edu.cn

Abstract   After a software evolution process is defined, its efficiency must be improved so that it can be executed efficiently. Evolving software concurrently is an effective way to shorten the evolution time and to speed up the evolution. In this chapter, an approach, which resembles a transplant operation on the human body, is proposed to dig down into an inefficient process segment from its process model, then to improve its efficiency and finally to put back the improved version into the original process model. In order to realise the approach, firstly, an algorithm to construct an entity dependence graph by means of analysing dependences between activities and between tasks is developed. Secondly, a method to localise dependences in an activity dependence graph is proposed. Thirdly, a method to simplify and preprocess an activity dependence graph is presented. Then an algorithm to construct a process segment from the preprocessed activity dependence graph is developed. Fourthly, an algorithm to refine an activity as an activity set is proposed. Fifthly, an algorithm to get two partition blocks and to analyse dependences between them is developed. Sixthly, an algorithm to extend concurrency in a bottleneck segment is presented based on the dependence analysis between two partition blocks. Finally, an algorithm to replace an inefficient process segment with an efficient process segment is also developed. It is proved that the interface consistency is preserved between before replacement and after replacement. In this way, when the reconstructed software process is executed, its efficiency is improved.

Key Words   efficiency improvement, concurrency, process, activity, task, entity, dependence, dependence graph, data dependence, control dependence, process segment, sequence relation, dependence analysis, preprocess, transformation rule, dependence relation, inflow, outflow, partition block, bottleneck segment, synchronisation relation, equivalence class, interface consistency.

Objectives

- To dig down into an inefficient process segment, then to improve its efficiency and finally to put back the improved one
- To present an approach to analysing dependence between activities and between tasks
- To propose an approach to capturing concurrency in software processes according to dependence analysis
- To propose an approach to extending the concurrency from the local into the global in software processes, and
- To realise the efficiency improvement by means of concurrent executions of software processes

9.1 Introduction

Concurrency has been widely accepted and applied in software development. As in software development, many activities can be executed concurrently. In actual software development projects, activities typically associated with multiple phases are performed concurrently (Aoyama 1993; Davis and Sitaram 1994; Kellner 1991). Concurrent activities exist at any stage in software development processes. These activities can be carried out in an unspecified concurrent fashion, such as by interleaving them (Humphrey and Kellner 1989). It is possible that the activities in the software development process overlap and parallel each other (Raccoon 1997; Ronald 1996). This chapter tries to answer how to evolve software systems concurrently, which are rarely discussed.

In 1966, Bernstein stated a sufficient condition for the independence of two programs. Dependence is the relationship of a program B to a program A. There are four types of dependence: true dependence, anti dependence, output dependence, control dependence (Bernstein 1966; Hawick 2005). The presence of dependence between two programs implies that they cannot be executed concurrently. The fewer the dependencies are, the greater the concurrency is.

After modelling a software evolution process, an important question is presented: how efficient is the software evolution process? Because the efficiency has not been paid any attention when modelling a software evolution process, the performance of the process might be unsatisfactory when it is enacted. In a software evolution process, many activities can be executed concurrently; however, in its model, these activities might have been defined as being executed sequentially. Consequentially, the evolution is inefficient and will take a long time. Obviously, the efficiency and performance must be improved.

In software evolution processes, the key to affect efficiency is at the process level. Therefore, after software processes are defined, their efficiency must be improved so that they can be executed efficiently in the future. The proposed approach in this chapter is to dig down into an inefficient process segment from its process model, then to improve its efficiency and finally to put back the improved version into the original process model. This work resembles a transplant operation on the human body.

Evolving software concurrently is an effective way to shorten the evolution time and increase the evolution speed. In this chapter, the objectives are focused on capturing concurrency in software processes so that activities which have the potential capability to be executed concurrently can be really executed concurrently. For achieving this objective, an approach to capturing concurrency in an inefficient process segment, which is dug down from a software process, is proposed. According to the dependence analysis between activities and between tasks, the approach searches for the factors of concurrency, captures activities that can be executed concurrently and reconstructs the inefficient process segment. If the concurrency in the process segment is local, an approach to extending the local concurrency into the global concurrency is also presented. According to the dependence analysis among partitions of activity sets, a process segment is reconstructed. Thus, the concurrency is extended from the local into the global. Finally, the new efficient process segment is put back into the original software process to replace the original inefficient process segment.

For the sake of simplicity, in this chapter, sometimes the term *entity* is used to denote either *activity* or *task*; the term *entity set* is used to denote either *activity set* or *task set*. However, it should be pointed out that a set which mixes activities and tasks is not an entity set.

9.2   Procedure of Efficiency Improvement

Using the approach proposed in Chapter 7, software processes can be modelled. The execution of each software process is carried out by the execution of its activities. If a software process is inefficient, the user modellers should search for the process segments which lead to the inefficiency. After capturing and extending concurrency, these process segments are replaced with improved process segments.

Definition 9.1   Input(a) denotes the *input data set* of entity a and output(a) denotes the *output data set* of entity a. Except for input(a) and output(a), all of the other data of entity a are *local* and have meaning only within entity a.

Definition 9.2   Let V be an entity set. For a_1, $a_2 \in V$, suppose a_1 is executed before a_2:

(1) a_2 is *true dependent* on a_1 iff output(a_1)$\cap$input(a_2) $\neq \emptyset$, which is denoted by $a_1 \, \delta \, a_2$;

(2) a_2 is *anti dependent* on a_1 iff output(a_2)$\cap$input(a_1) $\neq \emptyset$, which is denoted by $a_1 \, \bar{\delta} \, a_2$;

(3) a_2 is *output dependent* on a_1 iff output$(a_1)\cap$output$(a_2)\neq\varnothing$, which is denoted by $a_1\,\delta^o\,a_2$.

Definition 9.3   Let V be an entity set. For $a_1,a_2\in V$, a_2 is *control dependent* on a_1, denoted by $a_1\,\delta^c\,a_2$, iff whether a_2 can be executed is determined by the results of execution of a_1 and for $a_1,a_2,\cdots,a_n\in V$, if $a_1\,\delta^c\,a_2$, $a_1\,\delta^c\,a_3,\cdots,a_1\,\delta^c\,a_n$, then $\exists$ and only $\exists$ an entity $a_i\in\{a_2,a_3,\cdots,a_n\}$ must be executed.

If a_1 just determines whether a_2 can be executed, a virtual activity VA can be added such that $a_1\,\delta^c\,a_2$ and $a_1\,\delta^c\,VA$, either a_2 or VA must be executed.

Definition 9.4   True dependence, anti dependence and output dependence are called *data dependence*, denoted by $a_1\,\delta^d\,a_2$. Data dependence and control dependence are called *dependence*. Let V be an entity set. For $a_1,a_2\in V$, that a_2 is dependent on a_1 is also called that a_2 *depends on* a_1.

Definition 9.5   A *dependence graph* is a triple $DG=(V,D,R)$ where $V\neq\varnothing$ is an entity set; $D\subseteq V\times V$ is an *arc set*; $R\colon D\to\{\delta,\overline{\delta},\delta^o,\delta^c\}$ is called the *dependence function* of DG. If V is an activity set, the triple $ADG=(V,D,R)$ is called an *activity dependence graph*; if V is a task set, the triple $TDG=(V,D,R)$ is called a *task dependence graph*.

Dependences are shown in Fig. 9.1. In the figures of this chapter, " ", "/", "o" and "c" denote true dependence, anti dependence, output dependence and control dependence respectively. It is possible that several dependences exist between two entities.

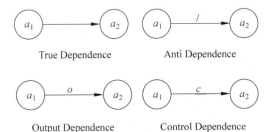

Figure 9.1   Four types of dependences

Definition 9.6   Let $p=(C,A;F,M_0)$ be a software process. $s=(C,A;F)$ is called a *process segment* of software process p iff $s.C\subseteq p.C$, $s.A\subseteq p.A$, $s.F\subseteq p.F$ and s is a net.

Definition 9.7   Let V be an entity set. $Rs\subseteq V\times V$ is a binary relation, the *sequence relation* on V iff $Rs=\{<a_1,a_2>|a_1$ is executed before $a_2(a_1\neq a_2)$ for some $a_1,a_2\in V\}$. $Rc\subseteq V\times V$ is a binary relation, the *control relation* on V iff $Rc=\{<a_1,a_2>|a_1$ determines whether a_2 will be executed $(a_1\neq a_2)$ for some $a_1,a_2\in V\}$.

The improvement procedure of software process $p=(C,A;F,M_0)$ is described by Procedure 9.1. This procedure integrates all procedures and algorithms proposed in this chapter to provide a unified process efficiency improvement approach.

Procedure 9.1 (Procedure of Efficiency Improvement)

```
PROCEDURE Efficiency_Improvement(p: software process);
BEGIN
  Analyse p to determine the process segment set S which results in the
  inefficiency of p;
  FOR each s'∈S DO /* For each s'=(C, A; F) loop */
    BEGIN
      Analyse s' to get the sequence relation Rs on s'.A;
      Analyse s' to get the control relation Rc on s'.A;
      Analyse s'.A to get input(aᵢ), output(aᵢ) for each aᵢ∈s'.A;
      Call Constructing_DG(s'.A, {input(aᵢ)}, {output(aᵢ)}, Rs, Rc, ADG);
  /* Call Algorithm 9.1 to get activity dependence graph ADG=(V, D, R). */
      Call Localising_Dependences(ADG); /* Call Procedure 9.2 to localise
  dependences of ADG=(V, D, R). */
      SADG:=ADG;
      Call Simplifying_ADG(SADG); /*Call Procedure 9.3 to simplify ADG as SADG.*/
      Call Preprocessing_SADG(SADG); /* Call Procedure 9.4 to preprocess SADG. */
      Call Constructing_Process_Segment(SADG, s); /* Call Algorithm 9.2 to
  construct process segment s from SADG. */
      FOR each a∈s.A DO /* For each a=(I, L, O, B), B={t₁, t₂, …} */
        IF a should be refined THEN
          BEGIN
            T:=a.B; /* a.B={t₁, t₂,…, tₘ} is the task set of activity a. */
            Analyse T to get the sequence relation Rs on T;
            Analyse T to get the control relation Rc on T; ·
            Analyse T to get input(tᵢ), output(tᵢ) for each tᵢ∈T;
            Refining_Activity(s, a, T, Rs, Rc, {input(tᵢ)}, {output(tᵢ)});
  /* Call Algorithm 9.3 to refine a in s. */
          END;
      Analyse s to get concurrency bottleneck segment set BS;
      FOR each bs∈BS DO /* For each bs=(C, A; F) loop */
        BEGIN
          Divide bs into set bs.A and bs.B;
          Construct synchronisation relation R_A on bs.A and R_B on bs.B;
          Analyse bs.A and bs.B to get input(aᵢ), output(aᵢ), input(bⱼ),
  output(bⱼ) for each aᵢ∈bs.A and bⱼ∈bs.B;
          Call Extending_Concurrency(bs, bs.A, R_A,{input(aᵢ)},{output(aᵢ)},
  bs.B, R_B, {input(bⱼ)}, {output(bⱼ)}, p'); /*Call Algorithm 9.5 to reconstruct
  the bottleneck segment bs into a new process segment p' to extend concurrency. */
          Replace bs with p' in s
        END; /* End of FOR each bs. */
      Call Reconstructing_Software_Process(p, s', s); /* Call Algorithm 9.6 to
  replace s' with s in p. */
    END /* End of the first FOR */
END.
```

If the efficiency of a software process is unsatisfactory, Procedure 9.1 is used to capture and extend the concurrency in the software process until the modellers are satisfied with the concurrency. Capturing and extending concurrency denotes that the activities and their tasks in a software process are rearranged for concurrent execution if and only if there is no dependence between corresponding activities and tasks.

In parallel processing, it is very complex to transform automatically sequential programs into equivalent parallel programs. It is not possible to find a solution for a general case. Similarly, to seek a general approach to capturing concurrency in software processes is also impossible. Therefore, many actions by human modellers must be involved in the work.

9.3   Dependence Analysis Between Entities

9.3.1   Constructing a Dependence Graph

In software evolution processes, there exist many entities (activities and tasks). Some of them can be executed concurrently and some of them cannot. Whether entities can be executed concurrently is determined by the dependences among them. Therefore, the dependences must be analysed.

Algorithm 9.1   (Constructing a Dependence Graph)

```
Algorithm Constructing_DG;
Input: entity set A={a₁, a₂, …, aₙ}, input(aᵢ), output(aᵢ) (i=1, 2, …, n), sequence
relation Rs on A, control relation Rc on A.
Output: dependence graph DG=(V, D, R).
BEGIN
  V:=A;  n:=|A|;  D:=Ø;  R:=Ø;
  FOR i:=1 TO n DO
    FOR j:=1 TO n DO
      BEGIN
        IF <aᵢ, aⱼ>∈Rs THEN
          BEGIN
            IF output(aᵢ)∩input(aⱼ)≠Ø THEN
              BEGIN
                D:=D∪{(aᵢ, aⱼ)};
                R:=R∪{<(aᵢ, aⱼ), δ>}
              END;
            IF output(aⱼ)∩input(aᵢ)≠Ø THEN
              BEGIN
                D:=D∪{(aᵢ, aⱼ)};
                R:=R∪{<(aᵢ, aⱼ), δ̄>}
              END;
            IF output(aᵢ)∩output(aⱼ)≠Ø THEN
```

```
        BEGIN
           D:=D∪{ (aᵢ, aⱼ) };
           R:=R∪{<(aᵢ, aⱼ), δᵒ>}
        END
      END;
    IF <aᵢ, aⱼ>∈Rc THEN
      BEGIN
         D:=D∪{ (aᵢ, aⱼ) };
         R:=R∪{<(aᵢ, aⱼ), δᶜ >}
      END
    END /* End of For j */
 END.
```

By Algorithm 9.1, a dependence graph for an entity set can be easily constructed. Respectively, if A is an activity set, then an activity dependence graph ADG is constructed; if A is a task set, then a task dependence graph TDG is constructed.

Because sequence relation Rs and control relation Rc do not include the elements with form (a, a), it is impossible that an entity depends on itself, i.e., in an entity dependence graph, there is no arc from an entity to itself. Dependence is described by a dependence graph. Generally, the less the dependence, the bigger the concurrency.

9.3.2   Localising Dependences

After an ADG is constructed, the modellers should take into account the need to improve the ADG. The basic improvement method is to localise dependencies in ADG. If an activity depends on another activity, they cannot be executed concurrently. However, in such a case, if each activity can be divided into finer activities and only the finer activities depend on other finer activities, the dependence might be localised so that the concurrency can be increased. The steps of localising dependences are described by Procedure 9.2.

Procedure 9.2   (Procedure of Localising Dependences)

```
PROCEDURE Localising_Dependences(VAR g: activity dependence graph);
/* g=(V, D, R) */
BEGIN
  FOR each a∈V DO
    IF a should be divided THEN
      BEGIN
        Divide a into a finer activity set A;
        V:=V-{a}∪A
      END;
  Analyse activities in V to get D and R;
  Let g=(V, D, R)
END.
```

For example, suppose that activity a_2 depends on a_1; therefore they cannot be executed concurrently. However, a_1 can be divided into three smaller activities v_1, v_2 and v_3, and a_2 into v_4, v_5 and v_6. Suppose there are dependences between v_1, v_2 and v_3 that stem from a_1 and dependences between v_4, v_5 and v_6 that stem from a_2, and also there is dependence between v_2 and v_5 that stems from the dependence between a_1 and a_2. Except for the dependences stated above, there are no dependences between these activities. In such a case, the activities can be executed concurrently. The activity dependence graphs of before and after dividing are shown in Fig. 9.2 (r denotes one of the four dependence types).

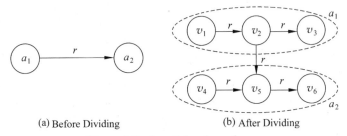

(a) Before Dividing   (b) After Dividing

Figure 9.2   Localising dependences

In Fig. 9.2(b), suppose v_2 depends on v_1, v_3 depends on v_2, v_5 depends on v_4, v_6 depends on v_5, v_5 depends on v_2, and all are true dependences. In this way, the dependence has been localised and more concurrency has been captured and the concurrency can be increased. In Fig. 9.2(a), a_1 and a_2 are executed sequentially. No part of them is executed concurrently. However, in Fig. 9.2(b), some activities can be executed concurrently, such as v_1 and v_4, v_3 and v_6.

9.4   Reconstructing Process Segments

In order to automatically parallelise an internal design representation for high-level synthesis of hardware structures, Grün et al. proposed an approach to transforming a dependence graph into a hierarchical control Petri Net, where the nodes of the dependence graph are transformed into places and the arcs into Petri Net transitions (Grün et al. 1996). Different from their approach, this section proposes a new transformation approach in which an activity is transformed as a transition (activity) of a Petri Net.

Because an *ADG* comprises many dependencies, it is very difficult to capture concurrency automatically. Similar to parallel processing, it is not possible to find a solution for a general case. In some situations, an *ADG* can be transformed into a process segment automatically. In the proposed approach, the activities in *ADG* are still activities in the process segment.

9.4.1   Preprocessing an ADG

Reconstructing process segments mean to transform an activity dependence graph into a process segment. However, a process segment just needs to describe the correct execution of activities; it does not need to preserve all dependence semantics. Therefore, the differences among true dependence, anti dependence and output dependence are meaningless when constructing a process segment. In addition, if an activity dependence graph is too complex, it will lead to transformation difficulty and unnecessary redundancy. Therefore, it is necessary to simplify the *ADG* to obtain a concise process segment. For this purpose, preprocessing the *ADG* must be carried out before transformation.

Definition 9.8   Let $ADG = (V, D, R)$ be an activity dependence graph. $\delta, \bar{\delta}$ and δ^o in R are replaced by δ^d. If $\exists\ v_1, v_2, \cdots, v_n \in V$, such that $((v_1, v_2), \delta^d) \in R$, $((v_2, v_3), \delta^d) \in R, \cdots, ((v_{n-1}, v_n), \delta^d) \in R$ and $((v_1, v_n), \delta^d) \in R$, (v_1, v_n) is called a *transitive data dependence arc*.

The data dependence of a transitive data dependence arc (v_1, v_n) has been described by (v_1, v_2), $(v_2, v_3), \cdots$, and (v_{n-1}, v_n). Therefore, the transitive data dependence arc (v_1, v_n) is redundant and should be removed from the *ADG* to reduce the complexity.

Procedure 9.3   (Procedure of Simplifying an $ADG\ g = (V, D, R)$)

```
PROCEDURE Simplifying_ADG(VAR g: activity dependence graph);
  BEGIN
    Replace all δ, δ̄ and δ° with δ^d in g.R;
    Remove all redundant elements in g.D and in g.R;
    Remove all transitive data dependence arcs in g.D
  END.
```

Definition 9.9   An *ADG* simplified by Procedure 9.3 is called a *simplified ADG, SADG* for short.

Definition 9.10   Let $SADG = (V, D, R)$ be a simplified activity dependence graph. A *cycle* in directed graph (V, D) is a path whose beginning and ending activities are the same and in which no arc occurs more than once.

Definition 9.11   Let $SADG = (V, D, R)$ be a simplified activity dependence graph. It is called an *acyclic data SADG* iff $R(D) = \{\delta^d\}$ and (V, D) does not contain any cycle.

Definition 9.12   Let $SADG = (V, D, R)$ be a simplified activity dependence graph. It is called a *basic control SADG* iff

(1) (V, D) does not contain any cycle;

(2) There are two activities sets V_1, $V_2 \subseteq V$, such that there are data dependences among V_1 and among V_2, and there is no dependence between the activities of V_1 and the activities of V_2, and there is no control dependence among V_1 and among V_2;

(3) There are a specified activity a_e whose indegree equals to 0 and two specified activities $v_{11} \in V_1$, $v_{21} \in V_2$, such that $a_e \, \delta^c \, v_{11}$ and $a_e \, \delta^c \, v_{21}$; a_e is called the *entrance* of *SADG*;

(4) There are a specified activity a_x whose outdegree equals to 0 and two specified activities $v_{1n} \in V_1$, $v_{2m} \in V_2$, such that $v_{1n} \, \delta^d \, a_x$ and $v_{2m} \, \delta^d \, a_x$; a_x is called the *exit* of *SADG*;

(5) $V = V_1 \cup V_2 \cup \{a_e, a_x\}$;

(6) Except for the dependences stated above, there is no dependence among V.

For directed graphs, the indegree of a vertex is the number of arcs pointing at the vertex; the outdegree of a vertex is the number of arcs pointing away from the vertex (Hein 2003).

Definition 9.13 A simplified activity dependence graph is called a *well-controlled SADG* iff it is constructed finite times only by the following rules (a and b are two activities):

(1) A basic control *SADG* is a well-controlled *SADG*;

(2) If $G = (V, D, R)$ is a well-controlled *SADG*, $(V \cup \{a\}, D \cup \{(a, a_e)\}, R \cup \{((a, a_e), \delta^d)\})$ (a becomes the entrance of the new graph) and $(V \cup \{b\}, D \cup \{(a_x, b)\}, R \cup \{((a_x, b), \delta^d)\})$ (b becomes the exit of the new graph) are also well-controlled *SADGs*;

(3) If $G_1 = (V_1, D_1, R_1)$ (a_{1e} and a_{1x} are the entrance and the exit respectively) and $G_2 = (V_2, D_2, R_2)$ (a_{2e} and a_{2x} are the entrance and the exit respectively) are two well-controlled *SADGs*, $G = (V_1 \cup V_2 \cup \{a, b\}, D_1 \cup D_2 \cup \{(a, a_{1e}), (a, a_{2e}), (a_{1x}, b), (a_{2x}, b)\}, R \cup \{((a, a_{1e}), \delta^c), ((a, a_{2e}), \delta^c), ((a_{1x}, b), \delta^d), ((a_{2x}, b), \delta^d)\})$ is a well-controlled *SADG*. a and b become the entrance and the exit of G respectively.

A function can be defined as a set (Hein 2003). For the sake of convenience, function R is regarded as a set and $z = R(x, y)$ is denoted by $((x, y), z) \in R$.

Definition 9.14 Let $SADG = (V, D, R)$ be a simplified activity dependence graph. It is called a *basic cyclic SADG* iff

(1) (V, D) includes and only includes a cycle $(v_1, v_2), (v_2, v_3), \cdots, (v_{n-1}, v_n), (v_n, v_1)$;

(2) $R(D) = \{\delta^d\}$;

(3) There are a specified activity a_e whose indegree equals to 0 and only one activity $v_1 \in V$, such that $a_e \, \delta^d \, v_1$; a_e is called the *entrance* of *SADG*;

(4) There are a specified activity a_x whose outdegree equals to 0 and only one activity $v_n \in V$, such that $v_n \, \delta^d \, a_x$; a_x is called the *exit* of *SADG*;

(5) $V = \{v_1, v_2, \cdots, v_{n-1}, v_n, a_e, a_x\}$.

Because a basic cyclic *SADG* only includes a cycle, the cycle will not exist if any arc in the cycle is deleted.

Definition 9.15 A simplified activity dependence graph is called a *well-cyclic SADG* iff it is constructed finite times only by the following rules (a and b are two activities):

(1) A basic cyclic *SADG* is a well-cyclic *SADG*;

(2) If $G = (V, D, R)$ is a well-cyclic *SADG*, $(V \cup \{a\}, D \cup \{(a, a_e)\}, R \cup \{((a, a_e), \delta^d)\})$ (*a* becomes the entrance of the new graph) and $(V \cup \{b\}, D \cup \{(a_x, b)\}, R \cup \{((a_x, b), \delta^d)\})$ (*b* becomes the exit of the new graph) are also well-cyclic *SADGs*;

(3) If $G_1 = (V, D, R)$ is a well-cyclic *SADG*, $G = (V \cup \{a, b\}, D \cup \{(a, a_e), (a_x, b), (a_x, a_e)\}, R \cup \{((a, a_e), \delta^d), ((a_x, b), \delta^d), ((a_x, a_e), \delta^d)\})$ is a well-cyclic *SADG*. *a* and *b* become the entrance and the exit of *G* respectively.

Definition 9.16   The acyclic data *SADG*, the well-controlled *SADG* and the well-cyclic *SADG* are called the *well-structured SADG*.

Procedure 9.4   (Procedure of Preprocessing a *SADG* $g = (V, D, R)$)

```
PROCEDURE Preprocessing_SADG(VAR g: simplified activity dependence graph);
BEGIN
  Try to adjust g into a well-structured SADG;
  IF g is a well-controlled SADG THEN
    FOR each exit activity aₓ∈V at different levels and any v∈V DO
    /* As shown in Fig.9.3.A well-controlled SADG might contain many finer
well-controlled SADGs. */
      Change ((v, aₓ), δᵈ)∈R into ((v, aₓ), δᵃᶜ)∈R;
  IF g is a well-cyclic SADG THEN
    BEGIN
      FOR each entrance activity aₑ∈V and each exit activity aₓ∈V at different
    levels and any v, v'∈V DO /* As shown in Fig. 9.4(a). A well-cyclic SADG might
    contain many finer well-cyclic SADGs. */
        Change ((aₑ, v'), δᵈ)∈R into ((aₑ, v'), δᵃᶜ), ((v, aₓ), δᵈ)∈R into ((v,
    aₓ), δᶜ);
      FOR each cycle DO /* As shown in Fig. 9.4(b). A well-cyclic SADG might
    contain many cycles. A virtual activity does nothing except for passing tokens.*/
        BEGIN
          Delete arc (vₙ, v₁) at different levels;
          Add virtual activity va into V;
          Add (vₙ, va), (va, v₁) into D;
          Add ((vₙ, va), δᶜ), ((va, v₁), δᵃᶜ) into R
        END
    END
END.
```

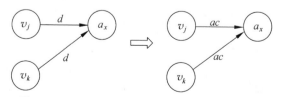

Figure 9.3   Preprocessing a well-controlled *SADG*

If an *ADG* cannot be adjusted into a well-structured *SADG*, this indicates the *ADG* is too complex. A feasible approach is to divide the corresponding process segment into several process segments to reduce the dependences or to re-dig down into another process segment from the original software process.

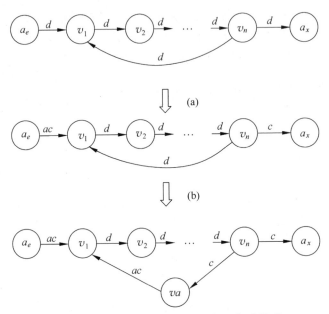

Figure 9.4   Preprocessing a well-cyclic *SADG*

If a well-structured *SADG* is embedded into another different well-structured *SADG* so that the whole is not a well-structured *SADG*, it can be regarded as an activity of the latter. After the latter is processed, the former can also be processed.

9.4.2   Transformation Rules

The following transformation rules transform a well-structured *SADG* preprocessed by Procedure 9.4 into a process segment.

Rule 9.1   Let $SADG = (V, D, R)$ be a preprocessed well-structured *SADG* and $s = (C, A; F)$ be a process segment. Each activity in V is transformed into an activity in A.

Rule 9.2   Let $SADG = (V, D, R)$ be a preprocessed well-structured *SADG* and $s = (C, A; F)$ be a process segment. If arc $(v_i, v_j) \in D$ and $R(v_i, v_j) = \delta^d$, then arc (v_i, v_j) is transformed into a conditions c_{ij} in C, arcs (v_i, c_{ij}) and (c_{ij}, v_j) in F, as shown in Fig. 9.5.

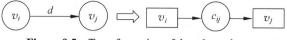

Figure 9.5   Transformation of data dependences

Rule 9.3   Let $SADG = (V, D, R)$ be a preprocessed well-structured $SADG$ and $s = (C, A; F)$ be a process segment. If (v_i, v_j), $(v_i, v_k) \in D$ and $R(v_i, v_j) = \delta^c$, $R(v_i, v_k) = \delta^c$, then two arcs (v_i, v_j) and (v_i, v_k) in D are transformed into a condition c_i in C and arcs (v_i, c_i), (c_i, v_j) and (c_i, v_k) in F, as shown in Fig. 9.6(a).

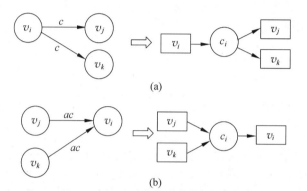

Figure 9.6   Transformation of control dependences

Rule 9.4   Let $SADG = (V, D, R)$ be a preprocessed well-structured $SADG$ and $s = (C, A; F)$ be a process segment. If (v_j, v_i), $(v_k, v_i) \in D$ and $R(v_j, v_i) = \delta^{ac}$, $R(v_k, v_i) = \delta^{ac}$, then two arcs (v_j, v_i) and (v_k, v_i) in D are transformed into a condition c_i in C and arcs (v_j, c_i), (v_k, c_i) and (c_i, v_i) in F, as shown in Fig. 9.6(b).

Obviously, the execution order of activities after transforming is the same as that before transforming.

9.4.3   Transformation Algorithm

Algorithm 9.2   (Constructing Process Segment s)

```
Algorithm Constructing_Process_Segment;
Input: preprocessed well-structured SADG=(V, D, R).
Output: process segment s=(C, A; F).
BEGIN
  A:=V; C:=Ø; F:=Ø; n:=|V|;
  FOR i:=1 TO n DO
    FOR j:=1 TO n DO
      BEGIN
        IF ((vi, vj)∈D) ∧(R(vi, vj)=δd) THEN
```

```
BEGIN
    C:=C∪{c_ij}; /* c_ij denotes a condition whose indexes are i and j. */
    F:=F∪{(v_i, c_ij), (c_ij, v_j)}
END ELSE
IF ((v_i, v_j)∈D) ∧(R(v_i, v_j)=δ^c) THEN
    BEGIN
        C:=C∪{c_i}; /* c_i might be added into C many times. Because C is a set,
only one c_i belongs to C. */
        F:=F∪{(v_i, c_i), (c_i, v_j)} /* (v_i, c_i) might be added into F many times.
Because F is a set, only one (v_i, c_i) belongs to C. */
    END ELSE
    IF ((v_i, v_j)∈D) ∧(R(v_i, v_j)=δ^ac) THEN
        BEGIN
            C:=C∪{c_j}; /* c_j might be added into C many times. Because C is a set,
only one c_j belongs to C. */
            F:=F∪{(v_i, c_j), (c_j, v_j)} /* (c_j, v_j) might be added into F many times.
Because F is a set, only one (c_j, v_j) belongs to C. */
        END /* End of FOR */
    END
END.
```

Algorithm 9.2 constructs a process segment from a preprocessed well-structured *SADG*. According to Algorithm 9.2, process segment s is constructed. In s, the activities which are executed either concurrently or sequentially are defined strictly. For control dependence, Algorithm 9.2 purposely makes a conflict in the corresponding activities so that the activities controlled by the conflict cannot be executed at the same time and only one activity can be executed. Thus, the control dependence has been described according to its semantics.

9.4.4　Examples

Example 9.1　Suppose r in Fig. 9.2 denotes data dependence. Activity a_1 and activity a_2 are divided into three smaller activities respectively. By capturing concurrency, a process segment shown in Fig. 9.7 is constructed according to the activity dependence graph shown in Fig. 9.2(b). In such a case, activities a_1 and a_2, which could just be executed sequentially before, can be executed concurrently now.

Example 9.2　Suppose seven activities a_1, a_2, a_3, a_4, a_5, a_6 and a_7 are executed sequentially; output(a_2)∩input(a_3) ≠ Ø, input(a_1)∩output(a_4) ≠ Ø, output(a_1)∩ output(a_2) ≠ Ø, output(a_5)∩input(a_7) ≠ Ø, output(a_6)∩input(a_7) ≠ Ø, and a_4 determines which one of a_5 and a_6 can be executed. Other intersections of any input data sets and output data sets are empty. According to Algorithm 9.1, the activity dependence graph, shown in Fig. 9.8, is constructed. According to

Algorithm 9.2, a process segment, shown in Fig. 9.9, is constructed. In Fig. 9.9, because there is a conflict at c_4, output(a_4) determines which one of a_5 and a_6 can be executed by making use of the token in c_4. In this way, the semantics of control dependence are realised.

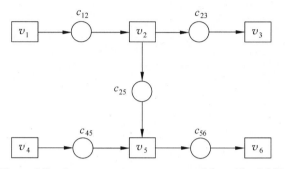

Figure 9.7 A process segment constructed from Fig. 9.2(b)

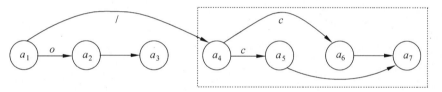

Figure 9.8 An activity dependence graph

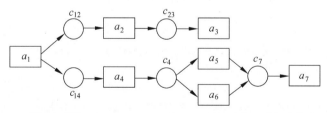

Figure 9.9 A process segment constructed from Fig. 9.8

In this example, the *ADG* shown in Fig. 9.8 is not a well-structured *ADG*. However, the components enclosed in dotted lines can be treated as an activity. Thus, the *ADG* becomes a well-structured *ADG*. After this *ADG* is transformed into a process segment, the components enclosed in dotted lines (it is also a well-structured *ADG*) can also be transformed into another process segment and these two process segments can be combined into a whole one. In this way, a non well-structured *ADG* is transformed into a whole process segment.

139

Example 9.3 A well-cyclic *SADG* shown in Fig. 9.10(a) is preprocessed into that shown in Fig. 9.10(b). The preprocessed well-cyclic *SADG* shown in Fig. 9.10(b) is transformed into a process segment shown in Fig. 9.11.

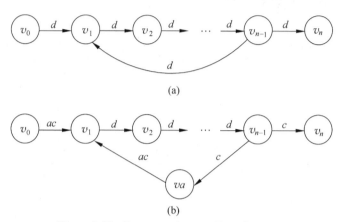

(a)

(b)

Figure 9.10 Preprocessing a well-cyclic *SADG*

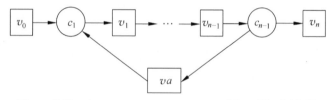

Figure 9.11 A process segment constructed from Fig. 9.10 (b)

9.5 Capturing Concurrency within an Activity

Definition 9.17 Let T be a task set in an activity. Relation R is called a *dependence relation* on set T iff R is constructed by and only by the following rules:

For $x, y \in T$,

(1) if x depends on y or y depends on x, $(x, y) \in R$;

(2) $(x, x) \in R$;

(3) if $(x, y) \in R$, $(y, x) \in R$;

(4) if $(x, y) \in R \wedge (y, z) \in R$, $(x, z) \in R$.

Obviously, because R is reflexive, symmetric and transitive, dependence relation R is an equivalence relation on T. Suppose $T = \{t_1, t_2, \cdots, t_m\}$ is the task set of activity a. Because R is an equivalence relation on T, the equivalence classes of R form a partition of T (Rosen 1998). The equivalence class set, denoted by $T/R = \{Tb_1, Tb_2, \cdots, Tb_n\}$, can be constructed and T/R is a partition of set T. Each $Tb_i \subseteq T$ $(i = 1, 2, \cdots, n)$ is called a *partition block*. The tasks in different partition blocks do not depend on each other and the tasks in the same partition block are dependent.

Each partition block Tb_i $(i = 1, 2, \cdots, n)$ is defined as a new activity $a_i = \{t_{i1}, t_{i2}, \cdots\}$, $t_{ij} \in Tb_i (j = 1, 2, \cdots)$. Because Tb_i $(i = 1, 2, \cdots, n)$ does not depend on each other, a_i $(i = 1, 2, \cdots, n)$ does not depend on each other and they can be executed concurrently. In this way, activity a is refined as an activity set $\{a_1, a_2, \cdots, a_n\}$ in which activities $a_1, a_2, \cdots, a_n$ can be executed concurrently.

Definition 9.18   To replace the occurrence a with occurrence a' is denoted as a/a'.

Algorithm 9.3   (Refining an Activity into a Concurrent Activity Set)

```
Algorithm Refining_Activity;
Input: process segment p=(C, A; F), activity a∈A, task set T of a, sequence
relation Rs on T, control relation Rc on T, {input(tᵢ)}, {output(tᵢ)} (tᵢ∈T).
Output: process segment p=(C, A; F).
BEGIN
  Call Constructing_DG(T, {input(tᵢ)}, {output(tᵢ)}, Rs, Rc, TDG); /* Call
  Algorithm 9.1 to get task dependence graph TDG=(V, D, R). T={t₁, t₂,…, tₘ} is
  the task set of activity a. */
  Get dependence relation Rₐ on T from TDG;
  Construct equivalence class set T/Rₐ={Tb₁, Tb₂, …, Tbₙ}; /* Each Tbᵢ (i=1, 2, …, n)
is a task set. */
  n:=|T/Rₐ|;
  FOR i:=1 TO n DO
      BEGIN
         Define Tbᵢ as activity aᵢ;
         Define the tasks in Tbᵢ as the tasks of activity aᵢ;
      END;
  A:=A∪{a₁, a₂, …, aₙ, a', a"}-{a};
  C:=C∪{c₁', c₂', …, cₙ', c₁", c₂", …, cₙ"};
  FOR i:=1 TO n DO
      F:=F∪{(a', cᵢ'), (cᵢ", a"), (cᵢ', aᵢ), (aᵢ, cᵢ")};
      F:=F-inflow(a)-outflow(a) ∪ inflow(a/a') ∪ outflow(a/a")
END.
```

For two specific activities $a', a'' \in A$, inflow $(a') = $ inflow $(a/a') \subseteq F$, outflow $(a'') = $ outflow $(a/a'') \subseteq F$. Namely, before and after refining activity a, the input flow and output flow preserve invariability. Thus, the interface consistency between activity a and process segment p is preserved.

According to Algorithm 9.3, the activity a enclosed in doted lines in Fig. 9.12(a) is refined as a process segment enclosed in doted lines in Fig. 9.12(b) in which activities $a_1, a_2, \cdots, a_n$ can be executed concurrently.

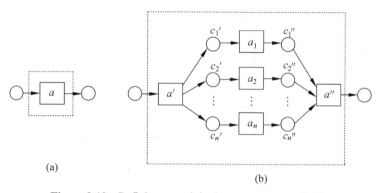

(a)

(b)

Figure 9.12   Refining an activity into concurrent activities

9.6   Analysing Dependences Between Partition Blocks

Using Algorithm 9.3, each of two sequential activities a and b shown in Fig. 9.13(a) is refined as many concurrent activities, as shown in Fig. 9.13(b). However, the concurrency is local.

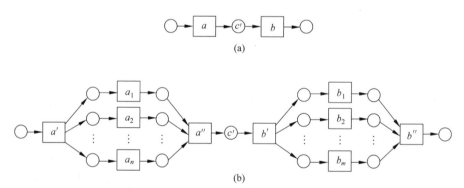

Figure 9.13   A concurrency bottleneck

In Fig. 9.13(b), there is a bottleneck between activity a'' and b' which blocks the concurrent execution of activities so that some activities which might originally be executed concurrently are executed sequentially. The process segment with a bottleneck is called a *bottleneck segment* $bs = (C, A; F)$, as shown in Fig. 9.13(b). Sometimes the sequence is necessary to ensure the execution correctness of a software process. However, sometimes it is also possible that these activities can be executed concurrently. In such a case, the concurrency must be extended from the local to the global. In the following, an approach to extending the concurrency in the bottleneck segment shown in Fig. 9.13 is discussed.

Definition 9.19   Let $A = \{a_1, a_2, \cdots, a_n\}$ be an activity set. Relation R is called a *synchronisation relation* on A iff R is constructed by and only by the following rules:

For $x, y \in A$,

(1) if x and y must be executed synchronously, $(x, y) \in R \wedge (y, x) \in R$;

(2) $(x, x) \in R$;

(3) if $(x, y) \in R \wedge (y, z) \in R$, $(x, z) \in R$.

Obviously, because R is reflexive, symmetric and transitive, synchronisation relation R is an equivalence relation on A. Because R is an equivalence relation on A, the equivalence classes of A can be constructed and a partition $\{Ab_1, Ab_2, \cdots, Ab_k\}$ can be obtained (Rosen 1998). Ab_i ($i = 1, 2, \cdots, k$) are called partition blocks. Analogously, a partition of activity set $\{b_1, b_2, \cdots, b_m\}$ can also be obtained. Obviously, there is no control dependence between Ab_i and Bb_j. Furthermore, the dependence between partitions is analysed as follows.

Suppose Ab_i is a partition block in $\{a_1, a_2, \cdots, a_n\}$ and Bb_j is a partition block in $\{b_1, b_2, \cdots, b_m\}$. By the dependence analysis, it can be determined whether the partition blocks Ab_i and Bb_j can be executed concurrently:

(1) if Bb_j depends on Ab_i, then Ab_i and Bb_j must be executed sequentially;

(2) if Bb_j does not depend on Ab_i, then Ab_i and Bb_j can be executed concurrently.

Algorithm 9.4   (Dependence Analysis between two Partition Blocks)

```
Algorithm Block_Dependence;
Input: activity set A={a₁, a₂, …, aₙ}, the synchronisation relation Rₐ on A,
       the input data set input(aᵢ) and output data set output(aᵢ) (i=1, 2, …,
       n), activity set B={b₁, b₂, …, bₘ}, the synchronisation relation R_B on
       B, the input set input(bⱼ) and output set output(bⱼ) (j=1, 2, …, m).
Output: array D that shows the dependence between partition blocks A/Rₐ and
       B/R_B, A/Rₐ, B/R_B.
BEGIN
Construct equivalence class set A/Rₐ={Ab₁, Ab₂, …, Ab_s};
Construct equivalence class set B/R_B={Bb₁, Bb₂, …, Bb_t};
s:=|A/Rₐ|; t:=|B/R_B|;
FOR i:=1 TO s DO
  FOR j:=1 TO t DO
    BEGIN
    D[i, j]:=false;
    na:=|Abᵢ|; /* na denotes the number of activities in Abᵢ. */
    nb:=|Bbⱼ|; /* nb denotes the number of activities in Bbⱼ. */
    FOR k:=1 TO na DO
      FOR l:=1 TO nb DO
        IF (output(aᵢₖ)∩input(bⱼₗ)≠∅) or (input(aᵢₖ)∩output(bⱼₗ)≠∅) or
        (output(aᵢₖ)∩output(bⱼₗ)≠∅) THEN D[i, j]:=true /*aᵢₖ∈Abᵢ, bⱼₗ∈Bbⱼ */
    END
END.
```

Algorithm 9.4 supposes the activities in A are executed before the activities in B. It analyses the dependence between every activity in every partition block in A

and every activity in every partition block in B. If there exists any activity in Bb_j which depends on any activity in Ab_i, Algorithm 9.4 indicates that partition block Bb_j depends on partition block Ab_i, denoted by $D[i, j]$ = true.

9.7 Extending Concurrency

After the dependence between partition blocks Ab_i and Bb_j of a bottleneck segment is analysed, the bottleneck segment is reconstructed to extend concurrency.

For the sake of simplicity, $D[i, 1..t]$ denotes the ith row of D. $D[i, 1..t]$ = false means that each block in B/R_B does not depend on the ith block in A/R_A. $D[1..s, j]$ denotes the jth column of D. $D[1..s, j]$ = false denotes the jth block in B/R_B does not depend on any block in A/R_A.

Algorithm 9.5 (Extending Concurrency)

```
Algorithm Extending_Concurrency;
Input: bottleneck segment p'=(C', A'; F') shown in Figure 9.13(b), activity
       set A={a₁, a₂, …, aₙ}, the synchronisation relation Rₐ on A, input data
       set input(aᵢ) and output data set output(aᵢ) (i=1, 2, …, n), activity
       set B={b₁, b₂, …, bₘ}, the synchronisation relation Rₑ on B, input data
       set input(bⱼ) and output data set output(bⱼ) (j=1, 2, …, m).
Output: a new process segment p=(C, A; F) whose concurrency has been extended
        from p'.
BEGIN
Call Block_Dependence(A, Rₐ, {input(aᵢ)}, {output(aᵢ)}, B, Rₑ, {input(bⱼ)},
{output(bⱼ)}, D, A/Rₐ, B/Rₑ); /*Call Algorithm 9.4 to get dependence array D,
partitions A/Rₐ and B/Rₑ. */
s:=|A/Rₐ|; /*There are s partition blocks in A/Rₐ={Ab₁, Ab₂, …, Abₛ} */
t:=|B/Rₑ|; /*There are t partition blocks in B/Rₑ={Bb₁, Bb₂, …, Bbₜ} */
A:=A'-{a″, b'};
C:=C'-{c'};
F:=F'-inflow(a″)-inflow(b')-outflow(a″)-outflow(b');
FOR i:=1 TO s DO
  BEGIN
    na:=|Abᵢ|; /* na denotes the number of activities in Abᵢ. */
    IF D[i, 1..t]=false THEN
      FOR k:=1 TO na DO F:=F∪{(lcᵢₖ, b″)} /* lcᵢₖ∈aᵢₖ˙ */
    ELSE
    FOR j:=1 TO t DO
      IF D[i, j] THEN
        BEGIN
          A:=A∪{bⱼ', aᵢ″};
          C:=C∪{cᵢⱼ};
          nb:=|Bbⱼ|; /* nb denotes the number of activities in Bbⱼ. */
          FOR l:=1 TO nb DO
            F:=F∪{(bⱼ', fcⱼₗ)}; /* fcⱼₗ∈˙bⱼₗ */
```

```
        F:=F∪{(aᵢ", cᵢⱼ), (cᵢⱼ, bⱼ')};
        FOR k:=1 TO na DO
            F:=F∪{(lcᵢₖ, aᵢ")}  /* lcᵢₖ∈aᵢₖ˙ */
        END; /* end of IF */
    END; /* end of FOR i */
FOR j:=1 TO t DO
  IF D[1..s, j]=false THEN
    BEGIN
        nb:=|Bbⱼ|; /* nb denotes the number of activities in Bbⱼ. */
        FOR l:=1 TO nb DO
        F:=F∪{(a', fcⱼₗ)} /* fcⱼₗ∈˙bⱼₗ */
    END /*end of IF */
END.
```

Algorithm 9.5 is shown in Fig. 9.14.

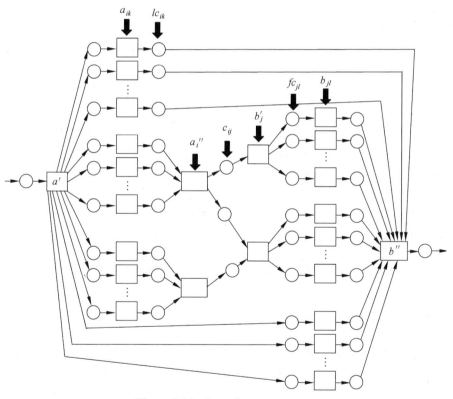

Figure 9.14   Extending concurrency

The key ideas of Algorithm 9.5 are discussed as follows:

(1) If any partition block in B does not depend on a partition block in A, the arcs which point at a'' are changed to point at b''.

(2) If a partition block in B does not depend on any partition block in A, the

arcs which point at the block from b' are changed into the arcs which point at the block from a'.

Example 9.4   In Fig. 9.15, activity set A is divided into two blocks Ab_1 and Ab_2, which have u activities and v activities respectively; activity set B is divided into two blocks Bb_1 and Bb_2, which have w activities and x activities respectively. Among these blocks, except that Bb_1 depends on Ab_1, there is no other dependence. By Algorithm 9.5, the concurrency can be extended from the process segment shown in Fig. 9.13(b) into the process segment shown in Fig. 9.15.

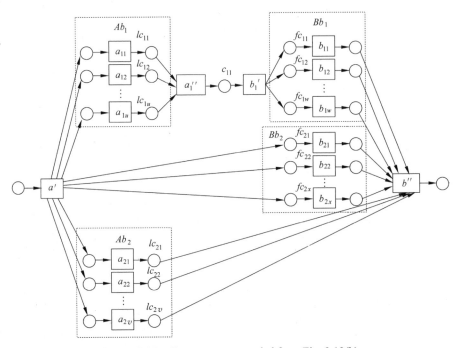

Figure 9.15   Concurrency extended from Fig. 9.13(b)

9.8   Reconstructing Software Processes

In the approach proposed in this chapter, firstly a process segment is dug down from a software process. In addition, the concurrency is captured in the process segment. Furthermore, the concurrency in the process segment is extended. Now there is a problem that must be solved: how is the process segment put back into the original software process?

In a software process, many new process segments whose concurrency have been captured and extended need to be put back to replace the old process segments. The process of putting back process segments is the process of reconstructing a software process.

However, this work is very complex. If a process segment has many relations (or interfaces) with the outside, it is almost impossible to put back the process segment because the new segment and the old one might have different interfaces. Therefore, the well-structured process segment with entrance and exit must be defined.

Definition 9.20 Let $(C, A; F)$ be a process segment of software process p. $s = (C, A; F, A_e, A_x)$ is called a *well-structured process segment* iff

(1) $A_e, A_x \subseteq A$ are called the *entrance* and the *exit* of s respectively if $\exists$ a step sequence $G_1 G_2 \cdots G_{n-1}$ $(G_1, G_2, \cdots, G_{n-1} \subseteq A)$ and $\exists$ cases $M_1, M_2, \cdots, M_n \subseteq C$, such that $[A_e > M_1, M_1[G_1 > M_2, \cdots, M_{n-1}[G_{n-1} > M_n$ and $M_n[A_x >$ and after A_x are executed, no token is left in C;

(2) $\dot{A_e} \cap C = \varnothing, A_e^\cdot \subseteq C, \dot{A_x} \subseteq C, A_x^\cdot \cap C = \varnothing$;

(3) $\dot{(A - A_e - A_x)} \subseteq C, (A - A_e - A_x)^\cdot \subseteq C$;

(4) $\dot{C} \subseteq A, C^\cdot \subseteq A$.

Theorem 9.1 Suppose process segment $(C, A; F)$ is generated by Algorithm 9.2. Let $A_e = \{a | a \in A \wedge \dot{a} = \varnothing\}$, $A_x = \{a | a \in A \wedge a^\cdot = \varnothing\}$. If $\exists$ a step sequence $G_1 G_2 \cdots G_{n-1}$ $(G_1, G_2, \cdots, G_{n-1} \subseteq A)$ and $\exists$ cases $M_1, M_2, \cdots, M_n \subseteq C$, such that $[A_e > M_1, M_1[G_1 > M_2, \cdots, M_{n-1}[G_{n-1} > M_n$ and $M_n[A_x >$ and after A_x are executed, no token is left in C, then $(C, A; F, A_e, A_x)$ is a well-structured process segment.

Proof According to the hypothesis, property (1) is obvious.

Property (2):

Since $A_e = \{a | a \in A \wedge \dot{a} = \varnothing\}, A_x = \{a | a \in A \wedge a^\cdot = \varnothing\}$, it follows that $\dot{A_e} = \varnothing, A_x^\cdot = \varnothing$, i.e. $\dot{A_e} \cap C = \varnothing, A_x^\cdot \cap C = \varnothing$.

According to Algorithm 9.2, the following properties are obvious:

Property (2): $A_e^\cdot \subseteq C, \dot{A_x} \subseteq C$.

Property (3): $\dot{(A - A_e - A_x)} \subseteq C, (A - A_e - A_x)^\cdot \subseteq C$.

Property (4): $\dot{C} \subseteq A, C^\cdot \subseteq A$. □

Algorithm 9.6 (Reconstructing Software Process)

```
Algorithm Reconstructing_Software_Process;
Input: software process p=(C, A; F, M0), well-structured process segment s'=(C,
    A; F, Ae, Ax), well-structured process segment s=(C, A; F, Ae, Ax).
Output: software process p=(C, A; F, M0) in which process segment s' is replaced
    with process segment s.
BEGIN
  p.C:=p.C-s'.C∪s.C;
  p.A:=p.A-s'.A∪s.A;
  inflow(s.Ae):={(x, y) | (x, z)∈inflow(s'.Ae)∧y∈s.Ae};
  outflow(s.Ax):={(x, y) | x∈s.Ax∧(z, y)∈outflow(s'.Ax)};
  p.F:=p.F-inflow(s'.Ae)-outflow(s'.Ax)∪inflow(s.Ae)∪outflow(s.Ax)
END.
```

Algorithm 9.6 is illustrated by Fig. 9.16. In Fig. 9.16, the process segment s' enclosed in dotted lines is replaced with process segment s.

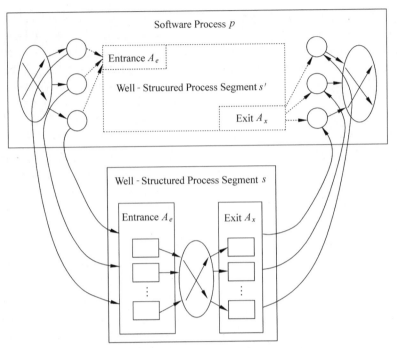

Figure 9.16 Reconstructing a software process

Theorem 9.2 Let $p = (C, A; F, M_0)$ be a software process. Let $s' = (C, A; F, A_e, A_x)$ and $s = (C, A; F, A_e, A_x)$ be two well-structured process segments of p. Using Algorithm 9.6 to replace s' with s, if $\exists M$, $M' \subseteq p.C$ such that $M[s'.A_e>$, $[s'.A_x>M'$, then $\exists$ a step sequence $G_1G_2\cdots G_{n-1}$ $(G_1, G_2, \cdots, G_{n-1} \subseteq s.A)$ and $\exists$ cases $M_1, M_2, \cdots, M_n \subseteq s.C$, such that $M[s.A_e>M_1$, $M_1[G_1>M_2$, $M_2[G_2>M_3, \cdots$, $M_{n-1}[G_{n-1}>M_n$, and $M_n[s.A_x> M'$.

Proof Suppose $M[s'.A_e>$, $[s'.A_x>M'$ $(M, M' \subseteq p.C)$.

Let $R = M - {}^{\bullet}(s'.A_e)$. The conditions in R are not used by s and s'.

Since After $s'.A_x$ are executed, no token is left in $s'.C$, $M' = (s'.A_x)^{\bullet} \cup R$.

Since ${}^{\bullet}(s.A_e) \cap s.C = \varnothing$, $(s.A_e)^{\bullet} \subseteq s.C$, $s.C \cap s'.C = \varnothing$ and $\text{inflow}(s.A_e) = \{(x, y)|$ $(x, z) \in \text{inflow}(s'.A_e) \wedge y \in s.A_e\}$, ${}^{\bullet}(s.A_e) = {}^{\bullet}(s'.A_e)$.

Therefore, if $s'.A_e$ is M-enabled, $s.A_e$ is M-enabled. It follows that $M[s.A_e>$.

Since s is a well-structured process segment, $\exists$ a step sequence $G_1G_2\cdots G_{n-1}$ $(G_1, G_2, \cdots, G_{n-1} \subseteq s.A)$ and $\exists$ cases $M_1, M_2, \cdots, M_n \subseteq s.C$, such that $M[s.A_e>M_1$, $M_1[G_1>M_2, \cdots, M_{n-1}[G_{n-1}>M_n$ and $M_n[s.A_x>$.

Since ${}^{\bullet}(s.A_x) \subseteq s.C$, $(s.A_x)^{\bullet} \cap s.C = \varnothing$, $s.C \cap s'.C = \varnothing$, and $\text{outflow}(s.A_x) = \{(x, y)|$ $x \in s.A_x \wedge (z, y) \in \text{outflow}(s.A_x)\}$, $(s.A_x)^{\bullet} = (s'.A_x)^{\bullet}$.

Since ${}^{\bullet}(s.A - s.A_e - s.A_x) \subseteq s.C$, $(s.A - s.A_e - s.A_x)^{\bullet} \subseteq s.C$, ${}^{\bullet}s.C \subseteq s.A$ and $s.C^{\bullet} \subseteq s.A$, if $M_n[s.A_x> M''$, then $M'' = (M_n - {}^{\bullet}(s.A_x)) \cup (s.A_x)^{\bullet} \cup R = (M_n - {}^{\bullet}(s.A_x)) \cup (s'.A_x)^{\bullet} \cup R$.

Since after $s.A_x$ are executed, no token is left in $s.C$, $M_n - {}^{\bullet}(s.A_x) = \varnothing$.
It follows that $M'' = (s'.A_x)^{\bullet} \cup R = M'$. $\square$

Theorem 9.2 indicates that when a well-structured process segment replaces a well-structured process segment (regarded as an activity in Definition 7.4) in a software process, the interface consistency is preserved between before replacement and after replacement. Namely a reconstructed software process preserves the interface consistency between the inefficient and the efficient well-structured process segments.

9.9   Summary

To capture and extend concurrency is an important approach to improving efficiency. In this chapter, an approach to improving the efficiency of software processes is proposed. As with a transplant operation on the human body, so the approach digs down into an inefficient process segment from a software process, improves its efficiency by means of capturing and extending concurrency, and then puts back the improved process segment into the original software process. Concretely, the following results are achieved:

Firstly, an algorithm to construct an entity dependence graph by means of analysing dependences between activities and between tasks is developed.

Secondly, a method to localise dependences in an activity dependence graph is proposed.

Thirdly, a method to simplify and preprocess an activity dependence graph is presented. Then an algorithm to construct a process segment from the preprocessed activity dependence graph is developed.

Fourthly, an algorithm to refine an activity as an activity set is proposed.

Fifthly, an algorithm to get two partition blocks and to analyse dependences between the two partition blocks is developed.

Sixthly, an algorithm to extend concurrency in a bottleneck segment is presented based on the dependence analysis between two partition blocks.

Finally, an algorithm to replace an inefficient process segment with an efficient process segment is also developed.

When a reconstructed software process is executed, it is expected that the time of evolution is shortened and the speed of evolution is increased. Namely, the efficiency of software evolution processes is improved.

References

[1] Aoyama M (1993) Concurrent-development process model. IEEE Software 10: 46 – 55
[2] Bernstein AJ (1966) Analysis of programs for parallel processing. IEEE Transactions on Electron Computer 15: 757 – 763

[3] Davis AM, Sitaram PA (1994) A concurrent process model of software development. ACM SIGSOFT Software Engineering Notes 19: 38 – 51

[4] Grün P, Eles P, Kuchcinski K, Pen Z (1996) Automatic parallelization of a Petri Net-based design representation for high-level synthesis. In: Proceedings of the 22nd EUROMICRO conference. IEEE Computer Society, Washington DC, pp 185 – 192

[5] Hawick K (2005) High performance computing and communications glossary 2.1. http://wotug.ukc.ac.uk/parallel/acronyms/hpccgloss

[6] Hein JL (2003) Discrete mathematics. Jones and Bartlett Publishers, Boston

[7] Humphrey W, Kellner MI (1989) Software process modeling: principles of entity process models. In: Proceedings of the 11th international conference on software engineering. ACM Press, New York, pp 331 – 342

[8] Kellner MI (1991) Software process modeling support for management planning and control. In: Proceedings of the 1st international conference on the software process. IEEE Computer Society, Washington DC, pp 8 – 28

[9] Raccoon LBS (1997) Fifty years of progress in software engineering. ACM SIGSOFT Software Engineering Notes 22: 88 – 104

[10] Ronald JN (1996) Object-oriented system analysis and design. Prentice Hall, New York

[11] Rosen KH (1998) Discrete mathematics and its applications. McGraw Hill, New York

10　Support Environment EPT

Tong Li

School of Software, Yunnan University, Kunming, 650091, China
Software Technology Research Laboratory, De Montfort University, Leicester, LE1 9BH, U.K
tli@ynu.edu.cn

Abstract　A Computer-Aided Software Engineering (CASE) environment is an effective tool supporting software evolution processes. In this chapter, a CASE environment EPT is designed and a prototype system of EPT is implemented. EPT can help software managers to model and control software evolution processes. EPT is designed with a three-level architecture: User Interface, Process Server and File Depository. EPT provides the following functions: Firstly, EPT supports modelling software evolution processes interactively and provides editors to edit models. An evolution process model in graph can be transformed into an EPDL program in text. Secondly, EPT provides a process package library to support the reuse of process packages. Thirdly, EPT compiles EPDL programs into data structures regarded as object codes and stored in Model Files. Fourthly, EPT runs EPDL programs and records the execution of the EPDL programs. Fifthly, EPT transforms the running processes into the visual representations by which users can execute, schedule, control and analyse the corresponding models. Sixthly, based on the execution records of an EPDL program, the statistics analysis can be processed. Seventhly, EPT supports the interactive efficiency improvement of software evolution processes based on an EPDL program. Finally, EPT supports the interactive decomposition of a 2-assertion into a series of finer 2-assertions.

Key Words　CASE, EPT, Process Reuse, EPDL Compiler, Process Engine, process interaction, process analysis, process improvement, functional decom-position, architecture, User Interface, Process Server, File Depository, Message Server, Modelling Manager, Decomposer, Knowledge Base, Runtime Manager.

Objectives

- To discuss the functions of EPT
- To present a three-level architecture of EPT

- To design the data structures of EPT, and
- To discuss the functions of User Interface, Process Server, Message Server and File Depository

10.1   Introduction

Computer-Aided Software Engineering (CASE) environments are effective tools supporting software development, of course, also supporting software evolution. Various process-centred software engineering environments (PSEEs) have been developed to support software processes (Pohl *et al.* 1999; Chou *et al.* 2005; Grundy and Hosking 1998; Padberg 2003; Lehman and Ramil 2002). The process models and process-based languages play important roles in PSEEs. These achievements have significantly promoted software process modelling, its execution, improvement and management. Enacting software processes using a PSEE is now well established (Fuggetta 2000). However, the CASE environments supporting software evolution processes are rarely discussed.

In order to effectively support software evolution processes, a CASE environment EPT (Evolution Process Tool) has been designed and a prototype system of EPT has been implemented. EPT transforms EPDL programs into visual Petri Net graphs on the screen; it also allows users to drive the activities of EPDL programs by means of the user interface. In addition, EPT can help the software managers to model and control software evolution processes. In detail, EPT provides the following functions:

(1) Modelling support: To support modelling software evolution processes interactively and to provide editors to edit models in graph and descriptions (EPDL programs) in text. An EPM in graph can be transformed into an EPDL program in text.

(2) Process reuse: To provide a process package library in which many process packages are stored, to support the reuse of process packages.

(3) EPDL compiler: To translate EPDL programs into data structures regarded as object codes and stored in Model Files.

(4) Process engine: To run EPDL programs. At the same time, when an EPDL program is executed, EPT also records the execution of the EPDL program using occurrence nets and stores these records in Process Files.

(5) Process interaction: To transform the running processes into the visual representations by which users can execute, schedule, control and analyse the corresponding models and descriptions.

(6) Process analysis: Based on the execution records of an EPDL program, the statistics analysis can be processed, especially for some important management attributes, such as time and cost.

(7) Process improvement: To support the interactive efficiency improvement of software evolution processes based on an EPDL program.

(8) Functional decomposition of tasks: To support the decomposition of a 2-assertion into a series of finer 2-assertions.

10.2   Architecture of EPT

EPT consists of three levels (or subsystems): User Interface, Process Server and File Depository. They interact with each other via Message Server. Both cooperation and communication between these subsystems are realised by message passing. The architecture of EPT is shown in Fig. 10.1.

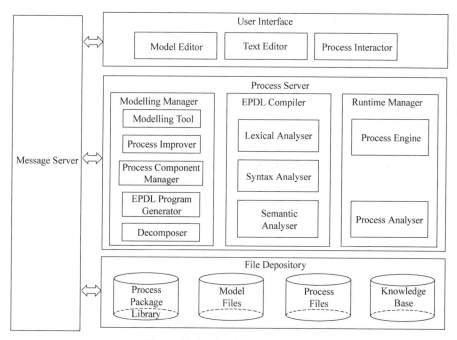

Figure 10.1   Architecture of EPT

File Depository provides services to store various files, including Process Package Library, Model Files, Process Files and Knowledge Base.

Process Server is a kernel subsystem of EPT. It provides support and services related with software evolution processes. It is composed of three subsystems: Modelling Manager, EPDL Compiler and Runtime Manager.

User Interface integrates Model Editor, Text Editor and Process Interactor into a unified user interface.

Message Server is a data bus which provides services for all subsystems in EPT. It also provides message services for EPDL programs which are being executed in Process Engine. Any entity can communicate with other entities if it defines the messages which can be identified and received by other entities. These messages are passed between entities by Message Server.

10.3   File Depository

10.3.1   Data Structures of EPDL Object Codes

Model Files store the data presentations of EPDL programs. In fact, these data presentations are the object codes which are generated by the EPDL compiler. Some important data presentations are shown as follows:

```
struct glossary /* The description of a glossary */
  {char *name; /* The name of a term */
   char *explanation; /* The explanation of the term */
  } glossary_set[]; /* The set of terms */
struct data_structure /* The description of a data structure defined by users*/
  {char *name; /* The name of the data structure */
   struct variable_declaration /* The variable declaration of the data structure */
     {char *name; /* The name of a data item in the data structure */
      char *data_type; /* The data type of the data item */
     }variable_declaration_set[]; /* The data item set included in the data
   structure */
  };
struct type_definition /* The description of data type defined by users */
  {char *name; /* The name of the data type */
   struct variable_declaration/* The variable declaration of the data type */
     {char *name; * The name of a data item in the data type */
      char *data_type; /* The data type of the data item */
     }type_definition_set[]; /* The data item set included in the data type */
  };
struct task /* The description of a task */
  {char *name; /* The name of the task */
   char *role[]; /* The role list who execute the task */
   struct receive_message /* The description of a received message */
     {char *name; /* The name of the message */
      char *variable[]; /* the variable list receiving the message */
     }receive_ message_set[]; /* The message list of received messages */
   struct decomposition_tree /* The description of the decomposition tree which
   describes the decomposition process */
   {char *name; /* The name of a vertex in the tree */
    char *vertex_type; /* One of sequence, selection and repetition */
    char *condition; /* The Boolean condition of selection decomposition or
       repetition decomposition */
    char *precondition, *postcondition; /* The 2-assertion describing the
       function of the vertex */
    struct send_message /* The message sent in the code segment */
```

```
       {char *name; /* The name of the message */
         char *process_name[], *activity_name[], *task_name[], *roles[],
           *condition[]; /* The massage receiver list */
         struct parameter /* The parameters of the message */
           {char *name; /* The parameter name */
            char *expression; /* The parameter expression */
            } parameter[]; /* The parameter set */
         } send_message; /* The message sent */
       struct decomposition_tree *left, *right; /* Pointing at left and right
         sub-tree */
       } decomposition_tree; /* The decomposition describing a code segment */
   };
   struct activity /* The description of an activity */
   {char *name; /* The name of the activity */
    struct activity *super_activity; /* The super activity which is inherited by
      the activity */
    struct data_structure input_data_structure[], output_data_structure[],
      local__data_structure[]; /* The declaration of the import, the export and
      the local data structures */
    union activity_body /* The description of the activity body */
      {struct software_process *name; /* If the activity is refined as a software
         process, it points at the process */
       struct task *task_set[]; /* The task set of the activity */
       } activity_body;
     };
   struct vertex /* The description of a vertex in a software process */
   {char *name; /* The vertex name */
    struct activity *activity; /* If the vertex is a condition vertex, then
      *activity is null */
    struct vertex *next; /* The pointer pointing at the next vertex */
   };
   struct vertexhead /* The description of the vertex head of a software process */
   { int count; /* The number of vertices which is adjacent to the vertex */
     char *name; /* The vertex name */
     char vertextype; /* The vertex type. "c" denotes condition vertex; "a" denotes
       activity vertex */
     short mark; /* for condition vertex, "1" indicates the vertex is marked; for
       activity vertex, "1" indicates the activity is being executed.*/
     struct vertex *first, *last; /* The pointers pointing at the first vertex
       and the last vertex in vertex adjacency list respectively */
     };
   struct software_process /* The description of a software process, not including
      the process package */
   {char *name; /* The name of the software process */
    struct software_process *super_process; /* The super software process which
      is inherited by the software process */
    struct type_definition data_type[]; /* The definition of a data type */
    struct vertexhead *vertexhead[]; /* The vertexhead of the software process */
    } software_process[];
   struct embedded_relation /* The description of embedded relation */
```

```
{struct software_process *first, *last; /* The software process at which pointer
    "last" points is embedded in the software process at which pointer "first"
    points. */
 };
struct global_model /* The description of a global model */
{char *name; /* The name of the global model */
 struct software_process *software_process_set[]; /* The software processes
    involved in the software evolution */
 struct embedded_relation embedded_list[]; /* The description of the embedded
    relation */
 };
```

In the data structures described above, the most complex data structure is the software process, which is stored in an adjacency list.

For example, the software process shown in Fig. 4.16 is compiled into the data structures shown in Fig. 10.2.

vertexhead [ ]

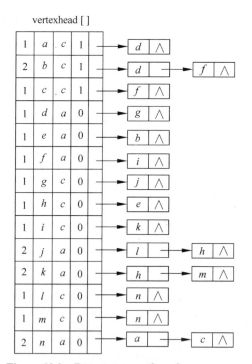

Figure 10.2 Data structure of a software process

10.3.2 Other Data Structures

In the Process Package Library, a software process package is composed of two parts: the definition of the package interface and the definition of the package body (a software process).

```
struct process_package /* The description of a process package */
{char *name; /* The name of the process package */
 struct data_structure input_data_structure[], output_data_structure[],
    local_data_structure[]; /* The declaration of the import, the export and
    the local data structures */
 char *mini_specification; /* The mini specification of the process
    package */
 char *key_word[]; /* The key words of the mini specification */
 struct software_process *body; /* The body of the process package is a software
    process */
} process_package_list[];
```

Process Files are used to store the execution records of an EPDL program using an occurrence net. The data structure of an execution record is defined as follows:

```
struct process_execution_record /* The description of an execution record of
    a software process which is an occurrence net */
{char *name; /* The name of the software process */
 struct software_process *process;/* A pointer which points at the recorded
    software process */
 struct vertexhead *vertexhead[]; /* Because an occurrence net is also a Petri
    Net, the data structure is the same as a software process */
} process_execution_record[];
```

The structures of the knowledge base are discussed in Chapter 8. The data structure of a predicate formula is described as a binary tree, defined as follows.

```
struct predicate_formula /* The description of a predicate formula */
{char quantifier; /* The quantifier of the predicate formula. "a" denotes "all";
    "e" denotes "exist" */
 struct variables /* The variable name list */
    {char *name;
     struct variables *next;
    }variables[];
 union tree_body /*The description of the predicate formula tree */
    {char *atom_operand; /* Vertex is a leaf of tree */
     struct operation /* Vertex is not a leaf of tree */
        {char *operator; /* The operator of the predicate formula. "not" denotes
           "¬"; "and" denotes "∧"; "or" denotes "∨"; "imply" denotes "⇒" and
           "iff" denotes "⇔". */
         struct predicate_formula *left, *right; /* Pointers pointing at operands
           */
        } operation;
    } tree_body;
} predicate_formula[]; /* The set of predicate formulae */
```

In addition, EPDL source programs, graph files of processes and documentation are also stored in Model Files.

10.4   Process Server

Process Server provides support and services related with software evolution processes. It is discussed in detail as follows.

10.4.1 Modelling Manager

Modelling Manager supports modelling and describing software evolution processes. It consists of five subsystems: Modelling Tool, Process Improver, Process Component Manager, EPDL Program Generator and Decomposer.

(1) Modelling Tool

Because many human factors are involved in the modelling process, fully formal modelling is very difficult. Modelling Tool provides the human modellers with an interactive means to support semi-formal modelling and describing formal software evolution processes with the aid of computers. It provides a top-down modelling approach using Procedure 6.1, Procedure 7.1, Procedure 7.2 and Procedure 8.1. A screenshot of Modelling Tool is shown in Fig. 10.3.

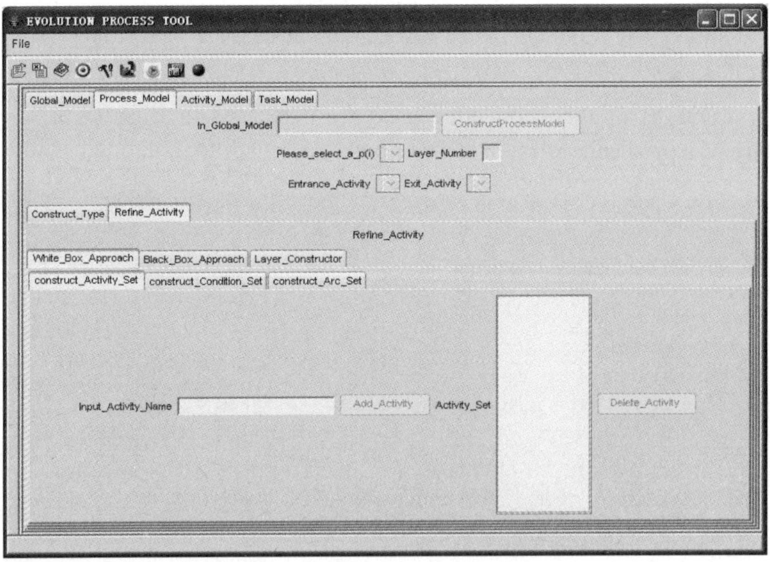

Figure 10.3   Screenshot of Modelling Tool

(2) Process Improver

Process Improver provides the human modellers with an interactive means to improve the efficiency of software evolution processes with the aid of computers. It realises the process improvement approach proposed in Chapter 9. Using Process Improver, the modellers can dig down into an inefficient process segment from a software process, improve its efficiency by means of capturing and extending concurrency, and then put back the improved process segment into the original software process. A screenshot of Process Improver is shown in Fig. 10.4.

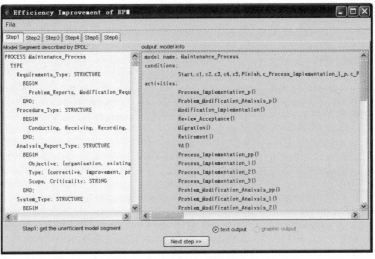

Figure 10.4　Screenshot of Process Improver

(3) EPDL Program Generator

Modellers can model software evolution processes in the form of a graph and describe these processes using EPDL programs. When modelling in graph, the EPDL Program Generator is used to generate an EPDL program, i.e. a software evolution process description, to preserve the consistency between the model in graph and the EPDL program.

(4) Process Component Manager

Process Component Manager manages the process packages (process components). If it finds a reusable process package in the library, Process Component Manager reuses the package. As modelling, when it needs to refine an activity, Modelling Tool sends a message to Process Component Manager, which retrieves the process packages from the Process Package Library. When the activity name matches one of the key words of a certain process package, Process Component Manager displays the Mini Specification of the process package on the screen and inquires of the modeller whether to refine the activity using the process package. If yes, Modelling Tool reuses it using the black box approach. A screenshot of Process Component Manager is shown in Fig. 10.5.

(5) Decomposer

Decomposer decomposes interactively a 2-assertion into a code segment with the support of the knowledge base. It includes the following modules: Knowledge Base Manager, Matching Detector and Decomposition Tree Manager. A screenshot of Process Component Manager is shown in Fig. 10.6.

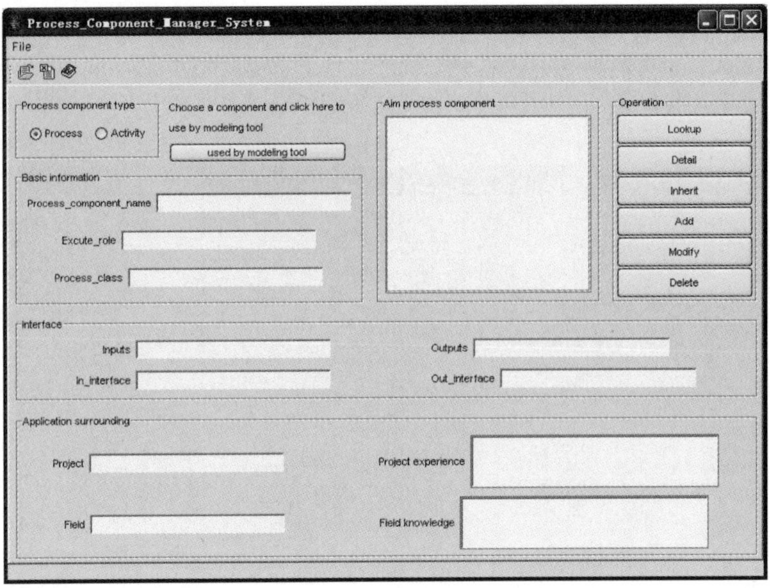

Figure 10.5 Screenshot of Process Component Manager

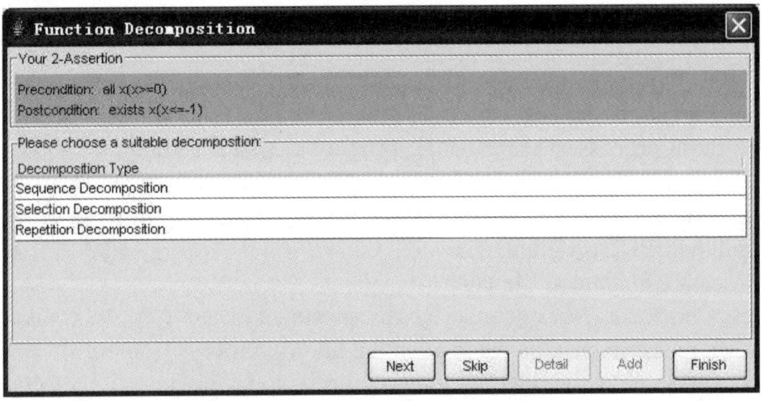

Figure 10.6 Screenshot of Decomposer

Knowledge Base Manager realises the management to the knowledge base, including adding, deleting, modifying and querying the cases, code segments and rules. The knowledge base consists of the case base, the segment base and the rule base. They are stored in a database.

The uses of the knowledge base depend on Matching Detector. When a 2-assertion is decomposed, the system needs to detect whether the 2-assertion matches cases or code segments in the case base and the segment base. If they match, Decomposer uses them directly. When they do not match, the decomposition rules are used. Therefore, the key to decomposition efficiency is the matching detection and decomposition rules.

Decomposition Tree Manager manages decomposition trees, especially their growth.

10.4.2   EPDL Compiler

EPDL compiler translates an EPDL program into data structures stored in Model Files. The architecture of EPDL Compiler is shown in Fig. 10.7.

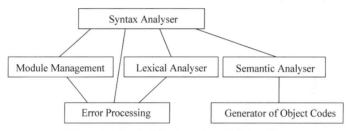

Figure 10.7   Architecture of EPDL Compiler

The Lexical Analyser identifies words and checks whether the words are legal or not. The legal words are stored in word list to support Syntax Analyser. The Lexical Analyser can be described as a deterministic finite automaton (DFA). It produces the legal words which the Syntax Analyser needs.

The Syntax Analyser checks EPDL source programs to confirm whether the programs fit the syntax definitions of EPDL. Syntax Analyser is composed of many recursive subroutines which check the correctness of EPDL programs.

The Semantic Analyser transforms a legal EPDL program into relevant data structures. The data structures can be regarded as the object codes of EPDL Compiler. The object codes are generated by the Generator of Object Codes.

10.4.3   Runtime Manager

Runtime Manager runs EPDL programs. When an EPDL program is executed, Runtime Manager also creates the corresponding execution records; it controls, supports and schedules the corresponding software processes. It consists of two subsystems: Process Engine and Process Analyser.

(1) Process Engine

Process Engine executes EPDL programs. It provides the modellers and the users of the software evolution process with visual Petri Nets. This provides the human users responsible for the evolution process with important information for scheduling and manipulating the remains of the process if necessary. A screenshot of Process Engine in which a software evolution process is executing is shown in

Fig. 10.8. Process Engine is implemented based on the open source software JARP (Padilha 2001).

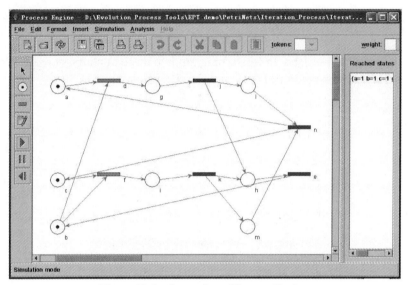

Figure 10.8 Screenshot of Process Engine

Executing an EPDL program can be viewed as a set of steps which need to be completed. When an EPDL program is executed, the roles are responsible for carrying out the real execution of a task. Therefore, a major challenge is to assure that there are excellent communications between human users and the Process Engine.

The time when an activity is scheduled is prescribed by the EPDL program. Human users drive the program to execute on the screen by mouse and keyboard. When an activity is enabled, i.e. can be executed, the human users announce the roles that will execute the tasks in the activity to execute the activity and its tasks. A role is an executor of a task of an activity. A role can be a person, a group of persons, a combination of both persons and computers and even computers only. When an activity is accomplished, the roles report this to the human users. After receiving the report, the human user updates the Model Files and drives the process to be in progress (changes the position of tokens) so that new activities can be executed until the software evolution process terminates. By the visual Petri Net, human users control and schedule the execution of processes according to their needs. The execution of an EPDL program is recorded in the Model Files as an occurrence net.

(2) Process Analyser

Process Analyser analyses the performance of software processes by analysing the execution records generated by Process Engine. It provides the statistical data of key attributes, such as time and cost. A screenshot of Process Analyser is shown in Fig. 10.9.

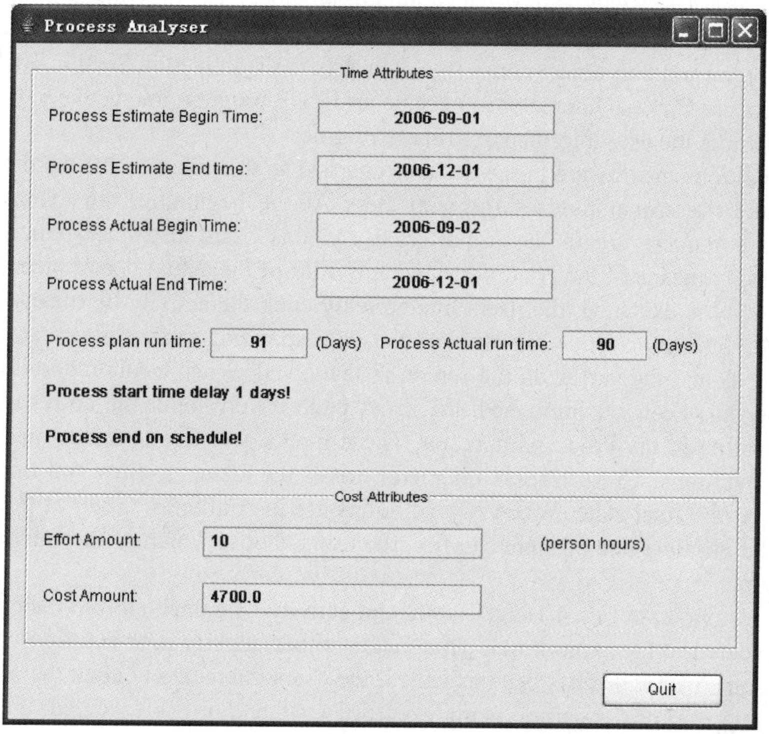

Figure 10.9   Screenshot of Process Analyser

Process Analyser can be used either before or after an EPDL program is executed. The use after a real execution is to sum up the experiences to improve the software process in the future. The use before a real execution is to simulate the execution of a real software evolution process and soon an execution result is obtained. By analysing the result, modellers can find faults in the EPDL program and improve them. As a result, when the EPDL program is actually executed, the performance and quality will be increased.

10.5   User Interface and Message Server

Model Editor provides users with a tool in the form of user interaction to edit graphs of software evolution processes. The graphs are composed of two kinds of elements: vertexes and arcs. Vertexes denote entities, such as tasks, activities and software processes. The attributes of vertexes store the attributes of these entities. Arcs denote the relations between entities, such as flow relations and embedded relations. These elements are displayed in graphical form on the screen and can be added, modified, removed and saved by the human users interactively. Users can also transform these graphs into EPDL programs.

Text Editor is used to edit EPDL source programs in text files and store them in Model Files. Users can send a message to the EPDL Compiler to translate an EPDL source program into object codes (the data structures defined in Section 10.3).

Users use Process Interactor to execute an EPDL program interactively. Process Interactor is the user interface of Process Engine.

Conditions in software processes are regarded as the milestone of the previous step and the cornerstone of the next step. At the beginning, the tokens of a software process are in the initial state. On this basis, users can control the process by means of the conditions and activities of the actual occurrence. When an activity is executed, the users interactively click the activity by means of the Process Interactor. Thus the state of the corresponding vertex is set to "being executed" and the vertex on the screen is shadowed. When a role reports that an activity has been accomplished, the users interactively input the corresponding information in the Process Interactor. These inputs give rise to tokens passed to new conditions. Thus, Process Interactor drives the tokens to flow and finally to arrive at the final state. When two activities are in conflict, i.e. two of them are enabled but only one of them can fire, the users choose which of the activities to execute.

For example, in Fig. 4.16, activity d and activity f are enabled (but they cannot be executed at the same time). This means either activity d or activity f can be executed. After d or f has been executed, the users interactively click the activity. The state of d or f is set to "being executed". After d or f is executed, the users again interactively input the information to Process Interactor, and thus the token is passed. In this example, if activity d has fired, the tokens is passed from $\{a, b, c\}$ to $\{g, c\}$.

Users can visually control a software evolution process by means of the corresponding Petri Net graph and can dynamically drive an EPDL program to execute. These formal and visual achievements improve the efficiency and correctness.

There are two message queues in Message Server: a free message queue and a full message queue. The sender firstly applies a free message box from the free message queue and then it fills the free message box with a new message. Finally, it sends the message box to the full message queue. The receiver firstly searches for its message in the full message queue. After getting the message, the receiver sends the message box to the free message queue to free it.

Message Server provides users with a unified communication platform. All the entities included in both EPT and software processes can communicate with each other on this platform. Thus, the module invoking directly between entities is avoided and the module coupling is reduced. As a result, the system complexity is decreased.

10.6   Summary

During software evolution, support environments play important roles. EPT supports software evolution processes effectively. EPT has been designed and a prototype system of EPT has been implemented. The following are discussed in this chapter.

(1) The three-level architecture of EPT is designed: User Interface, Process Server and File Depository. They interact with each other via Message Server.

(2) The important data structures are described, including Process Package Library, Model Files, Process Files and Knowledge Base.

(3) The functions of all subsystems are discussed. Process Server provides support and services related with software evolution processes. It is composed of three subsystems: Modelling Manager, EPDL Compiler and Runtime Manager. User Interface integrates Model Editor, Text Editor and Process Interactor into a unified user interface. Message Server is a data bus which provides services for all subsystems in EPT. It also provides message services for executing EPDL programs in Process Engine.

References

[1] Chou S, Hsu W, Lo W (2005) DPE/PAC: decentralized process engine with product access control. Journal of Systems and Software 76: 207 – 219

[2] Fuggetta A (2000) Software process: a roadmap. In: Proceedings of the conference on the future of software engineering. ACM Press, New York, pp 25 – 34

[3] Grundy JC, Hosking JG (1998) Serendipity: integrated environment support for process modelling, enactment and work coordination. Automated Software Engineering 5: 27 – 60

[4] Lehman MM, Ramil JF (2002) Software evolution and software evolution processes. Annals of Software Engineering 14: 275 – 309

[5] Padberg F (2003) A software process scheduling simulator. In: Proceedings of the 25th international conference on software engineering. IEEE Computer Society, Washington DC, pp 816 – 817

[6] Padilha R (2001) JARP. http://sourceforge.net/projects/jarp/

[7] Pohl K, Weidenhaupt K, Dömges R, Haumer P, Jarke M, Klamma R (1999) PRIME—toward process-integrated modeling environments. ACM Transactions on Software Engineering and Methodology 8: 43 – 410

11 Case Studies

Tong Li

School of Software, Yunnan University, Kunming, 650091, China
Software Technology Research Laboratory, De Montfort University, Leicester, LE1 9BH, U.K
tli@ynu.edu.cn

Abstract This chapter presents four case studies using the proposed approach and describes the results using EPDL programs. The first case study is about the classical waterfall model of the software life cycle. This case study aims to illustrate the proposed approach to modelling and describing classical software processes. The second case study is about a set of software processes which describe the evolution of a software system. This case study aims to illustrate the proposed approach to modelling and describing several software processes involved in the software evolution. The third case study is about the evolution of a certificate authority software SIS which provides the functions of encryption, decryption, digital signature and identity authentication. The case study shows the process of modelling the software evolution process and of describing the corresponding EPDL programs. This case study aims to illustrate the proposed approach to modelling and describing the software evolution process under which a security software system in Linux evolves into a cross-platform system in both Windows and Linux. The fourth case study is about the ISO/IEC 12207 Standard for Software Life Cycle Processes. This case study models and describes the maintenance process defined in this international standard. This case study aims to illustrate the proposed approach to modelling and describing software processes of the ISO/IEC Standard. These case studies are very different from each other. They cover different areas with various complexities and scales for showing the powerful modelling capacity of the proposed approach. These case studies try to indicate that the proposed approach is feasible and effective.

Key Words waterfall model, EPDL program, evolution process, support process, management process, SIS, ISO/IEC 12207 Standard, efficiency improvement, maintenance process, process implementation, problem and modification analysis, modification implementation, maintenance review/ acceptance, migration, software retirement.

Objectives

- To illustrate the approach to modelling and describing the classical waterfall model in the software life cycle
- To illustrate the approach to modelling and describing a software evolution which includes three software processes: Evolution Process, Support Process and Management Process
- To illustrate the approach to modelling and describing a software evolution process which evolves a security software system in Linux into a cross-platform system in both Windows and Linux
- To illustrate the approach to modelling and describing the maintenance process of the ISO/IEC 12207 Standard for Software Life Cycle Processes, and
- To indicate that the proposed approach is feasible and effective

11.1   Introduction

This chapter presents four case studies using the proposed approach and describes the results based on EPDL Language.

The first case study is about the classical waterfall model of the software life cycle. This case study aims to illustrate the proposed approach to modelling and describing the classical software processes.

The second case study is about a set of software processes which describe a software evolution. These software processes include three concurrent software processes: the Evolution Process, the Support Process and the Management Process. The Evolution Process includes two sub-processes which evolve software subsystems with different steps. This case study aims to illustrate the proposed approach to modelling and describing many software processes involved in the software evolution.

The third case study is about the evolution of a certificate authority software SIS (System Information Security) which provides functions of encryption, decryption, digital signature and identity authentication. The case study shows the process of modelling the software evolution process and of describing the corresponding EPDL programs. This case study aims to illustrate the proposed approach to modelling and describing a software evolution process which evolves a security software system in Linux into a cross-platform system in both Windows and Linux.

The fourth case study is about the ISO/IEC 12207 Standard for Software Life Cycle Processes. This international standard establishes a common framework for the software life cycle processes, which can be referenced by the software industry. It contains processes, activities and tasks that are to be applied during the acquisition of a system which contains software, a stand-alone software product and software service and also during the supply, development, operation, and maintenance of software products (ISO and IEC 1998). This case study models and describes the maintenance process of this international standard. Some researchers and practitioners use evolution as a preferable substitute for maintenance (Bennett and Rajlich 2000). Therefore, maintenance can be regarded as a special form of evolution. This case study aims to illustrate the proposed approach to modelling and describing software processes of the ISO/IEC standard, especially the software evolution process, although there is no software evolution process explicitly defined in the ISO/IEC standard.

These case studies are very different from each other. They cover different areas with various complexities and scales for showing the powerful modelling capacity of the proposed approach. These case studies try to indicate that the proposed approach is feasible and effective.

11.2   First Case Study: The Waterfall Model

The waterfall model is the first explicit model of the software life cycle process proposed by Royce in 1970 (Pressman 2000). This was enthusiastically accepted by software project management. This case study supposes that the software life cycle is divided into four phases: analysis, design, coding and test, as shown in Fig. 11.1. Using EPDL, the waterfall model can be described as follows (The comments are between /* and */).

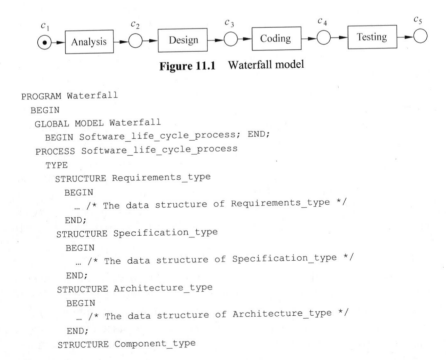

Figure 11.1   Waterfall model

```
PROGRAM Waterfall
  BEGIN
  GLOBAL MODEL Waterfall
    BEGIN Software_life_cycle_process; END;
  PROCESS Software_life_cycle_process
    TYPE
      STRUCTURE Requirements_type
        BEGIN
          ... /* The data structure of Requirements_type */
        END;
      STRUCTURE Specification_type
        BEGIN
          ... /* The data structure of Specification_type */
        END;
      STRUCTURE Architecture_type
        BEGIN
          ... /* The data structure of Architecture_type */
        END;
      STRUCTURE Component_type
```

```
      BEGIN
         … /* The data structure of Component_type */
      END;
   STRUCTURE Code_type
      BEGIN
         … /* The data structure of Code_type */
      END;
   STRUCTURE Test_case_type
      BEGIN
         … /* The data structure of Test_case_type */
      END;
   STRUCTURE Product_type
      BEGIN
         … /* The data structure of Product_type */
      END;
ACTIVITY Analysis
   IMPORTS
      User_requirements: Requirements_type;
   EXPORTS
      Specification: Specification_type;
   BEGIN
      … /* tasks */
   END;
ACTIVITY Design
   IMPORTS
      Specification: Specification_type;
   EXPORTS
      Architecture: Architecture_type;
      Component: Component_type;
   BEGIN
      … /*tasks */
   END;
ACTIVITY Coding
   IMPORTS
      Architecture: Architecture_type;
      Component: Component_type;
   EXPORTS
      Code: Code_type;
   BEGIN
      … /*tasks */
   END;
ACTIVITY Testing
   IMPORTS
      Specification: Specification_type;
      Architecture: Architecture_type;
      Component: Component_type;
      Test_case: Test_case_type;
      Code: Code_type;
   EXPORTS
      Product: Product_type;
   BEGIN
      … /*tasks */
```

```
    END;
  BEGIN
    CONDITION SET
      C:={c1, c2, c3, c4, c5};
    ACTIVITY SET
      A:={Analysis, Design, Coding, Testing};
    ARC SET
      F:={(c1, Analysis), (Analysis, c2), (c2, Design), (Design, c3), (c3,
  Coding), (Coding, c4), (c4, Testing), (Testing, c5)};
      MARKING {c1}
    END;
END.
```

11.3 Second Case Study: Three Software Processes Involved in Evolution

When a software system is evolving, there are many software processes involved in the evolution. This case study supposes that three software processes are involved in the software evolution, as shown in Fig. 11.2. The comments are between /* and */. "Config." is the abbreviation for "configuration" and "Mgt." for "management". The EPDL program, i.e. the description of the software evolution process, is as follows.

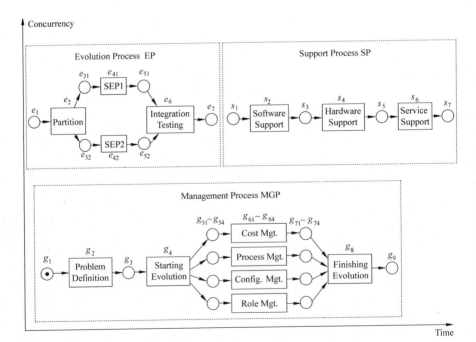

Figure 11.2 A software evolution process

```
PROGRAM Evolution_Process
#define e2: Partition;
#define e41: SEP1;
#define e42: SEP2;
#define e6: Integration Testing;
#define s2: Software Support;
#define s4: Hardware Support;
#define s6: Service Support;
#define g2: Problem Definition;
#define g4: Starting Evolution;
#define g61: Cost Management;
#define g62: Process Management;
#define g63: Configuration Management;
#define g64: Role Management;
#define g8: Finishing Evolution;
BEGIN
  GLOBAL MODEL Evolution_Process
    BEGIN EP; SP; MGP; END;
  PROCESS EP  /* Define software evolution process EP */
    ACTIVITY e2 …;  /* Define activity e2 */
    ACTIVITY e41 …;  /* Define activity e41 */
    ACTIVITY e42 …;  /* Define activity e42 */
    ACTIVITY e6 …;  /* Define activity e6 */
    BEGIN
      CONDITION SET
        EPC:={e1, e31, e32, e51, e52, e7};
      ACTIVITY SET
        EPA:={e2, e41, e42, e6};
      ARC SET
        EPF:={(e1, e2), (e2, e31), (e2, e32), (e31, e41), (e41, e51),
(e51, e6) ,(e32, e42), (e42, e52) , (e52, e6), (e6, e7)};
    END; /* End of PROCESS EP */
  PROCESS SP  /* Define software support process SP */
    ACTIVITY s2 …;  /* Define activity s2 */
    ACTIVITY s4 …;  /* Define activity s4 */
    ACTIVITY s6 …;  /* Define activity s6 */
    BEGIN
      CONDITION SET
        SPC:={s1, s3, s5, s7};
      ACTIVITY SET
        SPA:={s2, s4, s6};
      ARC SET
        SPF:={(s1, s2), (s2, s3), (s3, s4), (s4, s5), (s5, s6), (s6, s7)};
    END; /*End of PROCESS SP*/
  PROCESS MGP  /* Define software management process MGP */
    ACTIVITY g2 …;  /* Define activity g2 */
    ACTIVITY g4     /* Define activity g4 */
      LOCALS
        code: INTEGER;
        Execution, Set_token: MESSAGE;
      BEGIN
        TASK Main
          ON MESSAGES Execution(code)
```

```
                    BEGIN
                      SEND Set_token TO EP.e1, SP.s1(true)
                      END; /* End of task Main */
                  END; /* End of activity g4 */
              ACTIVITY g61 …; /* Define activity g61 */
              ACTIVITY g62 …; /* Define activity g62 */
              ACTIVITY g63 …; /* Define activity g63 */
              ACTIVITY g64 …; /* Define activity g64 */
              ACTIVITY g8 …;  /* Define activity g8 */
              BEGIN
                CONDITION SET
                  MGC:={g1, g3, g51, g52, g53, g54, g71, g72, g73, g74, g9};
                ACTIVITY SET
                  MGA:={g2, g4, g61, g62, g63, g64, g8};
                ARC SET
                  MGF:={(g1, g2), (g2, g3), (g3, g4), (g4, g51), (g4, g52), (g4, g53), (g4,
              g54), (g51, g61), (g52, g62), (g53, g63), (g54, g64), (g61, g71), (g62, g72),
              (g63, g73), (g64, g74), (g71, g8), (g72, g8), (g73, g8), (g74, g8), (g8, g9)};
                  MARKING {g1}
                  END; /*End of PROCESS MGP*/
              END.
```

The initial marking is in set {g1} of process MGP. It refers to starting firstly the software management process MGP. The starting of the software evolution process EP and software support process SP is determined by MGP in which task g4.Main sends a message to them to set their initial markings. Because e1 and s1 are set to "true" at the same time, EP and SP are executed concurrently.

Obviously, the process described above is very abstract. In EP, e41 and e42 can be furthermore refined by two sub-processes. Software processes SEP1, shown in Fig. 11.3, and SEP2, shown in Fig. 4.13, can be used to refine the activity e41 and e42 in EP using inheritance, respectively. The EPDL program is as follows.

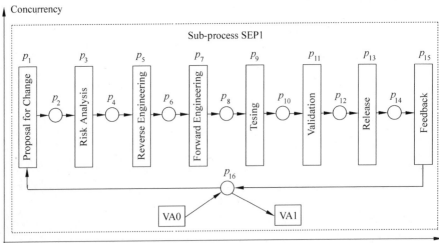

Figure 11.3   Sub-process SEP1

```
PROGRAM Evolution_Process_New
#define … /* all the #defines in Program Evolution_Process should be listed here. */
#define p1: Proposal for Change;
#define p3: Risk Analysis;
#define p5: Reverse Engineering;
#define p7: Forward Engineering;
#define p9: Testing;
#define p11: Validation,
#define p13: Release;
#define p15: Feedback;
#define d1: Requirements Analysis;
#define d2: Design;
#define d3: Prototype Construction;
#define d4: Prototype Execution;
#define d5: Prototype Verification;
#define d6: Prototype Optimisation;
BEGIN
  GLOBAL MODEL Evolution_Process
    BEGIN
      EP; SP; MGP; SEP1; SEP2;
      EMBEDDED RELATION (EP, SEP1); (EP, SEP2)
    END;
  PROCESS SP FROM Evolution_Process.SP
    BEGIN END; /* Completely inherit SP from Program Evolution_Process */
  PROCESS MGP FROM Evolution_Process.MGP
    BEGIN END; /* Completely inherit MGP from Program Evolution_Process */
  PROCESS SEP1 /* Define sub-process SEP1 as a process package */
  PACKAGE
    ENTRANCE VA0;
    EXIT VA1;
    ACTIVITY p1  …; /* Define activity p1 */
    ACTIVITY p3  …; /* Define activity p3 */
    ACTIVITY p5  …; /* Define activity p5 */
    ACTIVITY p7  …; /* Define activity p7 */
    ACTIVITY p9  …; /* Define activity p9 */
    ACTIVITY p11 …; /* Define activity p11 */
    ACTIVITY p13 …; /* Define activity p13 */
    ACTIVITY p15 …; /* Define activity p15 */
    BEGIN
      CONDITION SET
        SEP1C:={p2, p4, p6, p8, p10, p12, p14, p16};
      ACTIVITY SET
        SEP1A:={VA0, VA1, p1, p3, p5, p7, p9, p11, p13, p15};
      ARC SET
        SEP1F:={(p1, p2), (p2, p3), (p3, p4), (p4, p5), (p5, p6), (p6, p7), (p7,
p8), (p8, p9), (p9, p10), (p10, p11), (p11, p12), (p12, p13), (p13, p14), (p14,
p15), (p15, p16), (p16, p1), (VA0, p16), (p16, VA1)};
    END; /*End of PROCESS SEP1*/
  PROCESS SEP2 /* Define sub-process SEP2 as a process package, see Fig. 4.13. */
```

```
PACKAGE
  ENTRANCE VA0;
  EXIT VA6;
  ACTIVITY d1 …; /* Define activity d1 */
  ACTIVITY d2 …; /* Define activity d2 */
  ACTIVITY d3 …; /* Define activity d3 */
  ACTIVITY d4 …; /* Define activity d4 */
  ACTIVITY d5 …; /* Define activity d5 */
  ACTIVITY d6 …; /* Define activity d6 */
  BEGIN
    CONDITION SET
      SEP2C:={c1, c2, c3, c4, c5, c6, c7}; /* c0 is ignored. */
    ACTIVITY SET
      SEP2A:={d1, d2, d3, d4, d5, d6, VA0, VA1, VA2, VA3, VA4, VA5 VA6};
    ARC SET
      SEP2F:={(VA0, c1), (c1, d1), (d1, c2), (c2, d2), (d2, c3), (c3, d3),
  (VA1, c3), (VA4, c3), (d3, c4), (c4, d4), (c4, VA3), (c7, VA1), (VA3, c7), (VA5,
  c1), (c5, VA4), (c5, VA6), (c5, VA5), (d4, c7), (c7, d5), (d5, c6), (c6, d6),
  (d6, c5), (c7, VA2), (VA2, c1)}; /* (c0, VA0) is ignored. */
    END; /* End of PROCESS SEP2 */
  PROCESS EP FROM Evolution_Process.EP /* Inherit EP from Program
  Evolution_Process with changes */
    ACTIVITY e41
      BEGIN SEP1 END; /* Redefine e41, the descriptions of e41 is replaced with
  SEP1. */
    ACTIVITY e42
      BEGIN SEP2 END; /* Redefine e42; the descriptions of e42 is replaced with
  SEP2. */
    BEGIN
    END; /*End of PROCESS EP*/
  END.
```

In EP, the codes which are not newly described are inherited completely. Activities e41 and e42 are newly described and replaced by SEP1 and SEP2 respectively.

11.4 Third Case Study: An Evolution Process of an Information Security System

11.4.1 Background

In 2001, a certificate authority software SIS was designed and implemented in Linux by the author of this book and his colleagues. SIS includes two subsystems: SISCA which runs in server computers and SISUA which runs in client computers. SISCA realises the following functions: certificate management, key management, user registration and cross-certification of public keys. By interacting with its users, SISUA realises a user interface of encryption and decryption, digital signature and identity authentication. Both SISCA and SISUA call kernel algorithms, which are based on the elliptic curve cryptography, to realise the functions of encryption, decryption, digital signature and identity authentication.

Recently, some users requested SIS to support Windows and to improve the efficiency of the kernel algorithms. Therefore, SIS needs to evolve to meet these user requirements.

This case study illustrates modelling and describing the software evolution process at the global level and at the process level. Because the fourth case study shows mainly modelling and describing the software maintenance process at the activity level and at the task level in detail, in this case study, the descriptions at these two levels are omitted.

11.4.2 The Process of Modelling

Making use of the proposed approach, a series of software processes can be obtained. For the sake of simplicity, only one software process, SIS_Process, is included in the global model. At the process level, the process of modelling is shown in Fig. 11.4. The models SIS_Process(i) ($i = 1, 2, \cdots, 7$) are constructed by means of refinement. The number in parentheses denotes the level number of the software processes.

11.4.3 EPDL Program

The terms listed in the glossary are defined gradually with the process of modelling and describing. The EPDL program is as follows.

```
PROGRAM SIS_Evolution
#define c1: Start;
#define c2: Selected;
#define c3.1: Design Finished;
#define c3.2: Proposal Reviewed;
#define c3.3: Analysis Reviewed;
#define c3.4: Abstract Reviewed;
#define c3.5: Re-Design Reviewed;
#define c3.6: Re-Design Accepted;
#define c4: Reviewed;
#define c4.1: Kernel Design Reviewed;
#define c4.2: Interface Design Reviewed;
#define c5: Tested;
#define c5.1: Kernel Tested;
```

```
#define c5.2: Interface Tested;
#define c6: Finish;
#define a: Evolving to Windows;
#define a1: Technology Selection;
#define a1.1: Porting;
#define a1.2: By Virtual Machine;
#define a2.1: Design;
#define a2.2: Design Evolution;
#define a2.2.1: Proposal for Change;
#define a2.2.2: Risk Analysis;
#define a2.2.3: Abstract;
#define a2.2.4: Re-Design;
#define a2.2.5: Validation;
#define a2.2.6: Feedback;
#define a3: Review;
#define a4: Implementation;
#define a4.1: Kernel Algorithm Implementation;
#define a4.1.1: Kernel Algorithm Test;
#define a4.1.2: Kernel Algorithm Coding;
#define a4.2: User Interface Implementation;
#define a5: Integration;
BEGIN
GLOBAL MODEL SIS_Evolution
  BEGIN SIS_Process(6) END;
PROCESS SIS_Process(6)
    BEGIN
    … /* The description of software process SIS_Process(6) which will be
described in the following sections. */
    END;
END. /* End of EPDL program */
```

11.4.4 White Box Approach

The description of the software processes is level by level, from SIS_Process(0) to SIS_Process(6), shown as follows according to Fig. 11.4 using the white box approach.

```
PROCESS SIS_Process(0)
BEGIN
  CONDITION SET
    C:={c1, c6};
  ACTIVITY SET
    A:={a};
  ARC SET
    F:={(c1, a), (a, c6)};
  MARKING {c1}
END;
```

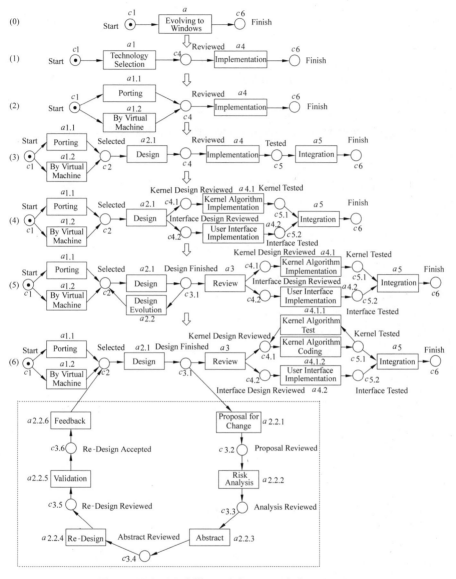

Figure 11.4   Modelling a software evolution process

By refining activity *Evolving to Windows* in software process SIS_Process(0), SIS_Process(1) is obtained using inheritance.

```
PROCESS SIS_Process(1) FROM SIS_Process(0)
  BEGIN
    CONDITION SET
    C:=C∪{c4};
    ACTIVITY SET
    A:=A∪{a1, a4}-{a};
```

177

```
      ARC SET
         F:={(c1, a1), (a1, c4), (c4, a4), (a4, c6)};
   END;
```

In SIS_Process(1), if something are not described, such as MARKING, then the original descriptions inherited from SIS_Process(0) are preserved. It should be pointed out that if a condition or an activity is removed from a set (using the "−" operation), then all the arcs attached to it are also removed automatically. In this way, other software processes are gradually described as follows.

```
   PROCESS SIS_Process(2) FROM SIS_Process(1)
   BEGIN
     ACTIVITY SET
       A:=AU{a1.1, a1.2}-{a1};
     ARC SET
       F:=FU{(c1, a1.1), (a1.1, c4), (c1, a1.2), (a1.2, c4)};
   END;
   PROCESS SIS_Process(3) FROM SIS_Process(2)
   BEGIN
     CONDITION SET
       C:=CU{c2, c5};
     ACTIVITY SET
       A:=AU{a2.1, a5};
     ARC SET
       F:=FU{(a1.1, c2), (a1.2, c2), (c2, a2.1), (a2.1, c4), (a4, c5), (c5, a5),
   (a5, c6)}-{(a1.1, c4), (a1.2, c4), (a4, c6)};
   END;
   PROCESS SIS_Process(4) FROM SIS_Process(3)
   BEGIN
     CONDITION SET
       C:=C-{c4, c5}U{c4.1, c4.2, c5.1, c5.2};
     ACTIVITY SET
       A:=A-{a4}U{a4.1, a4.2};
     ARC SET
       F:=FU{(a2.1, c4.1), (a2.1, c4.2), (c4.1, a4.1), (c4.2, a4.2), (a4.1, c5.1),
   (a4.2, c5.2), (c5.1, a5), (c5.2, a5)};
   END;
   PROCESS SIS_Process(5) FROM SIS_Process(4)
   BEGIN
     CONDITION SET
       C:=CU{c3.1};
     ACTIVITY SET
       A:=AU{a2.2, a3};
     ARC SET
       F:=F-{(a2.1, c4.1), (a2.1, c4.2)}U{(a2.1, c3.1), (c3.1, a2.2), (a2.2, c2),
   (c3.1, a3), (a3, c4.1), (a3, c4.2)};
   END;
   PROCESS SIS_Process(6) FROM SIS_Process(5)
   BEGIN
     CONDITION SET
       C:=CU{c3.2, c3.3, c3.4, c3.5, c3.6};
     ACTIVITY SET
       A:=A-{a4.1, a2.2}U{a4.1.1, a4.1.2, a2.2.1, a2.2.2, a2.2.3, a2.2.4, a2.2.5,
   a2.2.6};
```

```
ARC SET
  F:=FU{(c4.1, a4.1.2), (a4.1.2, c5.1), (c5.1, a4.1.1), (a4.1.1, c4.1), (c3.1,
a2.2.1), (a2.2.1, c3.2), (c3.2, a2.2.2), (a2.2.2, c3.3), (c3.3, a2.2.3),
(a2.2.3, c3.4), (c3.4, a2.2.4), (a2.2.4, c3.5), (c3.5, a2.2.5), (a2.2.5, c3.6),
(c3.6, a2.2.6), (a2.2.6, c2)}};
END;
```

In this case study, for the sake of simplicity, sometimes several refinements are merged into one refinement, e.g. from SIS_Process(4) to SIS_Process(5).

From this example, it is observed that modelling level by level simplifies the design of software evolution processes.

11.4.5   Black Box Approach

Now, suppose SIS_Process(5) has been obtained. SIS_Process(6) can be modelled using the black box approach to refining activity $a2.2$ and the white box approach to refining activity $a4.1$, shown as follows.

```
GLOBAL MODEL SIS_Evolution
  BEGIN
    SIS_Process(6);
    Design_Evolution_Package;
    EMBEDDED RELATION
      (SIS_Process(6), Design_Evolution_Package);
  END;
PROCESS Design_Evolution_Package
  PACKAGE
    ENTRANCE a2.2.1;
    EXIT a2.2.6;
  BEGIN
  CONDITION SET
    C:={c3.2, c3.3, c3.4, c3.5, c3.6};
  ACTIVITY SET
    A:={a2.2.1, a2.2.2, a2.2.3, a2.2.4, a2.2.5, a2.2.6};
  ARC SET
    F:={(a2.2.1, c3.2), (c3.2, a2.2.2), (a2.2.2, c3.3), (c3.3, a2.2.3), (a2.2.3,
  c3.4), (c3.4, a2.2.4), (a2.2.4, c3.5), (c3.5, a2.2.5), (a2.2.5, c3.6), (c3.6,
  a2.2.6)}};
  END;
PROCESS SIS_Process(6) FROM SIS_Process(5)
  ACTIVITY a2.2 /* Black box approach to refining activity a2.2 */
    BEGIN Design_Evolution_Package END;
  BEGIN
  ACTIVITY SET /* White box approach to refining activity a4.1 */
    A:=A-{a4.1}U{a4.1.1, a4.1.2};
  ARC SET
    F:=FU{(c4.1, a4.1.2), (a4.1.2, c5.1), (c5.1, a4.1.1), (a4.1.1, c4.1)}};
  END;
```

These descriptions specify the relationship among activities involved in SIS evolution. In these descriptions, activities, including some concurrent activities and iterations, are defined. Modellers can continue to refine these activities into finer activities until the granularity is suitable for use.

In the descriptions stated above, conflict is used to describe the selection behaviours. For example, there is a conflict in activity *Porting* and activity *By Virtual Machine*. The conflict indicates that these two activities are alternative. Moreover, activity *Design Evolution* in SIS_Process(5) is refined as a software process package *Design_Evolution_Package* in SIS_Process(6).

By means of this case study, it is also observed that when modelling an intricate process, the black box approach has a better abstract power than the white box approach.

11.4.6 Efficiency Improvement

In SIS_Process(6) of Fig. 11.4, the process segment encircled in dotted lines is executed sequentially. It is possible for it to be executed concurrently, discussed as follows.

Using the approach discussed in Chapter 9, the activity dependence graph of the process segment can be constructed, as shown in Fig. 11.5. According to Fig. 11.5, a new process segment can be reconstructed, as shown in Fig. 11.6. In Fig. 11.6, the concurrency is captured. Furthermore, within activity "Abstract" and within activity "Re-Design", the concurrency can also be further captured, as shown in Fig. 11.7. In Fig. 11.7, each of the preceding two activities is refined as two finer activities respectively. However, the concurrency is local. By means of extending the concurrency to the global, the process segment can be improved, as shown in Fig. 11.8.

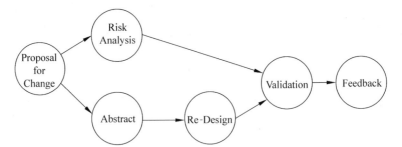

Figure 11.5 Activity dependence graph of Design Evolution

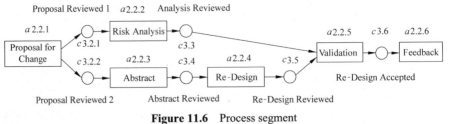

Figure 11.6 Process segment

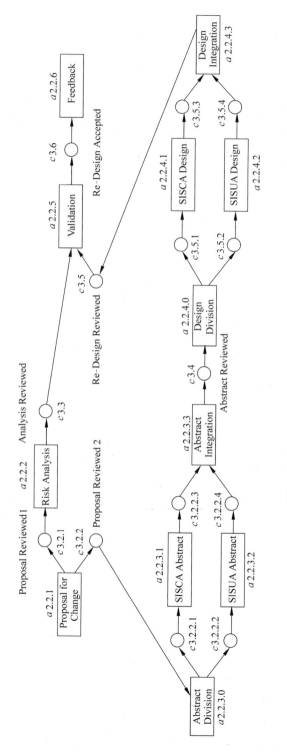

Figure 11.7 Capturing concurrency within activities

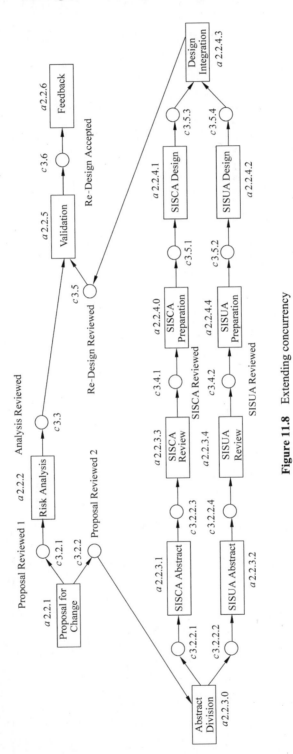

Figure 11.8 Extending concurrency

The reconstructed process segment can be put back to SIS_Process(6), named as SIS_Process(7). The description of SIS_Process(7) is listed as follows using the black box approach.

```
GLOBAL MODEL SIS_Evolution
  BEGIN
    SIS_Process(7);
    Design_Evolution_Package(2);
    EMBEDDED RELATION
      (SIS_Process(7), Design_Evolution_Package(2));
  END;
PROCESS Design_Evolution_Package(2)
  PACKAGE
    ENTRANCE a2.2.1;
    EXIT a2.2.6;
  BEGIN
    CONDITION SET
    C:={c3.2.1, c3.2.2, c3.2.2.1, c3.2.2.2, c3.2.2.3, c3.2.2.4, c3.3, c3.4.1,
    c3.4.2, c3.5, c3.5.1, c3.5.2, c3.5.3, c3.5.4, c3.6};
    ACTIVITY SET
    A:={a2.2.1, a2.2.2, a2.2.3.0, a2.2.3.1, a2.2.3.2, a2.2.3.3, a2.2.3.4,
    a2.2.4.0, a2.2.4.1, a2.2.4.2, a2.2.4.3, a2.2.4.4, a2.2.5, a2.2.6};
    ARC SET
    F:={(a2.2.1, c3.2.1), (a2.2.1, c3.2.2), (c3.2.1, a2.2.2), (a2.2.2, c3.3),
    (c3.3, a2.2.5), (c3.5, a2.2.5), (a2.2.5, c3.6), (c3.6, a2.2.6), (c3.2.2,
    a2.2.3.0), (a2.2.3.0, c3.2.2.1), (c3.2.2.1, a2.2.3.1), (a2.2.3.1, c3.2.2.3),
    (c3.2.2.3, a2.2.3.3), (a2.2.3.3, c3.4.1), (c3.4.1, a2.2.4.0), (a2.2.4.0,
    c3.5.1), (c3.5.1, a2.2.4.1), (a2.2.4.1, c3.5.3), (c3.5.3, a2.2.4.3), (a2.2.3.0,
    c3.2.2.2), (c3.2.2.2, a2.2.3.2), (a2.2.3.2, c3.2.2.4), (c3.2.2.4, a2.2.3.4),
    (a2.2.3.4, c3.4.2), (c3.4.2, a2.2.4.4), (a2.2.4.4, c3.5.2), (c3.5.2, a2.2.4.2),
    (a2.2.4.2, c3.5.4), (c3.5.4, a2.2.4.3), (a2.2.4.3, c3.5)};
    END;
PROCESS SIS_Process(7) FROM SIS_Process(6)
  ACTIVITY a2.2 /* Black box approach to refining activity a2.2 */
    BEGIN Design_Evolution_Package(2) END;
  BEGIN
  END;
```

Using software process SIS_Process(7), the efficiency of the corresponding software process based on SIS_Process(6) will be improved.

11.5   Fourth Case Study: The Maintenance Process of ISO/IEC 12207

11.5.1   Background

The ISO/IEC 12207 Standard for Information Technology—Software Life Cycle

Processes (ISO and IEC 1998) defines possible software processes in the software life cycle. By means of tailoring these processes, user-defined software processes which are suitable for a specified project are generated. The description of the maintenance process can be found in the ISO/IEC standard (ISO and IEC 1998).

In the following, the maintenance process, the process closest to the software evolution process (the standard does not define the software evolution process) of the ISO/IEC 12207 Standard, is described as a case study with EPDL. This case study also illustrates that all processes in the software life cycle can be described by EPDL. For the sake of widening points of view, all of the 17 processes of the ISO/IEC 12207 Standard are described at the global level.

Because the ISO/IEC 12207 Standard is just a framework for software processes, the relationships between software processes and between activities are not described explicitly by the standard. Therefore, some necessary information is provided by the author of this book when modelling and describing the maintenance process.

In addition, in this case study, functional decompositions of tasks have been achieved. For the sake of conciseness, the decomposition process is omitted. Of course, the functions of tasks can also be further decomposed depending on modelling and describing needs in some situations.

A maintenance process consists of the following activities (ISO and IEC 1998), as shown in Fig. 11.9:

(1) Process implementation,
(2) Problem and modification analysis,
(3) Modification implementation,
(4) Maintenance review/acceptance,
(5) Migration, and
(6) Software retirement.

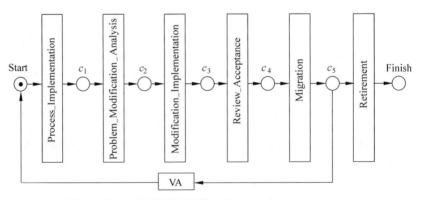

Figure 11.9   ISO/IEC 12207 software maintenance process

The iteration is provided by the author of this book. The detailed explanations can be found in ISO/IEC 12207 Standard (ISO and IEC 1998).

11.5.2   EPDL Program

In this case study, an EPDL program defines some terms and 17 processes.

```
PROGRAM ISO_IEC_12207
/* The predicates are symbolised as follows. */
#define Doc(x): x is documented;
#define Exe(x): x is executed;
#define Rec(x): x is recorded;
#define Enc(x): x is encountered;
#define Rea(x): x is ready;
#define App(x): x is approved;
#define Def(x): x is defined;
#define Ens(x, y): the property y of x is ensured;
#define Rev(x, y): the property y of x is reviewed;
#define Aff(x, y): x is affected by y;
#define Tra(x): x is trained;
#define Arc(x): x is placed in archives;
BEGIN
GLOBAL MODEL Software_Process
/* The global model lists the software processes involved in the software life
  cycle. */
  BEGIN
    Acquisition_Process; Supply_Process; Development_Process;
    Operation_Process; Maintenance_Process; Documentation_Process;
    Configuration_Management_Process; Quality_Assurance_Process;
    Verification_Process; Validation_Process; Joint_Review_Process;
    Audit_Process; Problem_Resolution_Process; Management_Process;
    Infrastructure_Process; Improvement_Process; Training_Process
  END;
/* The descriptions of other software processes are omitted except for
  Maintenance_ Process. */
PROCESS Maintenance_Process
/* TYPE clause declares the data types */
  TYPE
  Requirements_Type: STRUCTURE
    BEGIN
      Problem_Reports, Modification_Requests: STRING
    END;
  Procedure_Type: STRUCTURE
    BEGIN
      Conducting, Receiving, Recording, Tracking, Providing: STRING
    END;
  Analysis_Report_Type: STRUCTURE
    BEGIN
      Objective: {organisation, existing system, interfacing systems};
      Maintenance_Type: {corrective, improvement, preventive, adaptive};
      Scope, Criticality: STRING
    END;
  System_Type: STRUCTURE
    BEGIN
```

```
        Document, Data, Program: STRING
    END;
  Migration_Plan_Type: STRUCTURE
    BEGIN
       Requirement_Analysis, Tool_Development, Conversion, Execution,
Verification, Support: STRING
    END;
  Migration_Notification_Type: STRUCTURE
    BEGIN
        Reason, New_Environment, Other_Options: STRING
    END;
  Retirement_Plan_Type: STRUCTURE
    BEGIN
       Cessation_Time, Partial_Support_Time, Archiving, Responsibility,
Transition, Accessibility: STRING
    END;
  Retirement_Notification_Type: STRUCTURE
    BEGIN
        Replacement_Description, Upgrade_Description, Reason, Other_Options:
STRING
    END;
<Activity List>
/* All the activity descriptions should be listed here. However, for the sake
of convenience, they are listed in the following sections respectively. */
BEGIN
  CONDITION SET
  C:={Start, c1, c2, c3, c4, c5, Finish};
  ACTIVITY SET
  A:={Process_Implementation, Problem_Modification_Analysis,
Modification_Implementation, Review_Acceptance, Migration, Retirement, VA};
  ARC SET
  F:={(Start, Process_Implementation), (Process_Implementation, c1), (c1,
Problem_Modification_Analysis), (Problem_Modification_Analysis, c2), (c2,
Modification_Implementation), (Modification_Implementation, c3), (c3,
Review_Acceptance), (Review_Acceptance, c4), (c4, Migration), (Migration, c5),
(c5, VA), (VA, Start), (c5, Retirement), (Retirement, Finish)};
  MARKING {Start}
END; /* End of Maintenance_Process */
END. /* End of Program ISO_IEC_12207 */
```

In the following subsections, every activity in the software maintenance process is modelled and described. Each activity includes some tasks. Therefore, this case study focuses on modelling and describing at the activity level and at the task level.

11.5.3   Activity: Process Implementation

Activity *Process Implementation* includes three tasks: Main, Establish_Procedures and Configuration_Management.

```
ACTIVITY Process_Implementation
IMPORTS
  Requirements: Requirements_Type;
  Problem: STRING;
EXPORTS
  Plans: STRING;
  Procedures: Procedure_Type;
LOCALS
  Code: INTEGER;
  Start, Call, Execution, Finish: MESSAGE;
BEGIN
TASK Main
 ROLE: PM; /* PM denotes the Project Manager. */
 ON MESSAGES Execution(Code)
   BEGIN
    SEND Start TO Establish_Procedures, Configuration_Management(0);
    {PRECONDITION Rea(Requirements);
     POSTCONDITION Doc(Plans) and Doc(Procedures.Conducting) and Exe(Plans)
and Exe(Procedures.Conducting)};
    SEND Finish TO Process_Implementation(0)
    END; /* End of TASK Main */
TASK Establish_Procedures
 ROLE: PRM; /* PRM denotes the Process Manager. */
 ON MESSAGES Start(Code)
   BEGIN
     {PRECONDITION Rea(Requirements);
      POSTCONDITION Doc(Procedures. Receiving) and Doc(Procedures. Recording)
and Doc(Procedures.Tracking) and Doc(Procedures.Providing)};
     WHILE Enc(Problem) DO
      {PRECONDITION Rea(Requirements) and Enc(Problem);
       POSTCONDITION Rec(Problem)};
       SEND Call TO Problem_Resolution_Process.Start(true) OD;
   /* The start condition of Problem_Resolution_Process is set to true; Problem_
Resolution_Process will be executed. */
     SEND Finish TO Process_Implementation(0)
   END; /* End of TASK Establish_Procedures */
TASK Configuration_Management
 ROLE: PRM;
 ON MESSAGES Start(Code)
  BEGIN
    SEND Call TO Configuration_Management_Process.Start(true);
    /* The start condition of Configuration_Management_Process is set to true;
the Configuration_ Management_Process will be executed. */
    SEND Finish TO Process_Implementation(0)
  END; /* End of TASK Configuration_Management */
END; /* End of ACTIVITY Process_Implementation */
```

11.5.4   Activity: Problem and Modification Analysis

Activity *Problem and Modification Analysis* includes five tasks: Main, Verifying,

Options, Document and Approval.

```
ACTIVITY Problem_Modification_Analysis
 IMPORTS
  Problem_Report, Modification_Request: STRING;
 EXPORTS
 Analysis_Report: Analysis_Report_Type;
 Replicating_Report, Verifying_Report, Modification_Options: STRING;
 LOCALS
 Code: INTEGER;
 Start, Execution, Finish: MESSAGE;
BEGIN
TASK Main
 ROLE: MA; /* MA denotes the maintenance analyst. */
 ON MESSAGES Execution(Code)
  BEGIN
   SEND Start TO Verifying(0);
   {PRECONDITION Rea(Problem_Report) or Rea(Modification_Request);
    POSTCONDITION Rea(Analysis_Report)};
   SEND Start TO Options(0);
   SEND Finish TO Problem_Modification_Analysis(0)
   END; /* End of TASK Main */
TASK Verifying
 ROLE: MA;
 ON MESSAGES Start(Code)
  BEGIN
   {PRECONDITION Rea(Problem_Report);
    POSTCONDITION Doc(Replicating_Report) or Doc(Verifying_Report)};
   SEND Finish TO Problem_Modification_Analysis(0)
   END; /* End of TASK Verifying */
TASK Options
 ROLE: MA;
 ON MESSAGES Start(Code)
  BEGIN
   {PRECONDITION Doc(Analysis_Report);
    POSTCONDITION Rea(Modification_Options)};
   SEND Start TO Document(0);
   SEND Finish TO Problem_Modification_Analysis(0)
   END; /* End of TASK Options */
TASK Document
 ROLE: MA;
 ON MESSAGES Start(Code)
  BEGIN
   {PRECONDITION (Rea(Problem_Report) or Rea(Modification_Request)) and
Rea(Modification_Options) and Rea(Analysis_Report);
    POSTCONDITION (Doc(Problem_Report) or Doc(Modification_Request)) and
Doc(Modification_Options) and Doc(Analysis_Report)};
   SEND Start TO Approval(0);
   SEND Finish TO Problem_Modification_Analysis(0)
   END; /* End of TASK Document */
TASK Approval
 ROLE: PRM, PM, MA, USER;
```

```
ON MESSAGES Start(Code)
  BEGIN
    {PRECONDITION (Doc(Problem_Report) or Doc(Modification_Request)) and
Doc(Modification_Options) and Doc(Analysis_Report);
      POSTCONDITION App(Modification_Options)};
    SEND Finish TO Problem_Modification_Analysis(0)
  END; /* End of TASK Approval */
END; /* End of activity Problem_Modification_Analysis */
```

11.5.5   Activity: Modification Implementation

Activity *Modification Implementation* includes two tasks: Main and Implement_
Modifications.

```
ACTIVITY Modification_Implementation
 IMPORTS
  Analysis_Report: Analysis_Report_Type;
  Modification_Options, Original_Requirements: STRING;
 EXPORTS
  Modification_Decision, Modification_Requirements, Test_Criteria,
Evaluation_Criteria, Test_Result: STRING;
  Modified_System: System_Type; /* Produced by Development_Process */
 LOCALS
  Code: INTEGER;
  Start, Call, Execution, Finish: MESSAGE;
BEGIN
TASK Main
 ROLE: DR; /* DR denotes the Designer. */
 ON MESSAGES Execution(Code)
   BEGIN
    {PRECONDITION Doc(Analysis_Report) and Doc(Modification_Options);
      POSTCONDITION Doc(Modification_Decision) and Doc(Modification_
Requirements)};
    SEND Start TO Implement_Modifications(0);
    SEND Finish TO Modification_Implementation(0)
   END; /* End of TASK Main */
TASK Implement_Modifications
 ROLE: DR;
 ON MESSAGES Start(Code)
   BEGIN
    {PRECONDITION Doc(Analysis_Report) and Doc(Modification_Options) and
Doc(Modification_Decision) and Doc(Modification_Requirements) and
Doc(Original_Requirement);
      POSTCONDITION Doc(Test_Criteria) and Doc(Evaluation_criteria) and
Def(Test_Criteria) and Def(Evaluation_Criteria) and Ens(Modification_
Requirements, correctness) and Ens(Modification_Requirements, completeness)
and not Aff(Original_Requirements-Modification_Requirements,
Modification_Requirements) and Doc(Test_Results)}; /* Original_Requirements-
```

189

```
Modification_Requirements denotes original, unmodified requirements. "_"
denotes the minus sign.*/
    SEND Call TO Development_Process.Start(true); /* The start condition of
Development Process is set to true; Development Process will be executed. */
    SEND Finish TO Modification_Implementation(0)
  END; /* End of TASK Implement_Modifications */
END; /* End of ACTIVITY Modification_Implementation */
```

11.5.6   Activity: Maintenance Review/Acceptance

Activity *Maintenance Review/Acceptance* includes two tasks: Main and Approval.

```
ACTIVITY Review_Acceptance
 IMPORTS
   Modified_System: System_Type;
   Contract, Modification_Requirements: STRING;
 EXPORTS
   Review_Report, Approval_Report: STRING;
 LOCALS
   Authorising_Organisation: ROLE;
   Code: INTEGER;
   Execution, Start, Finish: MESSAGE;
BEGIN
TASK Main
 ROLE: PM, PRM, Authorising_Organisation;
 ON MESSAGES Execution(Code)
   BEGIN
   {PRECONDITION Rea(Modified_System) and Doc(Modification_Requirements);
    POSTCONDITION Rev(Modified_System,Integrity) and Doc(Review_Report)};
    SEND Start TO Approval(0);
    SEND Finish TO Review_Acceptance(0)
   END; /* End of TASK Main */
TASK Approval
 ROLE: PM, PRM, Authorising_Organisation;
 ON MESSAGES Start(Code)
   BEGIN
   {PRECONDITION Rev(Modified_System, Integrity) and Rea(Contract);
    POSTCONDITION App(Modified_System) and Doc(Approval_Report)};
    SEND Finish TO Review_Acceptance(0)
   END; /* End of TASK Approval */
END; /* End of ACTIVITY Review_Acceptance */
```

11.5.7   Activity: Migration

Activity *Migration* includes seven tasks: Main, Plan_Execution, Notification, Operation, Scheduled_Migration, Review and Data.

```
ACTIVITY Migration
 IMPORTS
   Migration_Request, ISO_IEC 12207_Standard: STRING;
   Old_System: System_Type;
 EXPORTS
   Migration_Notification: Migration_Notification_Type;
   Migrated_System: System_Type;
   Review_Report:STRING;
   Migration_Plan: Migration_Plan_Type;
 LOCALS
   Code: INTEGER;
   Appropriate_Authorities: ROLE;
   Start, Call, Execution, Notification, Report, Finish: MESSAGE;
 TASK Main
  ROLE: PM, USER;
  ON MESSAGES Execution(Code)
    BEGIN
     SEND Start TO Plan(0);
     {PRECONDITION Rea(Migrated_System) and Rea(ISO_IEC_12207_ Standard);
      POSTCONDITION Ens(Migrated_System, ISO_IEC_12207_Standard)};
     SEND Finish TO Migration(0)
    END; /* End of TASK Main */
 TASK Plan
  ROLE: PRM;
  ON MESSAGES Start(Code)
   BEGIN
    {PRECONDITION Doc(Migration_Request);
     POSTCONDITION Doc(Migration_Plan) and Exe(Migration_Plan) and
Rea(Migrated_System)};
    SEND Start TO Notification(Code);
    SEND Finish TO Migration(0)
   END; /* End of TASK Plan */
 TASK Notification
  ROLE: PRM, USER;
  ON MESSAGES Start(Code)
   BEGIN
    {PRECONDITION Doc(Migration_Plan);
     POSTCONDITION Doc(Migration_Notification)};
    SEND Notification TO USER(Migration_Notification);
    SEND Start TO Operation(Code);
    SEND Finish TO Migration(0)
   END; /* End of TASK Notification */
 TASK Operation
  ROLE: PRM, OP, USER; /* OP denotes the operator. */
  ON MESSAGES Start(Code)
   BEGIN
    {PRECONDITION Rea(Migrated_System) and Rea(Old_System);
     POSTCONDITION Exe(Migrated_System) and Exe(Old_System) and Tra(USER)};
    SEND Start TO Scheduled_Migration(Code);
```

```
      SEND Finish TO Migration(0)
    END; /* End of TASK Operation */
  TASK Scheduled_Migration
   ROLE: PRM, USER;
   ON MESSAGES Start(Code)
    BEGIN
     SEND Notification TO ALL("Migration Arrives!");
     {PRECONDITION true;
      POSTCONDITION Arc(Old_System)};
     SEND Start TO Review, Data(Code);
     SEND Finish TO Migration(0)
    END; /* End of TASK Scheduled_Migration */
  TASK Review
   ROLE: DR, OP;
   ON MESSAGES Start(Code)
    BEGIN
     {PRECONDITION Exe(Migrated_System);
      POSTCONDITION Doc(Review_Report)};
     SEND Report TO Appropriate_Authorities(Review_Report);
     SEND Finish TO Migration(0)
    END; /* End of TASK Review */
  TASK Data
   ROLE: PM, MA, DR, USER;
   ON MESSAGES Start(Code)
    BEGIN
     {PRECONDITION Exe(Migrated_System);
      POSTCONDITION Ens(Old_System.Data, Accessibility) and
  Ens(Old_System.Data, Protection) and Ens(Old_System.Data,
  Audit_Applicability)};
     SEND Finish TO Migration(0)
    END; /* End of TASK Data */
   END; /* End of ACTIVITY Migration */
```

11.5.8 Activity: Software Retirement

Activity *Software Retirement* includes five tasks: Main, Notification, Operation, Scheduled_Retirement and Data.

```
ACTIVITY Retirement
 IMPORTS
  Retirement_Request, Contract: STRING;
  New_System, Old_System: System_Type;
 EXPORTS
  Retirement_Plan: Retirement_Plan_Type;
  Retirement_Notification: Retirement_Notification_Type;
 LOCALS
  Code: INTEGER;
  Start, Call, Execution, Notification, Report, Finish: MESSAGE;
```

```
BEGIN
TASK Main
 ROLE: PM, USER;
 ON MESSAGES Execution(Code)
   BEGIN
    {PRECONDITION Rea(Retirement_Request);
     POSTCONDITION Doc(Retirement_Plan) and Exe(Retirement_Plan)};
     SEND Start TO Notification(Code);
     SEND Finish TO Retirement(0)
   END; /* End of TASK Main */
TASK Notification
 ROLE: PRM, USER;
 ON MESSAGES Start(Code)
   BEGIN
    {PRECONDITION Doc(Retirement_Plan);
     POSTCONDITION Doc(Retirement_Notification)};
     SEND Notification TO USER(Retirement_Notification);
     SEND Start TO Operation(Code);
     SEND Finish TO Retirement(0)
   END; /* End of TASK Notification */
TASK Operation
 ROLE: PRM, OP, USER;
 ON MESSAGES Start(Code)
   BEGIN
    IF Rea(New_System) THEN
      {PRECONDITION Rea(New_System);
       POSTCONDITION Exe(New_System) and Exe(Old_System) and Tra(USER)} FI;
     SEND Start TO Scheduled_Retirement(Code);
     SEND Finish TO Retirement(0)
   END; /* End of TASK Operation */
TASK Scheduled_Retirement
 ROLE: PRM, USER;
 ON MESSAGES Start(Code)
   BEGIN
     SEND Notification TO ALL("Retirement Arrives!");
     {PRECONDITION true;
      POSTCONDITION Arc(Old_System)};
     SEND Start TO Data(Code);
     SEND Finish TO Retirement(0)
   END; /* End of TASK Scheduled_Retirement */
TASK Data
 ROLE: DR, OP;
 ON MESSAGES Start(Code)
   BEGIN
    {PRECONDITION Rea(Contract);
     POSTCONDITION Ens(Old_System.Data, Accessibility) and
Ens(Old_System.Data, Protection) and Ens(Old_System.Data, Audit_
Applicability)};
     SEND Finish TO Retirement(0)
   END; /* End of TASK Data */
 END; /* End of ACTIVITY Retirement */
```

The maintenance process is an important process in the ISO/IEC 12207 Standard. Because it is the process closest to the software evolution process, this case study models and describes it to show the power of modelling software evolution process. It is also believed that all the processes of the ISO/IEC 12207 Standard can be modelled and described using the proposed approach.

Because the ISO/IEC 12207 Standard is too abstract, the maintenance process is coarse-grained. By means of capturing and extending concurrency and decomposing the functions of tasks, the model and the description will reach an ideal granularity.

11.6 Summary

In this chapter, four case studies are given to test and evaluate the proposed approach. The first, second and third case studies focus on the global level and on the process level; the fourth case study focuses on the activity level and on the task level.

The first case study illustrates how the classical waterfall model is described. This case study is simple but representative in the software life cycle. This case study indicates that the proposed approach is feasible and effective for modelling and describing the classical software life cycle process.

The second case study illustrates that many concurrent software processes involved in the software evolution can be modelled and described by the proposed approach. This case study is complex in concurrent software processes involved in software evolution. It mainly shows that concurrency can be modelled and described by the proposed approach. This case study indicates that the proposed approach is feasible and effective for modelling and describing many concurrent software processes.

The third case study illustrates how a software evolution process evolves an information security software system in Linux into a cross-platform system in both Windows and Linux. The modelling approaches, including the white box approach and the black box approach, are illustrated and the corresponding EPDL program is given. This case study mainly shows the inheritance characteristics and the process improvement approach proposed in Chapter 9. This case study indicates that the proposed approach is feasible and effective for modelling and describing industrial-scale software evolution processes.

The fourth case study shows that the proposed approach can be used to model and describe the maintenance process of the ISO/IEC 12207 Standard for Software Life Cycle Processes. The global model described by EPDL shows a bird's eye view of all the software processes defined by the standard. Furthermore, it focuses on the maintenance process. An EPDL program including various descriptions at the process level, at the activity level and at the task level is listed. This case study also shows how the 2-assertions are used to describe the functions of tasks. This case study indicates that the proposed approach is feasible and effective for modelling and describing the software life cycle processes of the ISO/IEC 12207 Standard. Because the maintenance process is the software process closest to the software evolution process (the ISO/IEC Standard does not define the software evolution process) in the ISO/IEC 12207 Standard for Software Life Cycle Processes, it is expected that the proposed approach is feasible and effective for modelling and describing software evolution processes similar to the maintenance process of the ISO/IEC 12207 Standard.

In summary, four case studies of various complexities and scales are used to test the main results proposed in this book. They indicate that the proposed approach is feasible and effective.

References

[1] Bennett K, Rajlich V (2000) Software maintenance and evolution: a roadmap. In: Proceedings of the conference on the future of software engineering. ACM Press, New York, pp 73 – 87

[2] ISO, IEC (1998) ISO/IEC 12207 Standard for information technology — software life cycle processes

[3] Pressman RS (2000) Software engineering: a practitioner's approach (ed5). McGraw Hill, New York

12 Conclusions

Tong Li

School of Software, Yunnan University, Kunming, 650091, China
Software Technology Research Laboratory, De Montfort University, Leicester, LE1 9BH, U.K
tli@ynu.edu.cn

Abstract This chapter validates the feasibility and effectiveness of the proposed approach described in this book. The success criteria listed in Chapter 1 are revisited to indicate that these criteria have been met by the proposed approach. The detailed comparison with Osterweil's work and Lehman's work, which are two of the most influential contributions in the areas of software process and software evolution process, can be referred to as sound verification of the success of the proposed approach. Some evaluations have also been made to verify the success of the proposed approach. These indicate that the approach proposed in this book is feasible and effective. Finally, the limitations to the proposed approach and the directions of future work for improving these limitations are also discussed.

Key Words success criterion, evaluation, comparison, Osterweil's approach, Lehman's approach, conclusion, limitation, future work.

As more and more software systems become legacy systems, software engineers must evolve them to meet increasing user requirements. A well-managed software evolution process can effectively support the software evolution. In this book, the software evolution process is closely investigated and an approach to modelling and describing a formal software evolution process is proposed to effectively support software evolution. This chapter validates the feasibility and effectiveness of the proposed approach.

12.1 Success Criteria Revisited

The research results meet the success criteria given in Chapter 1 as follows.

(1) Can the software evolution process models defined by EPMM embody the important properties of software evolution processes?

As stated in Section 4.7, an evolution process model (EPM) can effectively support the properties of software evolution. Firstly, the cycle is an effective description of iteration. The execution of a cycle realises a piece of iteration and a gradual evolution. Secondly, a cycle also effectively describes a feedback-driven evolution. Any activity in a cycle can be regarded as the operation which transfers the feedback of the previous iteration into the results which can then be submitted as an input to the next iteration. Furthermore, a task can send a message to conditions in other processes; this can drive the processes to be executed if the corresponding activities can fire. Thirdly, using Petri Nets, all of the concurrent phenomena in software evolution processes can be described precisely. Fourthly, continuous change and discontinuous change can also be described effectively by means of cycles and activities in non-cycles. Fifthly, because EPM has a four-level framework and an activity can be defined as a software process, a multi-level process framework can be constructed level by level.

(2) Can EPDL effectively describe software evolution processes defined by EPMM in detail?

EPDL is designed based on EPMM. Furthermore, it extends EPMM in order to describe software evolution processes in detail. EPMM is more abstract than EPDL. Even though some components are not important enough to a software evolution process so that they cannot be described by EPMM, they can also be described by EPDL. Besides, the structure of EPDL is the same as that of EPMM. Therefore, EPDL can effectively describe software evolution processes defined by EPMM.

(3) Is the framework of the software evolution processes reasonable? Does it support the descriptions of the software evolution processes at different levels and from different points of view?

The software evolution processes described by both EPMM and EPDL form a four-level framework: the global level, the process level, the activity level and the task level. Each level corresponds to the components at different granularities in EPM and EPD from different points of view. The framework accords with the structure of the ISO/IEC 12207 Standard for Software Life Cycle Processes. According to the characteristics of models at different levels, a top-down spiral meta-process for modelling software evolution processes, including four semi-formal procedures corresponding to different levels, is proposed.

(4) Can the approach effectively construct software evolution processes? Does it support the construction of industrial-scale processes? Can the interface consistency of the software processes over hierarchies be preserved?

Based on EPMM, an integrated modelling approach is proposed. It can construct all components of software evolution processes at different granularities. It supports the construction of EPMs level by level. Therefore, the modelling approach can effectively construct the software evolution process model on a large scale. Case studies indicate that the proposed approach also supports the modelling of industrial-scale processes. The interface consistency of software processes over different hierarchies has been proved using mathematical methods.

(5) Can the approach support the reuse of software processes?

In the proposed approach, three different process reuse methods are presented: reuse by inheritance, reuse of process packages (the black box approach) and reuse of basic blocks (the white box approach).

(6) Can the functions of tasks be further decomposed so that they are easily realised? Is the correctness of the decompositions preserved?

An approach is proposed to decompose a function into finer functions which are easy to realise. By means of matching the code segments in the segment base, matching the decomposition cases in the case base and executing the decomposition rules in the rule base, functional decomposition is carried out. The decomposition process continues until modellers consider that the granularity of functions is appropriate. The correctness of decomposition has been proved using mathematical methods.

(7) Does the approach support the efficiency improvement of the software evolution processes? Can the concurrency in software evolution processes be captured and extended?

According to the dependence analysis, the proposed approach captures activities that can be executed concurrently. Furthermore, it can also extend local concurrency into global concurrency. As a result, an inefficient software process can be reconstructed. Thus, the efficiency of the software evolution process is improved.

(8) Is the approach feasible and effective?

Four case studies, derived respectively from the waterfall model, a software evolution, a security system evolution and the ISO/IEC 12207 Standard for Software Life Cycle Processes, have validated that the proposed approach is feasible and effective.

12.2 Evaluations

Besides evaluations from success criteria, the following comparisons with the work of two of the most influential researchers in the areas of software process and software evolution process, Osterweil and Lehman, can be referred to as sound verification of the success of the proposed research.

12.2.1 Comparison with Osterweil's Approach

As stated in Chapter 2, Osterweil and his colleagues have researched into software processes for more than 20 years and have a record of considerable achievements in this area.

In 1987, Osterweil presented the now widely accepted view that "software processes are software too" (Osterweil 1987) and won the Most Influential Paper of ICSE9 Award in 1997 (Osterweil 1997). He suggested that the processes by which software is created are a particular type of software, and presumably this type is some sort of subtype of the larger universe of software (of which different application software systems are presumably instances of still different subtypes) (Osterweil 2003). He suggested that software processes might well themselves be merely subtypes of the more general class of all processes that humans perform. In that case, languages that are effective in defining software processes might well be effective in defining processes drawn from wider application domains (Osterweil 2003).

Based on these points of view, he and his colleagues designed a language APPL/A (Sutton *et al.* 1990, 1995) which demonstrated that processes could be defined using a procedural language, but that it was necessary also to provide reactive control constructs in that language.

Furthermore, they defined Little-JIL (Cass *et al.* 2000), a process definition language which attempts to stake out a more general view of what is needed in any language that is to be effective in defining processes. The principal contribution of Little-JIL is its suggestion of abstractions that seem particularly effective in communicating process thought. Thus, Little-JIL is a member of a newer family of process definition languages aimed at determining what these models and abstractions need to look like (Osterweil 2003).

Little-JIL is an executable, high-level language with a formal (yet graphical) syntax and rigorously defined operational semantics. The central abstraction in Little-JIL is the "step", which is the focal point for coordination, providing a scoping mechanism for control, data, and exception flow as well as for agent and resource assignment. Steps are organised into a static hierarchy, but can have a highly dynamic execution structure including the possibility of recursion and concurrency (Cass *et al.* 2000).

Little-JIL is based on two main hypotheses. The first is that coordination structure is separable from other process language issues. Little-JIL provides rich control structures while relying on separate systems for resource, artefact and agenda management. The second hypothesis is that processes are executed by agents that know how to perform their tasks but benefit from coordination support. Accordingly, each Little-JIL step has an execution agent (human or automated) that is responsible for performing the work of the step (Cass *et al.* 2000).

A Little-JIL program is a tree of step types, each of which can be multiply instantiated at runtime. The leaves represent the smallest specified units of work and the tree's structure represents the way in which this work will be coordinated. As processes execute, steps go through several states. Typically, a step is posted when assigned to an execution agent, and then started by the agent. Eventually, either the step is successfully completed or it is terminated with an exception. Little-JIL has been used to define a wide range of processes from domains as diverse as software engineering, robot control, and electronic commerce (Cass *et al.* 2000).

In comparison with Osterweil's approach, the approach proposed in this book shows significant differences as follows.

Firstly, the proposed approach defines a process meta-model and a process description language. The approach separates the process models from the process descriptions. The process model is more abstract and the process description is more concrete. This leads to an advantage that process design is separated from process implementation.

Secondly, different from Osterweil's approach which supposed a universal definition language, the proposed approach is focused on the software evolution processes. Therefore, the properties of software evolution processes are embodied sufficiently.

Thirdly, the process structure of the proposed approach accords with the ISO/IEC 12207 Standard; therefore, the standard is easily modelled and applied by the proposed approach.

Fourthly, Petri Nets have an excellent power to describe concurrency. The proposed approach is based on Petri Nets; therefore, the concurrency can be described rigorously.

Fifthly, the proposed approach is based on object-oriented technology. Therefore, the advantages of object-oriented modelling technology can be utilised.

Sixthly, the proposed approach can optimise and improve the efficiency of software processes based on the corresponding process models. This leads to a lower cost of process improvement.

Finally, Hoare Logic is used to define the function of a task. This strengthens the semantic descriptive power of the proposed approach.

12.2.2 Comparison with Lehman's Approach

As stated in Chapter 3, Lehman and his colleagues have researched into software evolution and software evolution processes for more than 30 years with considerable success. Their work is included in project FEAST/1 and FEAST/2 (Feedback, Evolution And Software Technology) (Lehman and Ramil 2000, 2002).

System dynamics models were proposed by Lehman *et al.* in FEAST/1 (Lehman and Wernick 1998). The objectives of system dynamics models are as follows (Lehman and Wernick 1998).

(1) To provide objective evidence that feedback phenomena and the consequent system dynamics have substantial impact in the software process

(2) To model global process feedback structures and mechanisms and identify their properties

(3) To demonstrate that feedback phenomena can be exploited in both managing and improving industrial processes, and

(4) To develop the foundations for a theory of software process and software evolution

Each model describes a specific, real-world industrial software process and its effects on its products. Whether a generic model over several systems within an organisation, or over more than one organisation, can be developed is, as yet, an open question. Each model is designed to reflect the actual evolution process associated with a single product (Lehman and Wernick 1998).

Recent progress is represented by FEAST/2. The goals of FEAST/2 are as follows (Lehman and Ramil 2002).

(1) To refine a set of models and their interpretations and formulate laws and rules derived from them

(2) To develop and refine FEAST methods and conclusions to forms suitable for transfer to industry

(3) To develop models of mechanisms underlying observed behaviour, and

(4) To monitor systems studied in FEAST/1 and extend techniques to new systems and data sets

Some significant results have been obtained in FEAST/2 (Lehman and Ramil 2002) as follows.

(1) Greatly increased understanding of software evolution, its regularities, patterns and constraints

(2) Support for refined version of the laws of software evolution

(3) System dynamics has significant impact on the software evolution process with regularities stronger within segments or stages of the life cycle

(4) Inflexion points in evolutionary trajectories possibly driven by changes in the domain (e.g. technology, demand) with resource level (e.g. team size) also playing a role

(5) Inverse square and related models and their pointing to complexity growth of applications and of implementing software as a significant constraint on continuing (and necessary) application and system evolution

(6) Incremental growth limits as a planning tool

(7) Advances in software process modelling, the application, analysis and interpretation of process metrics

(8) Simple SD (System dynamics) models can produce meaningful results and insights

(9) Approaches to and procedures for behavioural process modelling and exploitation of software process metrics

(10) Design principals and seeds for specific software process analysis, planning, management and control procedures, tools with long term potential for generic stand alone or integrated tools

(11) Emerging understanding of and design principals for tools for software process improvement

In comparison with Lehman's approach, the proposed approach shows significant differences as follows.

Firstly, in the proposed approach, a meta-model and a process description language are designed. The model and the language are not constrained to a specific software process or an organisation. Conversely, they can describe various software evolution processes because they are at the level of the meta-model and of the modelling language. However, they are also designed with different abstract levels so that the proposed approach can separate design from implementation.

Furthermore, in the proposed approach, not only the meta-model and process description language, but also the models and descriptions defined by them are formal and the consistency over hierarchies and the correctness of functional decomposition are proved by means of mathematical methods. Therefore, the proposed approach possesses a solid theoretical foundation.

In addition, the proposed approach is also different from Lehman's approach in other aspects. These differences are similar to from the 3rd point to the 7th point as elaborated in Section 12.2.1.

12.2.3 Evaluations

The following evaluations have been made to verify the success of the proposed approach.

(1) A search of important journals and conferences shows that one of the most influential pieces of research in the area of software processes has been carried out by Osterweil and his colleagues. As stated before, in comparison with their work, some aspects of the proposed approach are advantageous and innovatory.

(2) By means of searching for important journals and conferences, the most influential research in the area of software evolution processes has been identified as that by Lehman and his colleagues. As stated before, in comparison with their work, some aspects of the proposed approach to the software evolution processes are advantageous and innovatory.

(3) All the contributions listed in Section 1.2 are original. The proposed approach is innovative; some parts of the research in this book have proved difficult, but with hard work the job has been well accomplished.

(4) The structures of the proposed approach are tightly integrated into a whole. The methods in this book support each other.

(5) The support environment EPT provides the evidence of the feasibility of the proposed approach.

(6) The case studies have indicated that the proposed approach supports industrial-scale projects and the ISO/IEC standard.

(7) As stated in the success criteria revisited, the proposed approach has achieved the goals initially set up.

12.3 Summary

In this book, the following major progress has been made.

(1) From the point of view of software processes, five important properties in

the software evolution process have been analysed. Firstly, iteration describes the continuous changes and the processes to realise these changes. The continuous changes in evolution processes can be described by iteration at different abstract levels. Secondly, concurrency is another important property in software evolution processes. Many components in processes can be executed concurrently so that the efficiency of processes can be improved. Thirdly, the interleaving of continuous and discontinuous changes needs to be paid more attention during software evolution. Fourthly, software evolution is a feedback-driven system. It is impossible for an evolution to occur with no feedback from users or contexts. Finally, the framework of evolution processes must be multi-level. This leads to a modelling approach of successive refinement.

(2) A Petri Net is extended with object-oriented technology and Hoare Logic. Abstract data types and inheritance are added in order to define activities; Hoare Logic is added in order to define tasks. According to preceding properties, a formal evolution process meta-model, EPMM, based on the extended Petri Net is proposed. In EPMM, the structures and behaviours of all the important components in software evolution processes, such as tasks, activities and software processes, are formally defined. Using these definitions, the software evolution processes can be modelled. EPMM can represent software evolution process models at different abstract levels. Based on these models, the basis to simulate, control, analyse, measure and improve software evolution processes is established.

(3) Based on EPMM, an evolution process description language EPDL is designed. EPDL is a computer language that is more powerful and easier to apply by non-professional users than EPMM. An EPDL program is a software evolution process description which specifies a software evolution process in detail.

(4) Based on EPMM, an approach to modelling software evolution processes is proposed. A software evolution process possesses a four-level framework. The approach is used to construct software evolution process models at the global level, at the process level, at the activity level and at the task level in correspondence to the framework of software evolution processes. The approach supports the top-down white box modelling and the top-down black box modelling, which are proved to preserve the interface consistency over refinement hierarchies. Three different approaches are proposed to support the reuse of software evolution processes.

(5) In EPM, the function of a task is defined as a 2-assertion based on Hoare Logic. By means of repeatedly decomposing the function into one of the three basic control structures, an approach is proposed to decompose a function into a series of finer functions which are easily enacted. If the executions of all the decomposed finer 2-assertions terminate, the decompositions based on the proposed rules are proved to be totally correct.

(6) Based on dependence analysis, an approach to improving the efficiency of software evolution processes is proposed. As with a transplant operation on the

human body, the approach digs down into an inefficient process segment from a software process, improves its efficiency by means of capturing and extending concurrency, and then puts back the improved process segment into the original software process. It is proved that the consistency is preserved.

(7) A CASE environment EPT is designed and a prototype system of EPT is implemented.

(8) Four case studies also indicate that the proposed approach is feasible and effective.

12.4   Future Work

As with all research work, there are some limitations to the proposed approach. For improving these limitations, the directions of future work can be drawn.

12.4.1   Limitations

The limitations include the following aspects:

(1) Both EPMM and EPDL are confined to modelling and describing software evolution processes. EPDL is not a programming language. However, during software evolution, software systems need to be modelled and coded by modelling languages (e.g. UML) and programming languages (e.g. Java). In such a case, EPDL cannot cover all aspects. This leads to users having to use two or more different languages when implementing a software system so that system consistency becomes worse.

(2) Risks and uncertainties in the software evolution process are not addressed sufficiently. A risk is a potential problem. It might happen, it might also not. Risk analysis and management are a series of steps that help a software team to understand and manage uncertainty (Pressman 2000). Risk analysis and management is a special process during software evolution. How to model and describe the process and integrate it with other software processes are not discussed in this book. This will lead to risk analysis and management being ignored by the users.

(3) The metrics of software evolution processes are not addressed. Users have little quantitative guidance in software evolution processes from the proposed approach. When users try to improve software evolution processes, they have to search for the inefficient process segments by means of common sense. This leaves the users sightless. Process metrics help users gain quantitative evaluations of software evolution processes so that they can improve these processes insightfully.

12.4.2   Directions for Future Work

For improving the limitations stated above, further research will be focused on the following aspects:

(1) A wide-spectrum language which integrates EPDL with a ready-made programming language will be designed and the corresponding compiler and support environment will be developed. The language not only supports the definition of software evolution processes, but also the description of programs. Based on the language, the combination of the function of a task and software evolution automation, which makes use of the formal development technology, will be explored. Furthermore, the interface between the proposed approach and popular process technologies, e.g. UP, should be investigated so that the proposed approach can be widely applied in the software industry.

(2) An approach to modelling the risk analysis and management process will be proposed. Risks and uncertainties in the software evolution process are integral to software evolution processes. Lots of things in software evolution processes can go wrong. They are key activities during software evolution in order to understand the risks and to take proactive measures to avoid and manage them. Risks behave uncertainly. Although EPMM and EPDL can model and describe nondeterministic behaviours, the uncertainties in the model and the description potentially need to be explicitly defined in advance. This does not accord with the spirit of uncertainty. For modelling the risk analysis and management process, the properties of risks and uncertainty must first be analysed. Based on the properties, EPMM and EPDL will be extended so that the corresponding components are supplemented to model and describe risks and uncertainty. Furthermore, a metric method will be developed to determine the ranks of risks. Finally, based on this method, an improvement approach of the risk analysis and management processes will be proposed.

(3) An approach to measuring software evolution processes will be proposed. The metric objects will include: interaction, efficiency, concurrency, operability, repeatability, liveness, decomposability, reachability, safeness and deadlock freeness. The metric products will greatly promote the design, analysis and improvement of software evolution processes.

References

[1] Cass AG, Lerner BS, McCall EK, Osterweil LJ, Sutton SM, Wise A (2000) Little-JIL/ Juliette: a process definition language and interpreter. In: Proceedings of the 22nd international conference on software engineering. ACM Press, New York, pp 754 – 757

[2] Lehman MM, Wernick P (1998) System dynamics models of software evolution processes. In: Proceedings of international workshop on the principles for software evolution. Kyoto, Japan, pp 6 – 10

[3] Lehman MM, Ramil JF (2000) Towards a theory of software evolution and its practical impact. In: Proceedings of international symposium on the principles of software evolution. IEEE Computer Society, Washington DC, pp 2 – 11

[4] Lehman MM, Ramil JF (2002) Software evolution and software evolution processes. Annals of Software Engineering 14: 275 – 309

[5] Osterweil LJ (1987) Software processes are software too. In: Proceedings of the 9th international conference on software engineering. ACM Press, New York, pp 2 – 13

[6] Osterweil LJ (1997) Software processes are software too, revisited: an invited talk on the most influential paper of ICSE 9. In: Proceedings of the 19th international conference on software engineering. ACM Press, New York, pp 540 – 548

[7] Osterweil LJ (2003) Understanding process and the quest for deeper questions in software engineering research. ACM SIGSOFT Software Engineering Notes 8: 6 – 14

[8] Pressman RS (2000) Software engineering: a practitioner's approach (ed5). McGraw Hill, New York

[9] Sutton SM Jr, Heimbigner DM, Osterweil LJ (1990) Language constructs for managing change in process-centered environments. In: Proceedings of the 4th ACM SIGSOFT symposium on software development environments. ACM Press, New York, pp 206 – 217

[10] Sutton SM Jr, Heimbigner DM, Osterweil LJ (1995) APPL/A—a language for software-process programming. ACM Transactions on Software Engineering and Methodology 4: 221 – 286

Index